Inigo Jones

Complete Architectural Drawings

This exhibition and book have been made possible with the generous assistance of The Henry J. and Drue E. Heinz Foundation.

British Airways is the official airline of The Drawing Center.

The Drawing Center gratefully acknowledges grants from the American Express Family of Companies, the Samuel I. Newhouse Foundation, Inc. and Skidmore, Owings & Merrill.

We are grateful to the Helen Clay Frick Foundation for supporting the publication of the catalogue.

Public funds from the National Endowment for the Arts, the Institute of Museum Services and the New York State Council on the Arts assisted in making this exhibition possible.

An Indemnity has been granted by the Federal Council on the Arts and Humanities.

Inigo Jones

Complete Architectural Drawings

John Harris and Gordon Higgott

A. Zwemmer Ltd

Published in association with The Drawing Center, New York,
a nonprofit space for the study and exhibition of drawings

© 1989 The Drawing Center

First published 1989 for A. Zwemmer Ltd
by Philip Wilson Publishers Ltd
26 Litchfield Street, London WC2H 9NJ
in association with The Drawing Center

All rights reserved. No part of this publication may be reproduced, stored in a retrieval system or transmitted in any form or by any means, mechanical, electronic, photocopying or otherwise, without the prior permission of the Publisher

Distributed in the USA by Harper & Row, Publishers, Inc
10 East 53rd Street
New York, NY 10022

ISBN 0 302 00608 7

LC 88-062816

Organized by The Drawing Center, a nonprofit space for the exhibition and study of drawings, 35 Wooster Street, New York, NY 10013

Designed by Roy Cole
Typeset and printed by BAS Printers Limited,
Over Wallop, Hants
Bound by Dorstel Press Ltd., Harlow

Contents

Colour illustrations

Foreword

Since opening in January 1977, The Drawing Center, a nonprofit institution, has sought through exhibitions and educational events to express the diversity, quality and importance of drawing – the creation of unique works on paper – as a major art form. Each year the Center presents five exhibitions. Those of an historical nature complement the Center's *Selections* series – group exhibitions of drawings by promising artists whose work is shown by the Center for the first time in New York. These are chosen from the Center's Viewing Programme. Through this programme over 2500 artists each year are able to make appointments to show their drawings to curators or leave a portfolio for viewing by the curatorial staff. The Center shows drawings by architects, stage designers, film makers, sculptors and painters. Plans, sketchbooks, notebooks, models and maquettes as well as presentation drawings and works on paper complete in their own right are included in the exhibitions. The process of choosing the artists for the exhibitions is ongoing. Every four months the work of sixty artists is called back from the over 600 viewed. Seven to seventeen artists are chosen for each exhibition. In the past twelve years, 475 artists have been seen in 45 *Selections* exhibitions. Almost a hundred are now in the collections of museums around the world. These exhibitions are very special to the Center since every well-known artist – including Inigo Jones – was at one time promising and unknown.

This book wonderfully complements our other exhibition catalogues. Our very first historical catalogue was *The Drawings of Antonio Gaudi* written by the distinguished architectural historian George R. Collins. Dr. Collins was also the author of *Visionary Drawings of Architecture and Planning*. Vincent Scully was the author of *The Travel Sketches of Louis I. Kahn*. John Harris, Jill Lever and Margaret Richardson were the authors of *Great Drawings from the Royal Institute of British Architects* and Otto Graf was the author of *Masterdrawings of Otto Wagner*. Other exhibitions and catalogues for us have been: *Sculptors' Drawings Over Six Centuries* by Colin Eisler; *Reading Drawings: A Selection from the Victoria and Albert Museum* by Susan Lambert; *Drawings from Venice: Masterworks from the Museo Correr* by Terisio Pignatti and Giandomenico Romanelli; *The Northern Landscape: Flemish, Dutch and British Drawings from the Courtauld Collections* by Dennis Farr and William Bradford and *The Art of Drawing in France 1400–1900: Master Drawings from the Nationalmuseum in Stockholm* by Per Bjurström. Last year we published *Creative Copies: Interpretative Drawings from Michelangelo to Picasso* by Egbert Haverkamp-Begemann.

The appearance of this book has been a particularly happy event for The Drawing Center. The drawings and projects of Inigo Jones are landmarks in the history of architecture. The intelligence of the hand

and eye of this master cannot fail to captivate the imagination four centuries later. Thanks to John Harris and Gordon Higgott, who have brilliantly gathered together these drawings and discerningly written about them, stage designers, architects, city planners and all the rest of us now find the work of Inigo Jones easier to appreciate. The Drawing Center would like to extend its gratitude to the lenders of the drawings used in this book and exhibition and echoes the sentiments expressed by the authors in their acknowledgements.

Two people have made this exhibition and book possible. I would like to thank them here: Mrs Henry J. Heinz, II and Mrs Walter N. Thayer. Mrs Walter N. Thayer deserves double thanks. As Chairman of the Board, she brings a grace and quiet efficiency to all the efforts of The Drawing Center – from the visiting schools programme, to college and graduate school internships and conservation workshops. It is a pleasure to be with her. Gratitude goes to the entire Board for their day-to-day support: Michael Iovenko, Co-Chairman; Mrs Felix G. Rohatyn, Vice-Chairman; Dita Amory; James M. Clark, Jr.; Mrs Colin Draper; Colin Eisler; Werner H. Kramarsky; Abby Leigh; William S. Lieberman; Mrs Gregor W. Medinger; and Edward H. Tuck.

Members of the Advisory Board whom I would like to thank are Egbert Haverkamp-Begemann, John Langeloth, Loeb Professor of the History of Art at the Institute of Fine Arts, New York University; Per Bjurström, Director of the Nationalmuseum of Stockholm, Dennis Farr, Director of the Courtauld Galleries, John Harris, former Keeper of the Royal Institute of British Architects, C. Michael Kauffmann, Director of the Courtauld Institute, Giandomenico Romanelli, Director of the Civic Museums of Venice and Pierre Rosenberg, Conservateur en Chef, Louvre.

Special thanks go to my colleagues: Meryl Cohen, Registrar; Peter Gilmore, Director of Operations; Joanne Maynard, Administrative Assistant and Fraser Mooney, Director of Development.

A personal note of thanks goes to Sir Colin Marshall, John Lampl, Lilla Santullo and the many members of the cargo crew and flight personnel of British Airways who have handled the shipping of very fragile drawings from all over the world and the travel of couriers with skill, resourcefulness and unfailing courtesy.

Finally, I would like to thank the following people who helped in innumerable ways: Kahren Arbitman, David Bancroft, John Barelli, Michael Beirut, Huntington T. Block, Margaret Holben Ellis, Nadine Grabania, Laura Hillyer, Anne Jackson, Jane Bennett, Heather Jones, Michael A. McCarthy, DeCourcy E. McIntosh, Richard Oldenburg, Andrew Oliver, Richard Pribnow, Felix G. Rohatyn, Joe Saunders, Walter N. Thayer, Joline Tyhach, Lella and Massimo Vignelli, Alice Martin Whelihan, and Philip Wilson.

Martha Beck, Director

Preface

John Harris

Upon reflection it is extraordinary that there has been no comprehensive exhibition of the architectural drawings of Inigo Jones. A few were exhibited at the Royal Institute of British Architects at the tercentenary celebration of Jones's death in 1952, and more in the quatercentenary exhibition of Jones's birth – *The King's Arcadia: Inigo Jones and the Stuart Court* – in 1973. However, there have been cogent reasons for this omission, not the least that the drawings at Worcester College, Oxford, have been bound in two massive volumes, and only now are being disbound. Of course, it has been quite another matter with the masque designs. The first major exhibition of masque designs occurred at Chatsworth in the summers of 1965 and 1966, followed by *Festival designs by Inigo Jones*, circulated in the USA in 1967–8. The imprimatur to Jones as one of the greatest of all European festival designers was bestowed by Stephen Orgel and Roy Strong in their magisterial *Inigo Jones. The Theatre of the Stuart Court* in 1973. Not surprisingly, the festival designs have been more alluring than those for architecture as a subject for exhibition, although I suspect that the exhibition in 1967 can be seen as representative of that burgeoning of interest in stage and theatre design that reached a peak in the USA around 1970, and dropped away thereafter.

It has been quite different with architectural drawings. As a subject for study and presentation in exhibitions, it belongs to the 1970s and 1980s. Jones's drawings at the Royal Institute of British Architects were only published as a fully illustrated catalogue in 1972, and the Worcester College catalogue in 1979 was only a partial illustrated survey due to a publisher's decision. This growing study of architectural drawings can be seen as a corollary to the recognition of architectural history as a professional discipline. The focus of interest in architectural drawings is now astonishing, and the better for that.

In the past, an architectural drawing has been studied in three ways: for its aesthetic merit (the Old Master syndrome of colour and prettiness), for the building for which it was drawn, or as a representation of the drafting style of the architect. Unlike Old Master drawings, the non-specialist finds great difficulty in understanding architectural drawings, especially the changes in convention and the technical advances in drawing. Now each new generation brings new eyes that observe in wider and wider circles of comprehension (the stone in the pond analogy) with vision denied to earlier commentators. Had he lived, the great Rudi Wittkower would have readily acknowledged that in 1953 he had made demonstration with a design for a gateway that we now accept as not by Jones; and I now admit that in 1979 I catalogued Jones's designs for a theatre as of *c.* 1617 rather than twenty years later (cat. nos 91, 92). There is ample virtue in learning from one's mistakes.

What is happening to the study of architectural drawings is uncommonly interesting. Firstly, we are understanding office practice better; for example, the recognition that almost every major scenographic design by the Bibiena family is the product of at least three hands, or that nearly all the finely finished designs by Robert Adam are worked upon and coloured by others. Studies such as those by Professor Howard Burns of Palladio's drawings take account of paper, watermarks, handwriting, and the scientific study of the effect of drawing instruments on paper. This is transforming old-fashioned connoisseurship. Indeed, I believe this scientific approach to dating drawings and authenticating hand is being pioneered by architectural rather than art historians at the present time.

This historical exegis is necessary to introduce my young collaborator in this exhibition and catalogue, Dr Gordon Higgott. He belongs to that new generation of historians who can see Jones's drawings with added vision, born of a study of handwriting and drafting techniques. Thus is he able to interpret better the language of Jones's architecture.

Nevertheless, at the end of the day, with the drawing by the great master in front of one, what is surely important is that it raises the spirit, and this Gordon Higgott readily acknowledges. I will be bold to state that few exhibitions of drawings by one architect raise the spirit more than this, organised by The Drawing Center in New York. Out of ninety-three authenticated architectural drawings, no less than eighty-two are being exhibited. They confirm Horace Walpole's percipient remark of Jones that 'Vitruvius drew up his Grammar, Palladio showed him the practice, and Rome displayed a theatre worthy of his emulation'.

Acknowledgements

The authors would like to thank the trustees of the collections and those curators and librarians whose generous cooperation has made this catalogue possible: the British Architectural Library Drawings Collection, Royal Institute of British Architects, London – Jill Lever and Jane Preger; The Provost and Fellows of Worcester College, Oxford – Lesley Le Claire and David Landau; The Duke of Devonshire and the Trustees of the Chatsworth Settlement – Peter Day and Michael Pearman; The Visitors of the Ashmolean Museum, Oxford – Christopher White, Nicholas Penny and David Blayney Brown; the Pierpont Morgan Library, New York – Charles E. Pierce, Jnr., William Robinson and Cara Denison. Jane Preger and Lesley Le Claire have borne a particularly heavy burden of administrative work, for which we are greatly indebted, and the Duke of Devonshire and Peter Day have been exceptionally accommodating with many, often last-minute requests.

Warm thanks go to John Newman for much invaluable criticism of the Ph.D. research embodied in this catalogue, and to Howard Colvin and Peter Draper for many helpful and corrective comments. Among those to whom we are grateful for information or advice are Howard Burns, Edward Chaney, Kate Colleran (who restored the Worcester College drawings), Paul Davies, Lynda Fairbairn, David Hemsoll, David Hibler, Pamela Kingsbury, John Peacock (who has also contributed to the catalogue), Barbara E. Shapiro, Cinzia Sicca, Sir Roy Strong, Ruby Reid Thompson and Robert Williams. Perhaps our profoundest debt is to Howard Colvin and Sir John Summerson, whose masterly documentation of Inigo Jones's works and career in *The History of the King's Works*, has been of inestimable value. We would like to thank our meticulous editor, Charlotte Burri, and our indexer, Alice Mackrell. Geoffrey Fisher and his colleagues at the Conway photographic library, Courtauld Institute of Art, have been extremely helpful throughout.

We offer our sincere thanks to The Drawing Center for its enthusiastic support of the catalogue and exhibition. Our families also deserve recognition for their forbearance and their help in creating time for research; especially Gordon's wife, Suzanne, who has also offered much constructive criticism of the text.

Note to the Catalogue

The catalogue entries are divided into technical description and commentary. All technical descriptions were prepared by Gordon Higgott from first-hand study of the drawings in 1987–8. They give the known or approximate date of the drawing, the media and implement marks, the maximum dimensions of the sheet (height before width), together with any peculiarities in the make-up or appearance of the sheet, a brief description of the watermark (and countermark if shown) giving place of origin if known, handwritten inscriptions on both *recto* and *verso* of the sheet with media and authorship, the scale on the drawing (if marked, and in feet to inches, since Jones appears to have used an inch rule), the abbreviated name of the owning institution and the published catalogue or accession number, and finally a brief and essential bibliography which does not repeat the published catalogue reference above. The authors would like to acknowledge Mrs Ruby Reid Thompson, currently researching on 17th-century musical manuscripts at Cambridge University, for her help in providing descriptions of some of the watermarks and information on the origin of much of Jones's paper. She has also supplied the first published technical description of Jones's Roman Sketchbook (cat. no. 99).

The commentaries on drawings seek to establish secure dates and, where possible, attributions for all Jones's architectural drawings, and the catalogue is the first attempt at a complete chronology of these drawings. Entries are arranged by period, by theme and by individual building. Those drawings not shown in the Drawing Center exhibition are catalogued in the Appendix in chronological order. Many commentaries were jointly authored, others individually by John Harris or Gordon Higgott. The latter's Ph.D. thesis, 'The architectural drawings of Inigo Jones: attribution, dating and analysis' (London University, 1987), is the source for many revised datings, reattributions and reassessments published here for the first time (cat. nos 9, 14, 15, 20, 24, 25, 32, 39, 40–3, 46, 48–50, 57, 58, 62, 68, 78, 86–92, 114–16, 118, 122). The authors would like to repeat their acknowledgements to John Peacock for his major essay on Jones's figurative designs and his entry on the Roman Sketchbook, and to Howard Colvin for his commentary on cat. no. 123.

Anthony van Dyck. Portrait of Inigo Jones, *c.* 1640. Black chalk.
242 × 198 mm (ex catalogue)

Inigo Jones: Universal Man

John Harris

It may seem extravagant to propose that Jones is perhaps the single most important person in the history of the arts in seventeenth-century England; but this is so. He was a luminary, a meteor in a Court (of Charles I and Henrietta Maria) which was recognized as brilliant and cultured, until destroyed by the Civil War. Jones was painter, architect, festival designer, masque-maker, antiquarian, military engineer and collector. Indeed, he was a true *uomo universale* in the Renaissance mould, and perhaps the only man in England who could so be described.

Yet he is a mysterious figure, as mysterious as Shakespeare, whom he would have known. It is sometimes forgotten that these two geniuses were contemporaries, and that Jones was brought up an Elizabethan. The quality of genius must feature in any assessment of Jones, and this quality is as elusive and difficult to grasp as it is difficult to comprehend Jones. He was unique in his time, a giant in all things, and possessed an intellect rare even in continental Europe.

Jones's early life is shrouded in mystery, apart from his baptism on 19 July 1573. There are many legends about his upbringing. His father would seem to have been a clothworker of but moderate wealth, probably residing in Smithfield in the City of London. Jones's father died in 1597 when living near St Benet's, Paul's Wharf, where Jones would himself be buried. Apart from this, we know nothing more until the description of Jones as a 'picture-maker', that is, probably a painter of easel pictures, in the accounts of the 5th Earl of Rutland on 28 June 1603, where he is paid £10 for his 'paynes'. We now know that this payment immediately preceded the Earl's departure for Copenhagen to deliver the Order of the Garter to Christian IV of Denmark, Queen Anne of Denmark's brother. Jones was in his retinue and is mentioned as being at a dinner in Copenhagen. It is likely that he was present as a masque-maker.

A reference to Jones in 1605 as a 'great travellor', must not only refer to the voyage to Denmark, but to the years of travel in Italy following his father's death. Circumstantial evidence suggests that he left London in 1598 in the company of Francis Manners, Lord Roos, brother of the 5th Earl of Rutland. Their route took them through France, on to Germany and entertainments at the Courts of the Emperor Matthias and the Archduke Ferdinand, and then to Italy, where Jones may have spent five years. The death of Queen Elizabeth I on 24 March 1603 was an event that brought courtiers scurrying home to England.

We can only speculate on the reasons for Jones's travels and why this humble born 'painter' should have merited such exclusive treatment and patronage. In Italy he may have attached himself to the circles of Henry Wotton in Venice, and perhaps also to those of the homosexual dandified Earls of Essex and Southampton. Even if Jones's genius were apparent this early, he would have required powerful friendships to permit him to spend so long in Italy; it might be suggested then that Jones participated in an intimate relationship with his patrons.

A mystery that may never be solved is what artistic works Jones produced during the fourteen years, from the age of say seventeen, to *The Masque of Blacknesse* in 1604. Perhaps the reference to 'picture-maker' must be treated with caution, for it is surely significant that after 1604 not one work in oil can be associated with him. As for Italy, we can only speculate that Jones familiarized himself with the festivals and architecture of Bernardo Buontalenti at the Medici Court in Florence, and had discovered his love for the Italian Mannerist painters, such as Carracci, Parmigianino, and Schiavone.

If not a portrait painter of the conventional sort, Jones must surely have gone to Denmark to superintend, if not design, a Court spectacle. This fits in with preparations for Queen Anne of Denmark's *Masque of Blacknesse*, on which Jones was working in November and December 1603. As Orgel and Strong demonstrate, although Jones was not innovative in the masques of 1604–05, he was in the vanguard of the most advanced traditional techniques, such as concentrating the setting on a stage at one end of a hall. There was no turning machine, or *machina versatilis*, until the masque *Hymenaei* in 1606, when a proscenium arch to frame the scene is also first introduced. Two years later, Jones used a *scena ductilis*, or pair of painted shutters drawn back so as to reveal the hidden main scene, fully developed with *Oberon, The Fairy Prince* in 1611 (cat. nos 7, 8). In other words, Jones did not return from Italy fully versed in the latest Florentine or Parisian stage techniques. He was learning, and this only amplifies the enigma as to what he did produce in Italy before 1603. However, more important than any other aspect of masque design in England at this time, is the integration between Ben Jonson's text and Jones's spectacle. This was innovative, and lasted until poet and designer argued and fell out in the dispute as to whom credit for the success of the masque should be given.

So much for the masque designer, but where is Jones the architect in genesis? Of course, he is not yet an architect in the sense of being identified with a body of executed work. The designs for the Exchange in the Strand and for old St Paul's Cathedral in 1608 are the first evidence we have for his pretensions to be one (cat. nos 3, 4). Significantly, the patron for both was the Lord Treasurer, Robert Cecil, 1st Earl of Salisbury. If Cecil saw Jones's worth as an architect, so may the Earl of Arundel at this time. A precious clue to Jones's emerging role as an architect is the archway for the entertainment presented by Lord Salisbury to James I in May 1608 (fig. 2). Small it may be, but the arch is a pure piece of Italianate design of a sort rare in England, and in style not unlike Buontalenti's. Even then Cecil must have been regretting the huge, old-fashioned house that he had been building at Hatfield, Hertfordshire, since 1607. Hatfield represented the Establishment interest, and one suspects that already Jones had arrogantly made evident his superiority in design and intellect. He may have demonstrated his prowess to Cecil with the beautiful design for a stable (cat. no. 9) that would not look out of place at Fontainebleau.

As architect 'Mr Inico Joanes' came into his own when listed in May 1610 as Surveyor of the Works to Henry, Prince of Wales. Here for the first time his name is associated with an office that he would come to dominate for thirty years. This appointment may have boded well for Jones if that sad and brilliant Prince had not suddenly died in November 1612. In fact, it is difficult to associate Jones with any work for the Prince. There is mention of an ostrich house and buttery, and the fitting-up of a library and gallery at St James's Palace, but even these cannot unequivocally be given to Jones, as the bills were signed by Simon Basil, the Royal Surveyor. There is also some evidence that Jones had a competitor in Prince Henry's service in Constantino de Servi, a Florentine architect from the Medici Court who was in charge of considerable garden works at Richmond Palace undertaken with Salomon de Caus, the grotto and garden specialist.

Despite the opposition, Jones would triumph, and in the masques and entertainments enacted for the Prince, architecture was beginning to play a major role. There were numerous tilts and pageants, *Prince Henry's Barriers* (performed in January 1610), *Tethys' Festival* in June 1610, *Oberon, The Fairy Prince* in January 1611 and, barely a month later, *Love Freed from Ignorance and Folly* for Queen Anne of Denmark. The architectural episodes are of textbook or engraved derivation; not yet of pure invention.

The Prince's death caused havoc and grief, with focus upon Prince Charles as heir-apparent. There were still two masques to design associated with the tragic Prince: *The Lords' Masque*, performed in the Banqueting House on 14 February, 1613, and *The Middle Temple and Lincoln's Inn Masque* on the following day, but in the Great Hall of Whitehall Palace. Both commemorated the marriage of the Princess Elizabeth, Prince Henry's sister, to Frederick V, the Elector Palatine of the Rhine in 1613. It was on the *Middle Temple Masque* that its author, George Chapman, applauded Jones as 'our kingdom's most art-full and ingenious architect'. Alas that no drawings survive for this masque to display its architectural effects. Nevertheless, there was more to Chapman's comment than just eulogy, for on 27 April 1613 Jones was officially granted the reversion to the office of Surveyor of the King's Works to succeed the aging Simon Basil. By this time Jones was not in England, for he was accompanying the newly-wed royal couple to their castle at Heidelberg. With him was the Earl of Arundel, and both were ready for an extended tour of Italy which would last twenty-one months and have resounding effects upon the progress of the arts and architecture in Stuart England.

For both Arundel and Jones their travels in Italy were a shared education in antiquity, architecture and all the arts associated with connoisseurship and collecting. If Horace Walpole characterized Arundel as the 'Father of Virtu' in England, by association, Jones was its uncle. Their experiences in Heidelberg should not be discounted. Its castle incorporated some of the most impressive architecture of the northern Renaissance, and Jones must have been privy to the building of Princess Elizabeth's new wing, later significantly called the 'Englischer Bau'. It had probably been begun late in 1612 with one façade spanned by a giant order embracing an arcuated system of superimposed arches, worthy of Nicholas Hawksmoor, and the other the first example of a pure Palladian style north of the Alps. Long will controversy rage as to whether Jones influenced this design and the building of a court theatre in the adjacent tower. We can only speculate if Arundel and Jones made a detour, from, or on the way to Strasbourg, to see something of the remarkable Serlian architecture of Elias Holl and Joseph Heinz in Augsburg. Heinz's reputation as a painter-architect in the mould of Jones, and one admiring Palladio, might have reached Jones's ears in Heidelberg. However, all this is speculation and, after Strasbourg and Basle, the travellers arrived in Milan in the summer of 1613. Then came Venice and Vicenza, Padua and Florence, and they entered Rome in January 1614. The Italian tour might have lasted longer had Arundel's uncle, the Earl of Northampton, not suddenly died, obliging Arundel and Jones to journey back to London. Arundel was ill in Genoa, but that delay enabled Jones to pay one more visit to the Veneto, where he made that miraculous purchase of Palladio's drawings. He neither could have imagined what a shattering effect these would have upon the Palladian architecture in early eighteenth-century England, nor that through their association with his drawings, his own work would be discovered and catalogued by Lord Burlington.

In November 1614 both paid their respects to King James at Whitehall Palace. Jones would never again leave England's shores, but the travels were enough, for they had opened his eyes to a whole range of architecture, from Roman antiquity to the Mannerism of Florence and Bologna, and to Palladio and Scamozzi. He was now ready to be the British Vitruvius and to remake the old-fashioned Court architecture. His mind had become a huge and richly endowed resource out of which would emerge an architecture that can only be described as 'Jonesian'. It is doubtful if the subordinates in the Office of the Surveyor of the King's Works had the remotest idea of what would hit them. Their Jacobean world would be turned upside down.

Although Jones's achievement as the Royal Surveyor or chief architect to the Stuart Court is divisible between the two reigns of James I and Charles I, it was a continuous task, the later reign differing from the earlier by an increasing dependence on antique sources as well as a variety of eclectic ones, not the least due to the French influences brought to bear by Queen Henrietta Maria from her homeland. What is astonishing about the task as a whole is Jones's single-handed dedication to it, necessary because there was no-one in the 1620s capable of accepting design responsibility. Jones's architecture was simply incomprehensible to his colleagues during the period from 1615 until nearly 1630. Two examples may demonstrate the truth of this: in 1623, the year Jones designed the Queen's Chapel at St James's Palace, Thomas Baldwin, his Comptroller and principal under-officer, built Bray Hospital, Berkshire, as if Palladio or Serlio had never existed; or in 1638, the year Jones designed that minimal house for Lord

Maltravers (cat. nos 84, 85), Nicholas Stone, responsible for the masonry of the Banqueting House in Whitehall, built the north front of Kirby Hall, Northamptonshire, in a northern Mannerist style boasting no less than ten different window openings (fig. 95). Thus was the Surveyor an elevated figure who might just as well have been speaking a foreign language for all that his subordinates understood. This must be stressed time and time again, for we can look in vain for any work outside that for the Court by one of these subordinates that could even remotely be called Jonesian. One of the real distinctions to be made between Jones in 1615 and his colleagues, was their inability to read Palladio intelligently, and to draw on paper a building which is harmonious and rational from top to bottom and from back to front.

Jones's espousal of Palladio was related more to *I Quattro libri dell' architettura* than with the buildings themselves. His real achievement was to recognize in Book IV of Roman antiquity a grammar for the ornamental part of interior decoration, and to apply it rigorously to his designs from as early as 1619. In this it must be said cautiously that he was alone in Europe. For example, neither Palladio nor Scamozzi used Roman ornament so consistently, and no architects in the coming century seem to have responded to ancient Rome as did Jones. Indeed, it would be left to Lord Burlington to rediscover this neo-classical aspect of Jones's invention and to apply it to his own designs. It may well be as much for this, as for the Roman portico of old St Paul's Cathedral, that Webb called Jones the British Vitruvius.

Because Colen Campbell bracketed Jones with Palladio in his eulogistic introduction to *Vitruvius Britannicus* in 1715, Jones has been consistently seen as a Palladian. This is true to the extent that no one else in his time north of the Alps designed an architecture so generically Palladian. Nevertheless, neither the astylar design for the Prince's Lodging at Newmarket (cat. no. 31), nor the Banqueting House, nor the Queen's Chapel at St James's Palace, nor the Queen's House at Greenwich, would sit happily in a Vicentine situation. This is a mark of Jones's invention. Even when he uses Palladio's ratios, exterior elements, and ornament, the result is something quite alien to Palladio. This can be demonstrated by the houses for Sir Peter Killigrew (fig. 108) and Lord Maltravers, that Palladio would not recognize as Palladian, yet are quite alien to anything else in Europe. Indeed, they must be described as quintessentially English, even if peculiar to Jones alone, because of their plainness and simplicity of ornament. It is as if Jones had searched through and sifted the architecture of the Renaissance and the Renaissance textbooks, and then produced an architecture which can only be called Jonesian. Few architects achieved this level, this genius of invention.

So far in this introduction nothing has been said about Jones's draftsmanship, nor the character of his drawing. That pregnant comment in 1655, retold in 1665 by John Webb in *A Vindication of Stone-Heng Restored* (p. 11), that 'in designing with his Pen (as Sir *Anthony Vandike* used to say) not to be equalled by whatever great Masters in his Time, for *Boldness*, *Softness*, *Sweetness*, and *Sureness of his Touches*' could just as well refer to the delicate colour-washed masque designs, as to such masterpieces of orthography as the elevations for the Prince's Lodging at Newmarket Palace. Architectural drawing in Britain before 1604 was crude, as demonstrated by designs by the great Robert Smythson or John Thorpe. So often perspective was misunderstood, and wash, when used, applied without care for the containment of the lines; or the joining of one line to another is careless. There is also something else: like a figure study by a great artist, Jones's elevations when given body colour, are rendered with a feeling for the volume behind the façade. Thus does Jones think volumetrically, and for England in the later years of the Jacobean Court this was quite unknown. Of course, all this was accepted as part of the normal training of an Italian architect in the Renaissance. Jones recognized this, and brought the practice into this country.

The Surveyorship of the Office of Works was only one facet of Jones's achievement. His was a powerful voice on many official building commissions, and his role as an *éminence grise* may be detected behind the reformation of street architecture typified by the giant pilaster fronts of Great Queen Street and Lincoln's Inn Fields. Likewise, he must have played a leading role in the development of the Earl of Bedford's Covent Garden and the placing of the church of St Paul there. Although no designs by Jones survive for this pioneering example of urban planning, and both Isaac de Caus and Edward Carter were acting for Lord Bedford, Jones excercised a disciplined grip upon the design of the piazza, if not the exit streets with their many-gabled and balconied façades (figs 54, 91).

The primitive Tuscan or Vitruvian church of Covent Garden is a reminder of that other great Vitruvian work building through the early 1630s: the restoration of old St Paul's Cathedral. Jones responded to the great Romanesque nave by wrapping it up in ancient Roman costume, with ornamental cladding in the guise of rustication based upon Hieronymous Cock's engravings of the Baths of Diocletian and prefacing the whole by a noble Roman Corinthian portico based upon Palladio's reconstruction of the portico of the Temple of Venus and Rome in his Book IV (figs 75–8). It was as grand as the Pantheon's, grander than any other portico north of the Alps, and perhaps even the noblest of any Renaissance porticoes. It wasn't for nothing that his portico featured on Jones's tomb in St Benet's, Paul's Wharf.

That Jones was able to achieve all this is staggering. As a masque-maker alone, the equivalent of Buontalenti or Parigi at the Medici Court, or Antoine Caron at the Valois, his 450 surviving designs are only a fraction of what was required for the more than thirty masques and entertainments designed from 1605 to 1640. As Royal Surveyor, his Declared Accounts deal with nearly fifty works, to which must be added the urban commissions, St Paul's Cathedral, and at least fifteen private works. All were due to Jones and Jones alone, although from 1628 he had the help of John Webb as his personal assistant and sometimes clerk of works. Nevertheless, there is no evidence that he ever deputed to Webb anything more than minor jobs. In this execution of a monocracy we sense that Jones was a solitary, and of course solitude often accompanies genius. Despite the splendour and intellectual stature of the Court of Charles I and his Queen, one suspects that Jones stood head and shoulders above that courtly world as something of everything: a passionate collector of prints (Mariette remarked on his prints by Schiavone); a delicate judge of sculpture; a connoisseur who must have advised on the new 'cabinets' of Buckingham, Arundel, Pembroke, and the King; an antiquarian deputed by James I to unravel the mysteries of Stonehenge; and one whose drawings as works of art would not be surpassed until the great age of English architectural draftsmanship in the middle of the eighteenth century. Such was this extraordinary man, son of a humble clothworker, who was ignominously bundled away from the siege of Basing Castle in 1645, wrapped in a blanket.

1 Self-portrait of the architect and (on attached sheet below) sketch for cartouche with putti and (on *verso* of upper sheet) sketch of figure with hounds

c. 1620; the lower sheet late 1630s

Pen and brown ink

303 × 138 mm. In two attached sheets, with 4 mm overlap. Upper sheet is 163 × 137 mm, including 4 mm border added later; lower sheet is 143 × 138 mm

Watermark (on upper sheet): water-pot (top half cut off)

Inscribed by later hand in pen and brown ink, in right-hand corner of upper sheet border: *I*; and on *verso* of upper sheet by John Talman in pen and brown ink (upside down): 252: ♡ :

RIBA Jones & Webb 1

Fig. 1
Verso drawing of cat. no. 1, showing Diana the huntress(?), later 1630s

Jones wears a falling ruff of *c.* 1620 and a lace-edged nightcap, two garments seen on a portrait of the Duke of Richmond dated 1618–23 by Daniel Mytens. The loosely handled pen shading in unevenly spaced, hooked and scribbled lines belongs to Jones's early maturity as an architect, from about 1617 to 1620 (cf. cat. nos 18, 38). If drawn about 1620 Jones would have been fifty-seven, an indication that with the Banqueting House then building he had reached a plateau in his career. A more fluidly drawn, but rougher and perhaps more spontaneous self-portrait, also *c.* 1620, is at Chatsworth (Drawings VII, fol. 7*r.*) together with a third, dating slightly later, on a sheet with two head studies.

The cartouche is probably the centre-piece for a proscenium arch and belongs to the later 1630s, when Jones's figure drawing has a surer sense of anatomy and movement, and his pen shading is in thick, regularly slanted lines. The *verso* drawing (fig. 1) showing a female figure directing hounds, is presumably a study of Diana the huntress, and is similar in handling to Jones's masque designs of *c.* 1635–40.

Bibliography:
King's Arcadia, pp. 210–13

Provenance of Inigo Jones's Drawings

John Harris and Gordon Higgott

When Inigo Jones died in 1652 his drawings were part of a much larger corpus which he had amassed during his service to James I and Charles I as designer of Court masques and architect of the royal works. His collection included more than 250 architectural drawings by Palladio and his studio, acquired between 1612 and 1614,[1] at least 450 designs for stage costume and scenery, many hundreds of sheets of figurative sketches, and the ninety-three architectural drawings that have come down to us today. Many more final designs for major buildings such as the Banqueting House, the Prince's Lodging, Newmarket Palace, the Queen's House and the royal chapels at St James's Palace and Somerset House, must have existed, but were either consumed in the building process or destroyed during the Protectorate; although some, such as the final design for the west front of St Paul's Cathedral, survived into the eighteenth century to be copied by Henry Flitcroft for publication in William Kent's *The Designs of Inigo Jones* in 1727 (fig. 78).

Jones's executor and the principal benefactor of his will was his former assistant in the Office of Works, John Webb. Although there is no reference to the drawings in Jones's will, dated 22 July 1650,[2] we can safely assume that Webb inherited the entire collection because he added many hundreds of his own drawings to the corpus and these are found side by side with Jones's drawings in each of the four major holdings: the Royal Institute of British Architects in London, Worcester College and the Ashmolean Museum in Oxford, and Chatsworth House, Derbyshire.

The dispersal of the collection began after Webb's death in 1672, when he bequeathed his library and all his 'Prints and Cutts and drawings of Architecture' to his son William, with the proviso that nothing should be dispersed. Within a few years William died and his widow disregarded the stipulation. John Aubrey, writing in about 1682, recorded that all Inigo Jones's 'papers and designes, not only of St. Paul's Cathedral etc., and the Banqueting House, but his designe of all Whitehall'[3] were in the possession of John Oliver, a City Surveyor and Master in the Office of Works. Oliver seems to have acquired the bulk of Jones's Office of Works designs together with a large number in the hand of John Webb. This group appears to have passed from Oliver to William Talman. This may have occurred before Oliver's death in 1701 because there are Palladian episodes in some of Talman's designs for a Trianon at Hampton Court at the RIBA, for which the accepted scheme was made before September 1699. Meanwhile a second, smaller group of drawings by Jones and Webb, together with most of their library, passed by a different route to Dr George Clarke in Oxford, sometime in the first decade of the eighteenth century. Clarke may have bought the drawings through an intermediary such as Michael Burghers, who in 1694 noted his ownership on Jones's copy of Palladio's *I Quattro libri*, now at Worcester College.[4]

Clarke bequeathed his part of the Jones-Webb collection to Worcester College Library on his death in 1736. The nineteen architectural drawings which can be firmly attributed to Jones in this collection include a higher proportion of private house designs than among the drawings now divided between the RIBA and Chatsworth. There are also several drawings close in style to those of John Webb (e.g. cat. nos 86, 91, 92), whose own drawings at Worcester College vastly outnumber those by Jones. Possibly Clarke acquired a residue of Jones's Office of Works drawings (among them some overlooked because they resembled Webb's), along with the group of house designs which had been passed on to Webb in a separate batch. Also in the Worcester College Collection are some 130 small figurative drawings by Jones. These were probably cut from larger sheets by John Webb, and are now mounted in groups (cat. nos 100–13).

The larger part of Jones's collection passed from William Talman to his son, John, and it was he who catalogued many of the sheets with a system of numbers and code marks, of which the commonest among the architectural drawings of Jones and Palladio is 54: ⊩ :(e.g. cat. nos 11, 30, 31, 33, 34).[5] The next documented stage in the history of the collection occurs in 1720 and 1721 when John Talman, following his father's death in 1719, sold two lots of drawings to Lord Burlington, the first, 'a Book of Designs & Plains &c. by Inigo Jones' on 4 May 1720, and the second, 'a Parcell of Architectonicall Designs and Drawings by Palladio' on 7 April the next year.[6] Burlington made further substantial purchases of Jones drawings in the 1720s. The masque drawings had passed from John Talman to Elihu Yale (1648–1721), a magpie collector who had been governor of Fort St George, Madras, and almost all these came to Burlington in January 1723.[7] Burlington's collection at Chatsworth also includes two bound volumes of figurative drawings, the smaller of which, comprising about 260 cuttings compiled by John Webb, is inscribed on the flyleaf, 'Burlington May 5 1728'. The larger volume contains about 1,400 sketches by Inigo Jones (e.g. cat. no. 124), and some twenty figurative drawings by Italian, French and Netherlandish hands which must have come from Jones's collection.

Burlington was responsible for mounting and binding the drawings into folio volumes. His distinctive mark of collection is double red ruled border lines around the edges of the sheet or mount (e.g. cat. nos 9, 90). When he died in 1754 his collection passed into the Devonshire family at Chatsworth through his daughter Charlotte, who had married the 4th Duke. Greatly expanded by Burlington's own drawings, by those of followers such as William Kent, Isaac Ware and Henry Flitcroft, and by a further sixty Palladio drawings acquired by Burlington in Italy in 1719, the collection remained intact until 1894, when most of the architectural drawings were given 'in Trust' to the Royal Institute of British Architects in London. Sixty-five of Inigo Jones's architectural drawings, together with seventeen bound volumes of Palladio drawings and several hundred designs by Webb came into the RIBA Library, and within a few years the first modern scholars on Jones, J. Alfred Gotch and W. Grant Keith, had begun work attributing designs and cataloguing the collection. Chatsworth retained two of Jones's Banqueting House designs (cat. nos 33, 34), almost all the masque drawings and scores of John Webb's designs for Whitehall Palace. Among this holding are four further architectural drawings by Inigo Jones (cat. nos 22, 67, 117, 124).

It was W. Grant Keith who, in 1913, published a further set of Inigo Jones drawings discovered at the Radcliffe Library in Oxford.[8] These three drawings (cat. nos 57, 58, 71) are now in the Ashmolean Museum, Oxford, and were originally in a volume of ceiling and decorative designs by Jean Cotelle the Elder and others which the architect James Gibbs had acquired from John Talman. Gibbs probably bought the volume in the sale of Talman's collection after 1726 and he bequeathed it with the bulk of his collection to the Radcliffe Library in 1754.

Notes

1. See W. G. Keith, 'Inigo Jones as a collector', *RIBA Journal*, xxxiii (1925), pp. 94–108. Keith drew attention to notes in the lower margins of thirty-five pages of Jones's copy of *I Quattro libri* indicating that Jones had either seen or possessed Palladio's original drawings for the woodcuts of those pages. It is now realized that these drawings must have been acquired as early as 1612. The notes are in a style of handwriting predating Jones's Italian visit of 1613–14, and they contain references to Sir Henry Wotton who returned to England from his post as ambassador in Venice in 1612 and went back to Italy in 1616. Jones acquired the remainder of his Palladio collection in Italy in 1613–14, either from Palladio's sons, Silla and Marcantonio in Vicenza or from Giacomo Contarini in Venice (see D. Lewis, *The Drawings of Andrea Palladio*, pp. 7–9)
2. Probate Registers of the Provincial Court of Canterbury (now in PRO) 227 Bowyer. See *King's Works*, iii, p. 159, and J. Orrell, *The Theatres of Inigo Jones and John Webb* (Cambridge, 1985), pp. 17–18
3. J. Aubrey, *Brief Lives*, ed. A. Clarke (2 vols, Oxford, 1898), ii, p. 10
4. See B. Allsopp (ed.), *Inigo Jones on Palladio* (2 vols, Newcastle upon Tyne, 1970) [facsimile and transcription of Inigo Jones's annotated copy of Palladio's *I Quattro libri*], ii, 3rd flyleaf
5. The marks have never been fully analyzed. They were first discussed by W. Grant Keith in 'Inigo Jones as a collector', but Keith assumed they were in Webb's hand. See also P. Fraser and J. Harris, 'A Catalogue of the drawings by Inigo Jones (1573–1652), John Webb (1611–72) and Richard Boyle, 3rd Earl of Burlington (1694–1753) in the Burlington Devonshire Collection', RIBA typescript (1960), p. 86
6. Devonshire Collections, Chatsworth, 'Messrs Graham and Collier Joynt Accounts, June 23, 1719 to July 26, 1722'
7. O & S, i, pp. 29–30
8. W. G. Keith, 'Some hitherto unknown drawings by Inigo Jones', *Burlington Magazine*, xxii (1913), pp. 218–26

Style and Technique

Gordon Higgott

Inigo Jones was the first British architect for whom drawing was an essential medium for realizing ideas, as well as the means for communicating them attractively to patrons and subordinates. He was a self-taught architectural draftsman who came to the discipline as a figurative artist. This explains the freshness and vitality of all his architectural drawings and the remarkable stylistic development between the earliest designs of 1608, when Jones was still working chiefly as a stage designer, and the latest in the 1630s, when he had more than twenty years experience as Surveyor of the King's Works. An examination of this development is long overdue and will clarify the technical and stylistic qualities of the drawings.

In the early period from 1608 to 1613, Jones worked in a painterly manner, using heavy wash in several layers to convey effects of mass and volume (cat. nos 3, 4, 6, 9). Outlines are very tentative, the trembling straight lines betraying Jones's inexperience in the discipline of architectural drawing. He used his ruler only partially in this period, and on some drawings not at all. All four early architectural drawings have perspective features in the manner of the Elizabethan and Jacobean 'upright' drawings which combined a scaled frontal view of a building with elements shown in depth in a slanting view (e.g. fig. 25).

Jones's second tour of Italy from 1613 to 1614 transformed his architectural drawing method. He had already acquired some of Palladio's architectural drawings from Sir Henry Wotton, the English Ambassador in Venice who returned to London in 1612, but in Venice or Vicenza he bought many more, bringing the total in his possession to at least 250. Palladio had evolved a rational method of depicting a building on paper in which every feature was drawn to scale, without perspective aberrations. Many of his orthogonal drawings were published as woodcuts in *I Quattro libri* in 1570 and show plan, elevation and section juxtaposed on a single sheet. In this way all vertical, horizontal and receding parts could be understood, and their relationships to each other examined. During his tour of Italy Jones looked at Roman and modern buildings illustrated by Palladio in *I Quattro libri* and absorbed these conventions. His sketches and notes on the entrance hall to Palladio's Palazzo Thiene in Vicenza on a page in his own copy of the 1601 edition of *I Quattro libri* (fig. 13) show his understanding of the orthogonal methods and their value in elucidating visual and proportional relationships. He was also affected by the style and technique of Palladio's drawings, and in his first designs after returning from Italy we see a striking development over those of the previous decade. The signed and dated entrance-bay design of 1616 shows a strict elevational view in Palladio's manner, with all the main outlines ruler-drawn, and the wash evenly graded and subordinate to the outlines in the overall effect (cat. no. 21). Close dependence on Palladio is seen on the plan and façade designs for the Queen's House in 1616 at the RIBA (cat. nos 13–15). They embody such characteristic Palladio techniques as thorough under-scoring enhanced with graphite, and profiles of mouldings drawn with little freehand inset lines to join with the ruled horizontals of the moulding courses; indeed until quite recently both were mistakenly identified as Palladio originals. Jones also borrowed Palladio's conventions for showing the openings and staircases on plans and rusticated walling on elevations.

His own technique at this period was much bolder than Palladio's, less tidily handled, and not as sure in the freehand drawing. He took up the scoring implement with enthusiasm, using it, like Palladio, as the main under-drawing method on his finished designs. But where Palladio used a soft ebony or ivory stylus, Jones set out all his designs up to about 1619 with the sharp metal point of the dividers, which cut into the paper leaving dark traces in the wash (cat. nos 21, 28). The same heavy-handed technique characterizes Jones's pen drawing in the 1616–19 period. Lines were drawn with verve and great feeling for the strength of the outlines on the building itself, but uneven pen pressure and clumsy handling caused thickening, fading and overlapping of the outlines on the most meticulous presentation drawings before about 1620 (e.g. cat. no. 22). Wash was his favourite medium for shading in drawings of all types up to the end of the 1620s, but in this exploratory period he could not yet match Palladio's skill in grading the tones, and tended to lay on the wash too dry, creating a patchy and overworked effect (cat. nos 23, 40). His freshest and most vigorous drawings in the 1616–19 period are shaded in pen, a technique only employed by Palladio in a secondary way. Although the method is an untidy one, with much hooking and scribbling and uneven slanting and spacing of lines, it shows great sensitivity to the volume and texture of the façade (cat. no. 17).

A definite advance in Jones's style and technique inaugurates a third period in his draftsmanship from about 1620 to 1630. Drawings in this decade have firmer and cleaner pen outlines, a tidier scoring technique, and lighter, more smoothly handled wash than in the period from 1616 to 1619. Just as he developed a mastery of Palladian and Scamozzian sources in designs for Newmarket and the Banqueting House in 1619 (cat. nos 30–9), so his architectural drawing became more confident and fluent. In presentation designs for gateways in the early 1620s he was able to join up the ruled horizontals of moulding-courses neatly with the profiles, without need of the untidy freehand inset lines typical of the earlier period, and could draw tapering column shafts in cleanly ruled outlines (cat. nos 41, 42). Another technical advance was the adoption of a softer scoring implement with a rounded rather than sharp metal point. Scamozzi recommended an ivory or ebony tipped stylus for incised under-drawing in his treatise (*L'Idea della architettura universale* [Venice, 1615] Part I, p. 48), and it is significant that the first of Jones's drawings to show the broader indentations of this implement are Scamozzi-influenced elevations and plans for Newmarket Palace and the Banqueting House of 1619 (cat. nos 30, 33–

5). Although clear examples of the broader indentations of this type of stylus occur in the 1620s and 1630s, Jones continued to use the sharper point on the majority of drawings after 1619.

The 1620s also see changes in Jones's choice and handling of paper. Throughout his career Jones had access to a good-quality laid paper, thick and of creamy colour, which is often watermarked with a crested shield bearing a fleur-de-lys and ending in a '4WR' insignia. The '4WR' indicates Wendelin Riehel's mill in Strasbourg and is found on paper in England from the mid-sixteenth to the late eighteenth centuries. Among other watermarks on this type of paper is the Crozier of Basle ending in three spheres showing the initial 'D' for the Düring family mill in Basle. This exceptionally fine and rare paper was used by Jones for his two Banqueting House designs at Chatsworth and several other drawings (cat. nos 3, 33, 34, 52, 93). From the early 1620s, however, Jones began to use a poorer-quality paper, noticeably thinner than the first, more grainy in texture and often greyish in colour. The paper shows very clearly the close-set ridges left by the wires of the mould on which the paper was laid (cat. nos 44, 55, 84, 122). All visible watermarks on this paper consist of variants on a water-pot motif, often with a monogram, surmounted by a coronet, above which there is sometimes a crescent moon. This paper was of widespread origin in France and Italy and was very common in England from at least the early sixteenth century. Securely dated examples of the paper in Jones's work are all from 1622 onwards, with the exception of one drawing which is stylistically datable to *c.* 1617 (cat. no. 20).

It is significant that Jones turned to the poorer-quality paper at a time when he was becoming less concerned with meticulous 'presentation' effects. After the mid-1620s, far fewer presentation drawings survive than in the first half of Jones's career; there are many more sketches and preliminary drawings, and many final versions of his designs are not carried through to the last stage of elaboration (e.g. cat. nos 59, 86). He was also becoming more pragmatic in his handling of paper. He had been accustomed to folding the sheet vertically in the centre to establish a perpendicular on a single elevation (e.g. cat. no. 33), but in the mid-1620s he started to use the same technique to transfer the main points of the elevation to the plan by pricking through from one half of the sheet to the other, so that elevation and plan appear alongside each other rather than above and below (cat. no. 59). On two examples the elevation is on the *recto* and the plan on the *verso* of the folded paper (cat. nos 50, 55), a technique which did not lend itself to attractive display of the design.

The less tidy method of presentation from the mid-1620s is symptomatic of a change in Jones's attitude to architectural drawing in the second half of his Surveyorship. Having mastered the skills necessary to render a building accurately on paper, Jones increasingly viewed the drawing as a tool for realizing his ideas on paper rather than just as a medium for exhibiting the completed scheme to an interested patron. The change coincides with Queen Henrietta Maria's patronage of royal building and the complex interior decoration works at Somerset House from about 1626. Jones was now delegating many of the most sumptuous effects to experienced craftsmen such as Matthew Goodrich and Thomas de Critz, and was apparently trusted by both Henrietta Maria and Charles I to supervise the execution of chimney-pieces, doorways and other features without showing them polished final designs. From 1628 the young Webb was working as an assistant in Jones's office, and by 1633 both he and another assistant, Edward Carter, were employed under Jones on the restoration of St Paul's Cathedral. The confidence which Jones placed in his executant architects is illustrated by the design for the north and south nave doors at St Paul's in 1637 (cat. no. 80). This is a sketch which Jones was able to pass on as a final design ('The first draught Taken') by adding pencil instructions against some unresolved details.

Liberated from the need to work up every design to presentation standard Jones concentrated on the preliminary stages, and from the mid-1620s graphite and black chalk superseded the scorer as his main under-drawing techniques. With these media Jones could test out ideas more thoroughly before applying pen and ink. When he applied ink he continued to modify the outlines by shading over or redrawing them (e.g. cat. no. 69). Several late drawings, however, were left as finished designs in graphite or black chalk, and it is tempting to see a parallel between these designs and the tendency in Jones's late architecture to emphasize the bare ashlar or brick wall at the expense of applied ornament (cat. nos 79, 121, 122).

Jones's sketch and preliminary drawings in the 1630s are characterized by thick, dark outlines and regular pen shading. No longer loose and impressionistic, the late pen shading is in cleanly drawn lines, evenly spaced, and (especially from the mid-1630s) uniformly slanted across the sheet (cat. nos 70, 76, 80). The regularity of the pen shading in Jones's late architectural drawings provides the key to understanding the development of his figurative style. The drawings in his Roman Sketchbook (cat. no. 99) can be dated, by association with the handwriting style of their accompanying notes, either to Jones's stay in Italy in 1614 or much later to the 1630s, when his handwriting is more compact and italic in its letter forms, and when there is also a reference (on fo. 9*r*.) to paintings by Polidoro da Caravaggio in Whitehall, which were not acquired for the royal collection until 1637. All but three of the sketches in the Sketchbook can be assigned to the later period on grounds of style and they show that it was in the final decade of his career, rather than in Italy in 1614, that Jones flourished as a figurative draftsman. To this period belong almost all of the sketches of heads at Worcester College and Chatsworth (cat. nos 100–13), many of which can be related to studies after engravings in the Roman Sketchbook. The late figurative drawings prompted Van Dyck's praise, recorded by Webb, that Jones was not to be equalled by the great masters of his time for '*Boldness, Softness, Sweetness*, and *Sureness of his Touches*' (see above, p. 17), for they show great sensitivity in the modelling of features through outline and in the suggestion of form through pen shading. Jones based his pen-shading style on the Italian Mannerist engravings which he copied, but through firm pen handling and skilful cross-hatching was able to create a sense of movement and of light penetrating the shaded areas which is hardly apparent in the sources. In masque designs of the 1630s Jones turned to the pen-shading technique in preference to pen and wash for most scenery drawings and for all but the presentation costume designs. Although the technique is looser than in the figurative designs, the command of effects of light, recession and movement through inflections in the pen-shading lines is no less certain (cat. nos 96, 97).

The sureness and firmness of Jones's pen handling in the 1630s gave rise to a highly individual style of finished architectural drawing which bore no comparison with the examples by Palladio that he had so assiduously emulated in the period from 1616 to 1619. Nine drawings datable to or near 1638 (cat. nos 84–92) are distinguished by thick, fully ruled and precisely joined outlines and a minimal scoring technique. They show none of the blotting and fading that typify Jones's outline style up to 1619 and which are still present in designs of the 1620s. His complete command of the quill-pen is demonstrated by the fineness of details such as the metal railings on the seven-window house design (cat. no. 87), and the unwavering quality of freehand decorative details and profiles. With the exception of a design for a cupola (cat. nos 88, 89), all are drawn to a small scale, and contrast all the more strikingly with several elevations drawn to a large scale in 1616–19, where the handling of cornice profiles and other features is far less competent (cat. nos 22, 23). Washed shading, which on the earliest architectural drawings of 1608 is the dominant medium, is now wholly subservient to the outlines and is casually handled in places. Jones seems to have perfected his wash technique in the 1620s by applying the medium swiftly to avoid patchiness, and by narrowing the bands of cast shadow (e.g. cat. no. 45), but though it reached a peak of fluency in the early 1630s (cat. nos 57, 58, 95), his interest in the medium declined near the end of the decade as he concentrated almost exclusively on his pen style.

The meticulously ruled outline style of Jones's late architectural drawings corresponds with an extremely simple type of façade. Ornaments have been reduced to a few mouldings and the wall surface is left plain, without string-courses between the windows or quoins on the angles. We can now see a direct relationship between Jones's gradual mastery of the discipline of architectural draftsmanship and the evolution of his personal style between 1608 and 1638. Just as his richly eclectic and over-ornamented façades of 1608 gave way to more carefully proportioned Palladian elevations in 1616–19, and then, through a progressive reduction of detail, to the minimal elevations of the 1630s, so Jones gradually gained control of his medium, abandoning purely pictorial effects for a rational method of rendering the building on paper in which all the outlines were exactly defined. It was the command of the outline that gave Jones complete assurance in the handling of detail, and led him to distil the classical features of elevations to create a 'masculine and unaffected' architectural style.

The Emergent Architect, 1605–13

There is surely cause and effect between Jones's return from Copenhagen in the Earl of Rutland's retinue in the summer of 1603 and his work on the design of his first Court masque, *The Masque of Blacknesse*, performed for Queen Anne of Denmark in January 1604, for one must assume that Jones's talents and genius as 'picture-maker' had already been demonstrated in the Queen's own homeland. Two years later he designed the masque *Hymenaei* to celebrate the marriage of the Earl of Essex to Frances Howard, a daughter of the Earl of Suffolk (cat. no. 2). Then occurs that famous and pregnant inscription by Edmund Bolton in Bordino's *De Rebus praeclare gestis a Sixto V Pon. Max.* (Rome 1588, Worcester College) when he gave the book to Jones, hoping that through his agency, 'sculpture, modelling, architecture, painting, acting and all that is praiseworthy in the elegant arts of the ancients may one day find their way across the Alps into our England'.

When this was written in January 1606, Jones was thirty-three years of age. Apart from the two masques, and drawings only survive for the earlier one, there is not a scrap of visual evidence to support Bolton's eulogy. There must be more to this middle-aged man than the precious scraps we possess, and I suggest that Jones's reputation in 1605 as a 'great travellor', combined with Bolton's prophesies, imply that we are dealing with a man who stood above the common run of courtiers as a connoisseur, already versed in the polite arts. After all, what on earth did he produce with his pen during the formative years before 1604?

So far, of architecture we have nothing, and the prevailing Court style as characterized in the work of the Royal Surveyor Simon Basil (from 1606) was thoroughly old-fashioned, as demonstrated by Hatfield House begun in 1607. However, an event occurred in May 1608 that may portend change: Robert Cecil, 1st Earl of Salisbury, who was building Hatfield House, became Lord Treasurer, and began immediately to investigate the Office of Works. From this moment on, Jones as an emergent architect, the British Vitruvius in embryo, began to exert influence towards a reformation of style, even though without any official position. Indeed, he is acting, as so often in the future, as an *éminence grise*.

Cecil's role is crucial. He initiated the designs for his New Exchange in the Strand and for the tower of old St Paul's Cathedral in 1608 (cat. nos 3, 4), and it is surely significant that in this same year Jones designed his entertainment for James I with a fine classical archway (fig. 2). This, together with a similar arch dating *c.* 1608–9, is the first evidence we have of architectural representation in the masques (fig. 3). Finally, in February 1610, Cecil's 'Receivor-General' paid Jones £10 'for drawinge of some Architecture' at Hatfield House. This payment is a tantalizing one because it cannot be associated with any identifiable part of the house, unless it refers to modifications carried out to the south front, or to the wondrously beautiful stable design that would do credit to Philibert de L'Orme (cat. no. 9). What must be said of these attempts at architectural composition from 1608 to 1610 is that they are paper evidence of a new spirit in architecture, the first hints that Bolton's prophesies would be fulfilled.

It might have been expected that this fulfilment would have been initiated when 'Mr Inico Joanes' was appointed Surveyor of the Works to Henry, Prince of Wales, on 9 May 1610. Alas no, for not only had the Prince just two and a half years to live, but there is no real evidence of practical architecture apart from some alterations to a library and gallery in St James's Palace which in any case may well have been designed by Simon Basil. It was the same at Richmond Palace where the Prince's elaborate, Pratolinoesque, garden works were in the charge of the Frenchman Salomon de Caus, and a Florentine painter-architect Constantino de Servi, the latter clearly jealous of Jones and anxious to usurp him in the Prince's favours.

In order to grapple with Jones as the emergent architect it is still necessary to consult the masques. An unknown entertainment incorporates the Bramante-Belvedere concave-convex stairs from Serlio's Book III and the *Masque of Queens*, performed 2 February 1609, an interesting revolving octagonal 'House of Fame' (fig. 4), drawn with great fluency and brio. In effect this was a living *machina versatilis* turning round and round with the masquers and musicians. Then, in 1610, architecture begins to predominate, or at least more designs for architectural incidents survive. In *Prince Henry's Barriers*, performed on 6 January 1610, there are references to engraved sources for Roman ruins and monuments (Serlio, Hieronymous Cock etc.) plus excursions into a mixed Gothic style which evoke the type of Gothic architecture that Vignola or Giulio Romano offered for the façade of San Petronio in Bologna in the 1580s. Although a great deal of motif-mongering has

Fig. 2
Design for a rock and an archway, possibly for Lord Salisbury's entertainment of May 1608 celebrating his appointment as Lord Treasurer

Fig. 3
Design for an archway intended for an unidentified entertainment or masque, *c.* 1608–9

been done by Orgel and Strong, many more engraved sources need to be identified, for Jones was a passionate collector of prints, as testified by that redolent comment by the 5th Earl of Pembroke that Jones was 'so fond of Parmegiano [*sic*] that he bought the Prints of the Imperfect Plates, which are now [*sic*, not] here in this Book'. With *Oberon, The Fairy Prince* (performed on 1 January 1611), these engraved sources for architecture begin to abound (cat. nos 7, 8).

At this juncture it is necessary to make a journey, to the tiny church in the remote village of Norton-in-Hales, Shropshire, where the monument to Sir Rowland and Lady Cotton (the latter died in 1606) was adapted from a design by Inigo (cat. no. 6). Both the tomb and the surviving design are evocative; the sarcophagus to the tomb appears in the drawing for scene 1 of 'The Fallen House of Chivalry' of *Prince Henry's Barriers* (O & S 36), and the motif of columns with balls on top recurs in the scene of a 'Palace within a Cavern' in *Oberon* (fig. 9).

Fig. 4
Design for the 'House of Fame', for *The Masque of Queens*, performed 2 February 1609

Not until *Cupid's Palace*, an unknown masque of *c*. 1623 (cat. no. 94), would architecture be so strongly presented as in *Oberon, The Fairy Prince*. Again, although some sources have been identified – windows and dome from Bramante's Tempietto from Serlio, or the gateway to the Château of Anet from du Cerceau's *Les Plus excellents bastiments de France* (1576/9) – the interior of the palace, and 'Oberon's Palace' itself, hint at more esoteric or original sources, perhaps Buontalenti and Florentine design of the late sixteenth century. One senses with *Oberon* that the gap between it and the signed and dated 1616 elevation for the entrance bay of an unidentified house is not so wide. The unidentified stable design, suggestively made for Cecil, shares so many indiosyncrasies of drafting with *Oberon* that both must have been on the drawing-board at the same time (cat. no. 9). However, like *Oberon*, this is real architecture, and one can state unequivocally that there is nothing like this in English architecture before 1616.

Nothing has been said so far about the journey abroad made by Jones during this crucial period of his architectural career. In the summer of 1609 Jones went to Paris, carrying 'letters for his Majesty's service', and then on to the Roman antiquities of Provence. Perhaps, as with *Oberon*, one can associate these travels with an infusion of new ideas, but it would be dangerous to assume more.

On 6 November 1612 Prince Henry died in the presence of Frederick V, the Elector Palatine of the Rhine, who had come to London to marry Henry's sister Elizabeth. Their marriage was celebrated in the old Banqueting House on 14 February 1613 with *The Lords' Masque*, and on 15 February with *The Middle Temple and Lincoln's Inn Masque*, performed in the Great Hall of Whitehall Palace. Both were designed by Jones, and the latter was written by George Chapman, who described it as 'Invented, and fashioned with the ground, and special structure of the whole work by our kingdom's most artfull and ingenious architect Inigo Jones'. Alas, the important architectural scenes in both masques have not survived as drawings, but there can be little doubt that Chapman's words were not empty ones, and that Jones was now recognized as the rightful successor to the aged Simon Basil as Surveyor of the King's Works. On 27 April 1613 Jones was granted the reversion to this supreme post, just nine days after he had set out with the Earl of Arundel to escort the Elector Palatine and his bride to their castle at Heidelberg.

J.H.

Bibliography:

L. Stone, 'The Building of Hatfield House', *Archaeological Journal*, cxii (1955), pp. 100–28

—, 'Inigo Jones and the New Exchange', *Archaeological Journal*, cxiv (1957), pp. 106–21

King's Works, iii, pp. 121–7

G. Higgott, 'Inigo Jones in Provence', *Architectural History*, xxvi (1983), pp. 24–34

R. Strong, *Henry Prince of Wales and England's lost Renaissance* (London, 1986), pp. 110–13

2 Costume design for a winged masquer

c. 1605

Pen and brown ink over fine graphite or black chalk underdrawing, washed in blue, pink, pale orange, red, blue and brown watercolour, heightened with silver (now blackened), gold and white

278 × 178 mm. Laid down

O & S 5

The stiff formality of the pose and rich detailing of the jewelled costume in this very early drawing by Jones are characteristic of the Elizabethan full-length portrait tradition and betray his beginnings as an easel painter in the service of the 5th Earl of Rutland. As yet he shows little knowledge of Italian or French Mannerist figure drawing with its strong *contrapposto* and elongated proportions (cf. cat. nos 6, 7, 9).

The costume of this dancing masquer resembles that in a portrait by John de Critz at Woburn Abbey of Lucy Harrington, Countess of Bedford, as she appeared in the masque *Hymenaei* (performed 5 January 1606), with a billowing veil flowing down from a coronet, horizontally braided sleeves and a layered striped skirt. The present drawing may be a preliminary design for the ladies' costumes or for another of the female participants. If so, the wings on the costume would refer to the central spectacle of the masque: the descent from the clouds of Juno and her ladies to confirm the union of the marriage between the Earl of Essex and Frances Howard, daughter of the Earl of Suffolk.

See colour illustration on p. 145

3 Elevation for the New Exchange in the Strand, London

1608

Pen and brown ink, washed in brown, over scorelines and faint black chalk under-drawing

492 × 732 mm. Very thick paper with central vertical fold, torn at top of sheet

Watermark: large coat of arms above a D and three circles: the mark of the Düring family mill, Basle

Inscribed on *verso* in pen and brown ink by John Webb in centre: *ffor y*[e] *new Exchange* and repeated in graphite

Worcester College H & T 9

The design for the New Exchange, or 'Britain's Burse' as John Donne called it, is celebrated in the annals of Jones because it is his earliest for a piece of pure architecture. Indeed, even in the history of masques it is early, for architecture in them only first appears in an entertainment presented by Robert Cecil, 1st Earl of Salisbury, between 6 and 11 May 1608 in the library of Salisbury House in the Strand, probably to mark his appointment as Lord Treasurer (fig. 2).

Adjacent to Salisbury House was Durham House, which after the death of Queen Elizabeth in 1603 was eyed by Cecil for acquisition to enlarge his own accommodation. Commercial interests were also involved, for on the Strand frontage Cecil determined to build an Exchange meant to rival Gresham's in the City. There was to be a stock exchange, shops and a bazaar. Once all legal impediments were ruthlessly eliminated, building was effected with astonishing speed. The first stone was laid on 10 June 1608, by the end of August the arches of the main façade were up and, by 11 April 1609, it was ready to be formally opened by James I.

Clearly, Jones's design must predate June 1608. However, for reasons unknown it was not executed, and the Exchange as built is shown in a drawing (fig. 5) made by Robert Smythson when he came to London from Nottingham in 1609 to view the latest fashions in building. Although his drawing is crude, it must be reasonably accurate. Above the two main floors of the Exchange he shows gables of wild extravagant shape, characteristic of north European Mannerism. However, the façades below are of considerable purity, quite uncharacteristic of Simon Basil's Court style. The suggestion is here made that Jones revised Basil's design, substituting a more Italianate arched and window system.

Although Jones's design has been described by Sir John Summerson as 'the work of somebody who had had little to do with architecture and nothing with building', this is unfair. After all, Jones's experience of architecture was coloured by what he had seen in Denmark in 1603, and his design compares well with north European Classicism of the Amsterdam Exchange type, a building also of 1608. For details Jones turned to his much-thumbed Serlio. Here for the first time in English architecture appears the Serliana, or as it was called in the eighteenth century, the Palladian window.

The technique of shading in several layers and tones of wash, using a deep tone for the openings, is found on the St Paul's Cathedral tower design of the same year (cat. no. 4), and can be

Fig. 5
Robert Smythson. The New Exchange in the Strand, London, drawn in 1609

compared with some masque costume and set designs of 1605–10 (e.g. *Prince Henry's Barriers* in 1609–10). In this period Jones is happier with the brush than the pen. His ink outlines are extremely shaky and uncertain, the ruled being used only for the main horizontal lines and not for the vertical elements such as columns and wall edges. He uses the scorer to guide his pen lines, but not to mark the central axes of the columns and bays, as he invariably does on drawings after 1614 (e.g. cat. nos 30, 34). His concern is less with an underlying proportional grid of bay units or column diameters than with the overall volumes. This is apparent from the way in which Jones composed his façade dividing the space between the top of the steeps and the straight roof-line into five equal squares, $5\frac{1}{8} \times 5\frac{1}{8}$ in., and then subdivided the ground floor into arches, two squares high, so that the columns and entablatures are extraneous to the main proportional system. There is, however, a cohesive effect in the use of continuous dado rails and string-courses to offset the vertical accents of the columns, and it is only above the roof-line that Jones allows an element of pure fantasy to take control.

See colour illustration on p. 146

Bibliography:
L. Stone, 'Inigo Jones and the New Exchange', *Archaeological Journal*, cxiv (1957), pp. 106–21
J. Summerson, *Inigo Jones* (Harmondsworth, 1966), pp. 26–7

4 Elevation for a new termination to the tower of old St Paul's Cathedral, London

1608

Pen and grey ink washed in grey; faint black chalk under-drawing; under-scoring

755 × 513 mm. Single sheet of thick paper previously mounted in bound volume and folded horizontally in centre

Watermark: large coat of arms with rampant lions and crest, below which three balls: Düring family mill mark, Basle

Worcester College H & T 13

The old spire of the thirteenth-century tower of St Paul's Cathedral had been struck by lightning in 1561. Nothing had come of efforts to reinstate the upper stage of the tower in Queen Elizabeth's reign, and in 1608 James I invited the Lord Mayor and Bishop of London to survey the cathedral and have the spire rebuilt. Robert Cecil, 1st Earl of Salisbury, was a commissioner, and must have been the promoter of this design by Inigo Jones. It would not be incongruous if it did not sit so unhappily upon the Gothic tower. Jones was no less eclectic in his borrowings from printed sources than on the New Exchange design earlier the same year (cat. no. 3). The range of Serliana windows comes from Palladio's Basilica at Vicenza in Book III of *I Quattro libri*, and the pinnacles and spire from Labacco's illustration of Antonio da Sangallo the Younger's design for St Peter's in Rome. The lunettes are like those on Michelangelo's dome at St Peter's, but are on an octagonal spire with the profile of a classical scroll. However, there are details that exonerate Jones of the charge of adolescence in design, not least the fine lateral windows.

In technique, the drawing is very similar to the New Exchange design, executed a few months earlier in the same year. It is a monochrome drawing, in grey rather than brown ink, with several layers of wash over nervously applied pen outlines. The wash, however, is not as dense as on the New Exchange drawing and Jones has exercised greater discipline in the design of his turrets. Not only are these in strict elevational view but the scale and proportion of the various decorative elements are more carefully considered.

Both the New Exchange and the St Paul's tower designs were abortive, but nevertheless are icons in the development of Jones's personal style. Their production must have led to his intervention in the progress of Cecil's house at Hatfield, in 1610.

See colour illustration on p. 147

Bibliography:
J. Summerson, 'Inigo Jones: lecture on a master mind', *Proceedings of the British Academy*, l (1965), pp. 182–92

5 Study of the Pont du Gard, near Nîmes, France

c. 1609

Pen and light brown ink, over some incised lines. Later red ink ruled border lines around edge of sheet

430 × 577 mm. Central vertical fold

Watermark: fleur-de-lys flanked by P and G initials; countermark: large bunch of grapes

Inscribed by Jones in pen and brown ink at the top of the sheet *Ill Pont du Gartt./*, and below to the right of the drawing in two columns:
The first order hath 6 arches / ye Bayse of ye Arch is 58 foote / ye Pillasters ar in breadth 18 foote / The hole breadth of this under order is 438 foot / and the heayght is 83 foot / ye Space or cornice betwene ye first order and y^{e} / Second is 7^{foo} 11^{yn} / Ther is in ye Second order 11 arches / ye Space of ye arch is 56 foote / Thear is 11 Pillasters and every on is 13 foot brode / The Breadth of all This Second order is 746 foot / The Breadth of ye Arch inwardes which is y^{e} / Breadth of y^{e} Pillaster is 21 foot / and every arch is in heygh 67 foote / The Space betwene y^{e} Second order and y^{e} thirde / is 6^{foo} 8^{yn} heygh / The thirde order whear y^{e} Acquiducte was / hath 35 arches / y^{e} Spaces are 17 foote / y^{e} Pillasters ar Brode 5^{foo} $\frac{1}{2}$ / and heygh 6 foote / This uppermost order is / in all 504^{foo} $\frac{1}{2}$ in breadth / The holle acquiduct and arches is in / heygh 182^{foo} / y^{e} Aquiducte allone / is 3^{foo}./; and below in dark brown ink, added slightly later;
I obserued that ouer y^{e} 6th arch / frō y^{e} Left hand which is somwhat / Broder thē y^{e} Rest is foure / Littell arches of y^{e} upper order / and all ye Rest have but 3 arches / ouer thē; and inscribed on *verso* by John Talman in pen and brown ink: *257* ☿

RIBA Jones & Webb 102

Once described as a topographical sketch made during Jones's return from Italy in 1614, this drawing is in fact not an on-site study but a modified copy of a perspective view of the famous Roman acqueduct published in Jean Poldo d'Albenas's *Discours historial de l'antique et illustre cité de Nismes* (Lyon, 1560), and the inscription is little more than a translation of that beneath the original (fig. 6). Moreover, the drawing must be considerably earlier than 1614, for Jones's handwriting in the inscription is immature. There are Elizabethan 'secretary'-style characters such as the lower-case 'r', written with a double-footed stem (as in the word 'ar', third line), and the 'p' written as a loop preceded by a figure '2' (as in 'Space', sixth line). Jones began to suppress these features in his writing in about 1610 and tried consciously to replace them with modern 'italic' equivalents when he was in Italy from 1613 to 1614. On this evidence the drawing must date to 1609, the year Jones travelled to Paris bearing diplomatic letters from James I. The tour was probably made in the company of the Earl of Cranborne, son of Robert Cecil, and took Jones to the Château de Chambord, to Bordeaux and to the antiquities of Provence. The few notes in his copy of *I Quattro libri* concerning the visit to Provence are all retrospective in character and reveal a well-informed historical awareness: Jones looked enquiringly for evidence of the original function and appearance of buildings,

Fig. 6
The Pont du Gard, Nîmes. Woodcut from Jean Poldo d'Albenas, *Discours historial de l'antique et illustre cité de Nismes* (Lyon, 1560)

as in a note about holes in the frieze indicating an inscription on the Maison Carrée in Nîmes. His observation at the end of the note on this drawing is in the same vein. In it he recalls that one of the arches was wider than the rest, a crucial aspect of the Roman monument which the author of the woodcut had failed to notice.

By redrawing the perspective as an elevation, Jones could evaluate the arch construction and massive stonework of the Roman monument. These two themes are found in his work at Covent Garden (*c.* 1631) and for the St Paul's Cathedral restoration (1633–42). But the drawing had a more immediate purpose. Soon after he had returned from France Jones was at work on designs for the tournament *Prince Henry's Barriers*, performed 6 January 1610 to celebrate the martial prowess of Prince Henry (O & S 36, 37). The first scene is an agglomeration of decayed Roman structures, which has on the left a set of broken arches like Jones's rendering of the Pont du Gard. The steep bank of the Pont du Gard drawing appears in the second scene of *Barriers* and is a motif in shutter designs for *Oberon, The Fairy Prince* performed a year later (cat. no. 8). Thus it was for the settings of masques rather than for the realities of architecture that Jones sought to recreate the Pont du Gard on paper.

Bibliography:

G. Higgott, 'Inigo Jones in Provence', *Architectural History*, xxvi (1983), pp. 24–34

J. Peacock, 'Jonson and Jones collaborate on *Prince Henry's Barriers*', *Word & Image*, iii, no. 2 (1987), pp. 172–94

E. Chaney, review A. C. Fusco, *Inigo Jones Vitruvius Brittannicus: Jones e Palladio nella cultura architettonica inglese 1600–1740* (Rimini 1985), *Burlington Magazine*, cxxx (1988), pp. 633–4

6 Elevation/perspective of a monument to Lady Cotton in St Chad's Church, Norton-in-Hales, Shropshire

c. 1610

Pen and brown ink, washed in brown; some under-scoring

264 × 200 mm. Trimmed on all sides

Inscribed by Jones in pen and brown ink on central plaque: *Heare lyeth one y[t] / heauen sent to earth / To see no doubt her pu= / rer soule conjoyned / wth mortall mans, she / findes a dearth, / virtue so spent, that she / at first resigned / Her mortall weedes, and / as at first addressed / wth Immortalitye— / Borne wth desyre her wings / alreddye pressed, / she finds eternitye—*; and in modern pencil, top right *B4/46*; RIBA accession stamp on top left; inscribed on *verso* by John Talman pen and brown ink: *296: VII*

RIBA: shelf L5/1

This small drawing, the only one by Inigo Jones for a monumental tomb, passed unrecognized into the RIBA Library when the Institute acquired the Burlington-Devonshire Collection of architectural drawings on permanent loan from Chatsworth in 1894, and it was not published until 1973. It was made for a monument which still stands in a remote Shropshire church, somewhat modified in execution by a Burton-on-Trent master mason. The tomb itself (fig. 7) bears the effigies of Sir Rowland Cotton, his wife and new-born child, but the design commemorates only Lady Cotton, who died in childbirth in 1606. She is shown half reclined, as if rising from a sleep, a shroud covering her legs. In the words of the poem on the plaque, she has 'resigned/Her mortall weedes' and 'finds eternitye', a theme of resurrection that is also implied by the symbolic use of columns on each side of the sarcophagus. John Newman has shown that these almost certainly represent the two pillars Jachin and Boaz, which stood in the porch of the Temple of Solomon (II Kings, 7:15–22). In the early seventeenth century the Temple was equated with the Church of Christ, so in this context they would signify that the lady had entered Heaven. Such learned biblical references are hardly surprising in the decade which saw the preparation of King James's Authorized Version, but are of particular interest here because Sir Rowland Cotton was himself well versed in biblical Hebrew and has apparently based the iconographic programme on writings about the Temple by his mentor, the Rabbinical scholar, Hugh Broughton.

Sir Rowland, born about 1577, was attached to the Court of Henry, Prince of Wales, where Jones was Surveyor from June 1610 until the prince's death in November the following year. The drawing was probably made in 1609 or 1610 for it is close in style to Jones's designs for *Barriers* (performed 6 January 1610). Both

Fig. 7
Monument to Sir Rowland and Lady Cotton in St Chad's Church, Norton-in-Hales, Shropshire, *c.* 1610 (completed after 1634)

sets of drawings have gentle brown ink pen lines, with dense and suggestive brown wash shading, reinforced in places with pen. On the backcloth design for 'The Fallen House of Chivalry' (O & S 36) there appears part of a sarcophagus of similar shape, decorated with a harpy and a heavy fruit swag. These motifs were unknown on English tomb chests at the period but were common in carvings on Roman sarcophagi in the necropolis of Les Aliscamps at Arles, which Jones visited during his tour of Provence in 1609. For his central motif of a reclining figure beneath a pair of cupids holding a plaque Jones turned to an engraving by Angelo Falcone of the *Tomb of a Young Man*, after a design by Parmigianino.

Even in a sculptural setting Jones could not overlook the role of proportion and visual harmony. The drawing is set out on simple ratios of 1 : 1 and 2 : 1. The width of the sill of the sarcophagus equals the height from the sill to the underside of the main cornice, and is twice the height of the sarcophagus and twice the width of its base. By a perspective convention Jones made it clear that the columns were to stand in line with the effigy at the centre of the sides of the tomb. Reverting to an elevational view he showed the alignment of the sill and the mouldings on the column shafts. The figure was thus linked visually to the columns that symbolized Lady Cotton's entrance into Paradise.

Bibliography:

J. Sumner Smith, 'The Italian sources of Inigo Jones's style', *Burlington Magazine*, xciv (1952), fig. 22 [showing Falcone's engraving]

J. Newman, 'An early drawing by Inigo Jones and a monument in Shropshire', *Burlington Magazine*, cxv (1973), pp. 557–61

O & S i, pp. 158, 163

G. Higgott, 'Inigo Jones in Provence', *Architectural History*, xxvi (1983), p. 30

R. Strong, *Henry Prince of Wales and England's lost Renaissance* (London, 1986), pp. 135–6

7 Scenery design for the masque *Oberon, The Fairy Prince* (1611): interior of the Palace within the *machina versatilis*

1610

Pen and brown ink with grey wash over faint black chalk underdrawing and scorelines

470 × 388 mm. Laid down

Chatsworth O & S 62

This Mannerist scene is related by Orgel and Strong to their no. 60, an outcrop of rocks arranged around a *machina versatilis*. Essentially the masque explores the relationship between the rough and natural and the civilized and man-perfected. The shutters would have drawn back to reveal the 'Palace within a Cavern' (O & S 60, 61; figs 8, 9), and this would turn around to reveal the interior presented here. Peacock has convincingly demonstrated the peculiar architectural interest of these *Oberon* scenes. Engraved sources are conflated into a design of astonishing originality. The general idea comes from John Harington's *Ariosto* (1591) with its

Fig. 8
'Scene of Rocks', for *Oberon, The Fairy Prince*, constructed around a *machina versatilis*, 1610

Fig. 9
'Palace within a Cavern', the scene following the Rocks, but with side wings withdrawn, 1610

cavern and arcading. The stag and baying hounds are found in Du Cerceau's engraving of the gateway at Anet from *Les Plus excellents bastiments de France* (1576/9). In O & S 61 these hounds were accompanied by putti aiming with arrows and spears, borrowed from Vredeman de Vries's *Artis perspectivae* of 1568.

Bibliography:
J. Peacock, 'Inigo Jones's stage architecture and its sources', *The Art Bulletin*, lxiv (June 1982), pp. 199–205

8 Scenery design for the masque *Oberon, The Fairy Prince* (1611): scene 2: 'Oberon's Palace'

1610

Pen and light brown ink with grey wash, reinforced with dark brown ink, over black chalk and scorelines

331 × 386 mm. Heavy paper with deep fold down centre of sheet

Watermark: coat of arms surmounted by coronet; below shield is a golden fleece

Inscribed by John Webb in pen and brown ink at bottom right: *2 sceane K: oberons Pallace*

Chatsworth O & S 63

The palace is here a revision of Orgel and Strong 61 where the palace was within the cavern, and it follows Ben Jonson's text that 'the whole scene opened' to reveal the palace. Unlike the more delicate and emphemerally festive look of the 'Palace within a Cavern' (fig. 9), this new design is more dramatic, theatric and symbolic, composed of an extraordinarily wide-ranging number of sources. The building is no longer in opposition to nature with the rock pressing in, but now grows out of nature, out of the bedrock. The dome hints of Bramante's Tempietto from Serlio; the battlements and rustication come from the Londinium and New World Arches of Stephen Harrison's *Arches of triumph in London* (1604); and the satyr terms from Vredeman de Vries via Du Cerceau's interior of the Château de Madrid in *Les Plus excellents bastiments* (1576/9). Acknowledgement is also made to grotto work by Salomon de Caus, possibly at Richmond Palace, whose quasi-romantic Tudor medievalism, Jones may have responded to. Paraphrasing John Peacock, 'Oberon's Palace' presents a form of chivalric architecture – a blend of the classical architecture of Italy and France with a native style (the idea of Elizabethan fairy palaces and the architecture of the Progress) – which speaks the language of Oberon appropriate to Spenser's mythology of Albion.

See colour illustration on p. 148

Bibliography:
J. Peacock, 'Inigo Jones's stage architecture and its sources', *The Art Bulletin*, lxiv (June 1982), pp. 199–205

9 Elevation for a stable

c. 1610

Pen and brown ink, washed in brown, over slight graphite underdrawing and some incised lines. 18th-c. red ink ruled border lines around edges of sheet

325 × 416 mm. Including a later (18th-c.) strip pasted at bottom (57 × 412 mm, with 10 mm overlap). The original sheet is 279 × 415 mm, and has a deep central vertical fold

Watermark: shield with diagonal band surmounted by fleur-de-lys; beneath is a tailpiece and part of a monogram (rest cut off)

Inscribed by an 18th-c. hand in pen and brown ink in top right-hand corner: *29.*; and on *verso* by John Talman in pen and brown ink: *296*: ⍂

RIBA Jones & Webb 58

Although previously associated with a stable built at Newmarket Palace between 1616 and 1617, it can now be shown that this drawing dates before Jones's second Italian visit, and belongs around the year 1610. Typical of the 1610 period are the nervously handled pen outlines, the absence of ruler drawing, the horizontal pen shading in the wash, and the elongated, half-turned pediment figures in the manner of Parmigianino or Primaticcio (cf. cat. nos 3, 6–8). In its sources the design draws heavily on a woodcut of Philibert de L'Orme's house in the rue de la Cerisaie in Paris, from his *Le Premier tome de l'architecture* (1567) (fig. 10). Prints by de L'Orme and Du Cerceau inspired Jones's designs for 'Oberon's Palace' in the masque *Oberon, The Fairy Prince* prepared late in 1610, and show the influence of Jones's visit to France in the previous year. The French, rather than Italian, influence on this elevation is particularly clear from the rusticated quoins, which are round-cornered and almost undifferentiated, a style of dressing which recalls the stone *chaînes* ('chains') running up between the windows at the Place Royale (Place des Vosges) in Paris, begun in 1605 and just completed when Jones was in the city in 1609.

There is no record of Jones having designed a stable at this early period, but we know that he was in the 1st Earl of Salisbury's service at Hatfield, first on 30 October 1609 and again 28 February the following year, when he was paid for 'drawinge of some Architecture'. This may be an unexecuted proposal for a stable at Hatfield House or for Salisbury's London house in the Strand.

Fig. 10
Philibert de L'Orme's house in the rue de la Cerisaie, Paris, 1554–8. Woodcut from *Le Premier tome de l'architecture* (Paris, 1567) [fol.253*v*.]

Bibliography:
E. Auerbach and C. Kingsley Adams, *Painting and sculpture at Hatfield House* (London, 1971), p. 24 (citing Hatfield archives SPD, JI, 57/82)

10 Costume design for a torchbearer: a fiery spirit, for *The Lords' Masque*

1612–13

Pen and brown ink over black chalk, washed with red, brown and blue watercolour, heightened with white gouache

295 × 160 mm. Inlaid on Whatman paper marked 1832 and reinforced on back

Inscribed on *verso* by John Talman in pen and brown ink: *296 : VII*

Chatsworth O & S 81

The Lords' Masque was performed on 14 February 1613 in the old Banqueting House, Whitehall (built 1606–9), to celebrate the marriage of Princess Elizabeth (daughter of James I) to Frederick V, the Elector Palatine. According to the poet Thomas Campion, Jones was responsible for 'the whole invention'. Technically it was his most advanced production so far, involving three complete changes of scene, an upper and a lower stage, a revolving set (*machina versatilis*) and sliding shutters (*scena ductilis*).

This is one of three highly accomplished costume designs for the masque, and is among the most beautiful of all Jones's drawings before his second Italian visit. It depicts the masquing Lords' attendants who were 'like fiery spirits, all their attires being alike composed of flames, with fiery wings and bases, bearing in either hand a torch of virgin wax'. John Peacock has shown that the costumes for the *Lords' Masque* were almost certainly inspired by those for the Florentine *intermedii* of 1589, known through descriptions by Bastiano de'Rossi and probably from original drawings by the designer, Bernardo Buontalenti, which may have passed through the Stuart Court in 1611 or 1612 at the time of the proposed match between Prince Henry and the sister of the Grand Duke of Tuscany, Cosimo III. This particular costume echoes those for Platonic demons of fire in the fourth *intermedio*, which, in de'Rossi's words, had 'wings, made of flaming red sarsenet, splashed with silver [. . .]. Their hair was very long and curled, a fiery colour mixed with silver, and their faces shining and beautiful; they were dressed mid-thigh in fire cloth of silver and red'. Jones's emulation of Buontalenti's art would explain the enormous development in his technique since the earliest costume designs of 1605 (cat. no. 2). There is a surer sense of anatomy, a greater feeling of movement, and a bolder, more fluid pen and brush technique. In designing for an attendant rather than a lord Jones was also freed from the constraints of the Jacobean portrait tradition, which demanded that the pose and costume of a subject should reflect his or her status and wealth.

No scenery design for the *Lords' Masque* has survived, but Campion lavishly praised Inigo Jones and described a remarkable setting of gem-studded pilasters, the capitals 'of a new invention', its upper 'bastard order with cartouses reversed, coming from the capitals of every pilaster'; above was 'a cornice, which returned over every pilaster, seeming all of gold and richly carved'. This scene changed to 'a prospective with porticos on each side, which seemed to go in a great way [. . .]'. The splendours of the *Lords' Masque* confirmed Inigo Jones's position as the central artistic personality of the Stuart Court, and on 27 April 1613 he was granted the reversion to the post of Surveyor of the King's Works. By then, however, he was in the retinue of the Elector and his new wife on their journey to their castle at Heidelberg.

See colour illustration on p. 145

Bibliography:
J. Peacock, 'Inigo Jones and the Florentine Court Theater', *John Donne Journal*, v (1986), pp. 201–34

The Making of an Architect: Inigo Jones's Second Tour of Italy, 1613–14

Gordon Higgott

Inigo Jones's tour of Italy with Lord Arundel from July 1613 to September the following year was the turning point in his development as an architect, for it was through first-hand study of buildings by Palladio in Venice and Vicenza, and Roman architecture in central Italy and the Bay of Naples, that Jones grounded himself in principles of classical design that were to be the mainspring of his creative endeavour over the next twenty-five years.

The tour is chronicled in notes by Jones in his copy of Palladio's *I Quattro libri* at Worcester College, Oxford,[1] and the Roman Sketchbook at Chatsworth (cat. no. 99), and in the correspondence between Lord and Lady Arundel, who often travelled separately.[2] Apart from a period in August and September 1614 when Arundel was detained by illness in Genoa, Jones would seem to have stayed with the Earl's retinue and was presumably required to assist him in his investigations of painting and sculpture. Jones is never mentioned in Arundel's correspondence and little is known in detail of Arundel's activities as a collector and connoisseur. In Jones's notes, however, we see growing appreciation of qualities in classical and modern Italian architecture that were to be fundamental in his mature work: variety and textural contrast in ornaments and materials, and visual correspondence between the parts of a building or decorative scheme.

A striking feature of the on-site annotations in Italy is that Jones wrote little before he travelled with Lord Arundel to the Bay of Naples in late February and early March 1614. In Vicenza on 23 and 24 September 1613 he had looked at Palladio's Teatro Olimpico and Villa Rotunda,[3] and in early January he was in Rome examining the Temples of Vesta, Fortuna Virilis, Nerva Trajanus and Hadrian (Palladio's 'Temple of Mars').[4] These notes are mostly very brief and methodical and are concerned more with isolated details than the overall effect of a building. When travelling to Naples, however, Jones's interest was caught by the rich textural quality of Roman brick-and-stone construction. Writing retrospectively when he was back in London in January the following year, he recalled having seen much *opus reticulatum* on the Via Appia and an 'Antike house' with walls of polygonal masonry which 'did well'.[5] At the Palatium Imperiale at Baia, on the north side of the Bay of Naples, he remembered variations from the usual type of brick-bonded walling:

> Like wise at ye Thearmi at Baia thear ar many wales wth mor courses of Brick and Sum great Bricke amongst for ye Romans varied thes things according to thear Cappriccio mingling on wth another. so yt sheaud well.[6]

In Naples itself Jones admired the richly carved Corinthian capitals and finely jointed column shafts of the Temple of Castor and Pollux. 'This', he wrote on Saturday 8 March 1614, 'is on[e] of the best things that I haue seen',[7] adding of the capitals on a second visit 'This I obsearued Sonday ye 23 March and indeed thes capitels are Exelent'.[8] The note is a gloss on an earlier annotation of *c*. 1610 in which Jones had paraphrased Palladio's praise of the unusual intertwined acanthus stalks beneath the central flower on the abacus, a 'dilicatt inuension and sheaues thatt wch is doo[n] by reason and is gratious Though yt varry fro[m] the useual way is good and to be folloed'.[9]

Jones's fullest study of a Roman building was at the Pantheon on 31 May 1614. He was now attuned to the importance of colour and texture in the overall effect of the building. He made detailed notes of types of marbling used for the panelling of the portico walls and internal tabernacles,[10] and speculated about materials which had disappeared, observing of the vaulting of the dome: 'I Do thinke that all this volt was Ciuered [Covered] with Stuco O for on may yt Perceaue ytt in Som places'.[11] Jones's awareness of larger relationships in a building, rather than individual features, is apparent from his comment that the main niche of the central chapel was similar in shape to the entrance arch on the opposite side of the rotunda; the chapel was therefore likely to be of the same date as the rest of the buildings and not later, as some had thought:

> This Chapell must needs be antike for yt accompaith the cheef enterance and I wonder thear shu[ld] bee any doubt made of yt.[12]

The comment illustrates another aspect of Jones's thinking about architecture in Italy. Many of his enquiries were motivated by an antiquarian interest in the original appearance of the building. Two weeks later Jones suggested that the circular Temple of Vesta at Tivoli had been erected on the foundations of an earlier building,[13] and at the Temple of Clitumnus at Trevi, on 16 June 1614, he concluded that the pediment was modern because of the cross and inscription in the frieze.[14]

Jones's notes about Palladio's buildings during his second visit to the Veneto in August 1614 show a keen sensitivity to the effects of materials and a well-developed awareness of how the parts of a building relate to each other in space. At the Palazzo Thiene in Vicenza, on 14 August, Jones compared types of material on the inside and outside of the building and explored the effects of textural contrast and spacial harmony in the entrance hall (figs 11–13). He demonstrated that the vaulted bays of the entrance hall and the adjacent loggia were the same size (commenting above the drawing: 'thes Pillors do maak ye Crochera in the midest Squar and equal to thos of ye Portico G'), and noted the contrasting types of rustication. Later, when he was back in London and reviewing the notes he had made in Italy, Jones observed an 'admirable discretion' in the rusticated columns supporting the vault of the hall, 'for ye Scapi [shafts] Q being sllender the pillar answers to ye heyght of the Placce and the adiuncte of ye Bozzi answers to ye strength and rusticke of the reste'. That is to say, he saw that the interior was unified by two contrasting characteristics: slenderness in the proportions of the column shafts and in the height of the hall, and strength and roughness in the applied rustication. The notion that good design resides in a harmony of effect, whether in 'strength' or 'slenderness', is fundamental to Jones's mature architectural thinking, and is found in many of his evaluations on Roman details illustrated by Palladio (see below, pp. 124–5). The idea can be traced to passages in Lomazzo's *Trattato dell' arte, della pittura, scoltura, et architettura* (Milan, 1585), annotated by Jones at about this time, in which the theorist, praising the richness of Roman ornament, recommended strong contrast between carvings, provided that the ornaments agreed in the essential characteristics of their orders, be it the 'heavy and solid' of the Tuscan and Doric, or the 'pretty and slender' qualities of the Corinthian and Composite.[15]

For Jones, the Palazzo Thiene was a textbook of Palladio's building techniques. He must have been surprised to discover that the rusticated walling was in brick, and that stone was used only for the decorative details. Jones observed the two types of rustication, rough-cut below and 'a flatt rusticke aboufe or rather a [sw]eet rusticke to be imitated', and commented on the flatness of the upper-floor pilasters.[16] Thus he supplemented the woodcut with information on the modelling, colour and texture of the building, and returned to England with a store of knowledge to draw on for his own designs.

During this second stay in Vicenza Jones visited all Palladio's extant palazzi illustrated in Book II of *I Quattro libri*, looking chiefly at the materials employed, and noting how the buildings differed from the woodcut plans, elevations and sections.[17] Outside Vicenza he saw the incomplete Villa Valmarana at Lisiera[18] and the Villa Thiene at Quinto, where he sketched the courtyard loggia (since disappeared)

Fig. 11
Palazzo Thiene, Vicenza, by Andrea Palladio. East façade, from *c.* 1542

Fig. 12
Palazzo Thiene, Vicenza, by Andrea Palladio. Entrance hall, from *c.* 1542

and the vault types shown on the plan.[19] He probably rejoined Lord Arundel in Genoa later in the month and stayed in the city for two or three weeks. Writing in his *I Quattro libri* in London the following January, he recalled the typical Genoese use of loggias at the ends of the elevations rather than in the middle, as on Palladio's palaces and villas. The Genoese arrangement had some advantages, but he concluded that 'on ye outside on is more gracefull for bringing a frontispiece in the midest wch is ye greatest ornament a house cann haaue'[20] By the middle of September 1614, the Arundel party was in Turin on a homeward journey through the Mont Cenis pass to reach Paris by about 12 October. Detained in Paris for three weeks awaiting an audience with the King, they probably returned to London in November.

In addition to those places mentioned in his notes in *I Quattro libri* we know that Jones visited Padua, Bologna, Florence and Siena while travelling slowly from Venice to Rome in the summer and autumn of 1613. In Rome Jones began annotating his sketchbook now at Chatsworth, but it was not until he was in London in January the following year that he wrote his famous statement on the design and use of ornament in architecture. The note is worth quoting in full because it draws together all the threads of his thinking on architecture at the outset of his career as Surveyor:

> friday y^{e} 20 January 1614
> In all inuencions of C[a]ppresious ornaments on must first designe

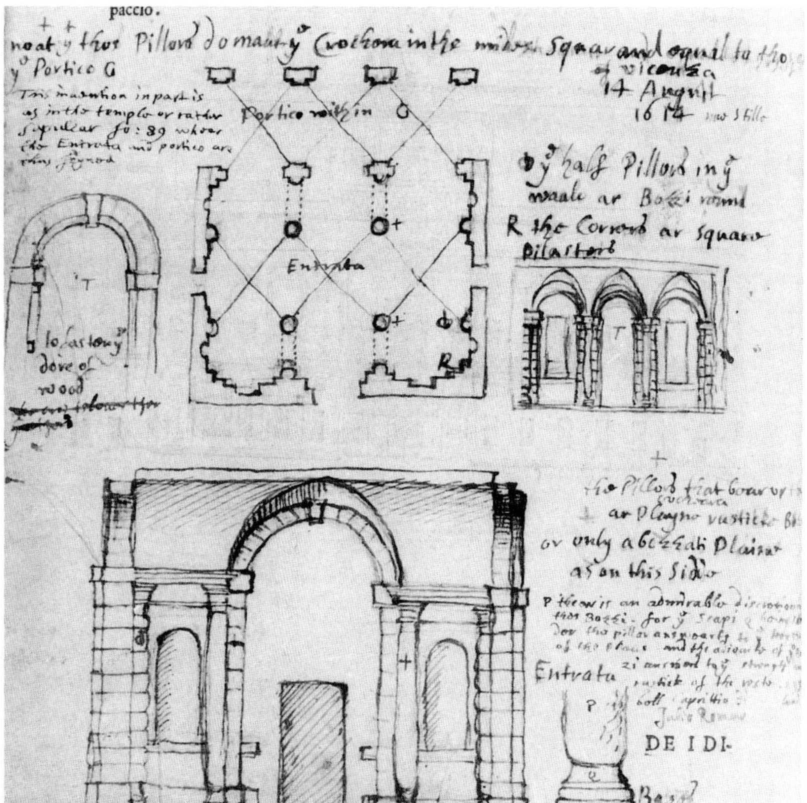

Fig. 13
Inigo Jones. Sketches and annotations in Book II, p. 12 of his *I Quattro libri*

y^e^ Ground, or y^e^ thing plaine, as y^t^ is for youse, and on that, varry yt, addorne yt. Compose yt wth deccorum according to the youse, and ye order yt is of, as in the Cartouses I haue of Tarquinio ligustri of Vitterbo.

and to saie trew all thes Composed ornamentes the wch Proceed out of ye aboundance of dessignes, and wear brought in by Mihill Angell and his followers, in my oppignion do not well in sollid Architecture and ye facciati of houses, but in gardens loggis, stucco or ornamentes of chimnie piecces, or the innerparts of hoases thes composisiones ar of necesety to be youced, for as outwardly euery wyse ma[n] carrieth a grauiti in Publicke Places, whear ther is nothing els looked for, & yt inwardly hath his Immaginacy set free, and sumetimes licenciously flying out, as nature hirsealf doeth often tymes Strauagantly, to dellight, amase us sumtimes moufe us to laughter, Sumtimes to Contemplatio[n] and horror, So in architecture ye outward ornamentes oft to be Sollid, proporsionable according to the rulles, masculine and unaffected

whears within the Cimeras yoused by the ansientes the[y] varried and Compoced ornamentes both of the house yt Sealf and the mouables within yt ar most commendable.[21]

After noting in the first paragraph that ornaments should be designed with decorum, in keeping with the function for which they are intended and the order of architecture to which they belong, Jones goes on to emphasize the appropriateness of certain types of ornament to certain situations. All 'Composed' (i.e. fanciful or capricious) ornaments should only be used on the insides of houses or on garden buildings such as loggias. On the outsides of the houses, and in 'sollid Architecture' (i.e. in the structural parts), the ornaments should be 'sollid, proporsionable according to the rulles, masculine and unaffected'. The concluding sentence provides an instance of the correct use of 'Composed ornamentes': the rooms ('Cimeras') of the ancients had fanciful ornaments on both the fixed architecture and the movable furniture, creating a commendable effect. The essential theme of the note is that ornaments should always be designed with their situation in mind, fanciful ornaments being suitable to one place and plain ornaments to another. A design will succeed when, as in the ancient rooms, the ornaments agree in their fundamental characteristics. This philosophy, rooted in the experience of Italy, was to guide Jones in his architectural practice for the next quarter of a century.

Notes

1. See J. A. Gotch, *Inigo Jones* (London, 1928), pp. 71–83 and 'Inigo Jones's principal visit to Italy in 1614. The itinerary of his journeys', *RIBA Journal*, xlvi (1938), pp. 85–6. A facsimile edition of Jones's annotated copy of Palladio's *I Quattro libri dell' architettura* (Venice, 1601) was published by B. Allsopp (ed.), *Inigo Jones on Palladio* (2 vols, Newcastle upon Tyne, 1970). The first volume has a transcription of all the notes based on a typescript by Gotch but is unfortunately inaccurate in places. Many pages from Jones's *I Quattro libri* are reproduced and discussed by Annarosa Cerutti Fusco in *Inigo Jones Vitruvius Britannicus: Jones e Palladio nella cultura architettonica inglese 1600–1740* (Rimini, 1985), but the notes are not considered chronologically. See also G. Higgott, 'Inigo Jones in Provence', *Architectural History*, xxvi (1983), pp. 24–6

2. See M. F. S. Hervey, *The Life, correspondence and collections of Thomas Howard, Earl of Arundel* (Cambridge, 1921), ch. 7
3. Notes in *I Quattro libri*, 10th flyleaf *verso* and Book II, p. 19
4. Ibid., Book IV, pp. 53, 49, 24, 56
5. Ibid., Book I, p. 12 [undated note but in same style of handwriting as note on Baia, discussed below].
6. Ibid., Book I, p. 11. This comment is dated '1614/Baia/17 January', but cannot have been written when Jones was in Italy. It belongs to a sequence of notes sharing a similar handwriting style in Books I and II, some of which have the words 'london' or 'lond' and are dated more or less chronologically from January to February '1614', the latest being a note of 22 February 1614 on page 39, Book II. When Jones returned from Italy in November 1614 he reverted to the 'Old Style' or Julian Calendar still current in England which began the New Year not on 1 January (as in the 'New Style' or Gregorian Calendar then used in Italy and still used today), but on 25 March. Thus his notes of January and February 1614 in Books I and II of *I Quattro libri* were in fact written a year after he was in Italy. The same applies to his famous note about architecture in his Roman Sketchbook dated 20 January 1614 (see below)
7. *I Quattro libri*, Book IV, p. 96
8. Ibid., Book IV, p. 97
9. Ibid., loc. cit. Palladio writes on p. 95, 'non è vietato all'Architetto partirsi alcuna volta dall'vso commune, pur che tal variatione sia gratiosa, & habbia del naturale.' ('the architect is not restrained from departing sometimes from the common custom, provided such a variation be graceful and natural')
10. Ibid., Book IV, pp. 79–81
11. Ibid., Book IV, p. 81
12. Ibid., Book IV, p. 73, headed 'Roma 1614'
13. Ibid., Book IV, p. 90
14. Ibid., Book IV, p. 98
15. Jones's, copy of Lomazzo's *Trattato* is in a private collection. Lomazzo's comments on Roman ornament are in Book VI, chapter xlvi, headed 'Composizione de gli edifici in particolare' and annotated by Jones on pp. 410 and 411. While in Italy, Jones studied Lomazzo's instructions on the proportions of children in Book I, chapters xvii–xix and translated some passages into his Roman Sketchbook (cat. no. 99). For a modern edition of Lomazzo see R. P. Ciardi (ed.), *Gian Paolo Lomazzo: Scritti sulle arti* (2 vols, Florence, 1974), ii
16. *I Quattro libri*, Book II, p. 14
17. Notes in Book II, pp. 6–7 (Palazzo Chiericati), 8–10 (Palazzo Iseppo Porto), 16–17 (Palazzo Valmarana), 22–3 (Palazzo Barbarano)
18. Ibid., Book II, p. 59
19. Ibid., Book II, p. 64. See also A. A. Tait, 'Inigo Jones – architectural historian', *Burlington Magazine*, cxii (1970), p. 235
20. *I Quattro libri*, Book I, p. 52
21. Roman Sketchbook, Chatsworth, fol. 76*r*. See below, cat. no. 99. The words 'set free', line 15, have in the past been mistranscribed as 'set on fire'

11 Andrea Palladio. Alternative elevations with plan (on *verso*) for the Palazzo Iseppo Porto, Vicenza

c. 1546/7

Pen and brown ink with brown wash over scorelines. Single red ink ruled border lines on left and bottom sides of sheet. On *verso* is a preliminary plan for the palazzo in pen and brown ink with brown wash over graphite, accompanied by a castle-villa plan entirely in graphite

282 × 406 mm. Single sheet of thick paper with two strongly marked central vertical folds, the left one dividing the two halves of the elevation

Watermark: Anchor in circle surmounted by crossed bar motif

Inscribed by Palladio on *recto* and *verso* in pen and brown ink with dimensions in Vicentine feet, and on verso by John Talman in pen and dark brown ink: *54:* [illegible]*:*

Scale: 10 ft = 50.5 mm (2 Roman inches); scale on *verso*: 10 units = 18 mm

RIBA Palladio XVII/9*r*.

Jones acquired this beautiful presentation drawing during his second tour of Italy from 1613 to 1614 in a batch of more than 250 sheets of designs by Palladio and his studio. The design belongs to Palladio's early maturity as an architect, before his final visit to Rome in 1554 and the onset of a richly ornamented external style. Typical of the earlier phase is the dependence on a type of palace front initiated by Bramante for the Palazzo Caprini ('Raphael's house') in Rome from about 1509. This consists of a ground floor treated as a rusticated podium and a grand upper floor, or *piano nobile*, articulated with an applied order and balconied windows, and surmounted by an entablature and an attic storey.

In this drawing Palladio presented his client, Iseppo Porto, with two differing solutions for the façade, of which the more complex and deeply modelled scheme on the left was essentially the one chosen. This scheme shows a dynamic interplay between primary architectural members – columns, entablature, rusticated walling and quoins – and the secondary window and balcony elements, the latter squeezed against the former and competing for attention with them. On the executed front some of this tension is dissolved through the absence of window frames on the ground floor and the use of wider spacing between the columns and windows above. Jones, in his elevation for Sir Fulke Greville's house of *c.* 1617 (cat. no. 22), emulated both the smoothly washed technique of the drawing and the Bramantesque scheme, but avoided any feeling of conflict by setting his windows on a plain wall and using straight cornices rather than pediments.

Palladio's preliminary plan on the *verso* of the sheet is based on Vitruvius' description of the Greek private house, adapted here to a deep urban site, with front and back ranges for the family and guests separated by a peristyle courtyard with giant-order columns. As Jones observed when he saw the palace in August 1614, only the front range was built. The distinguishing feature of this block is the large entrance hall with four columns, similar to the one at the earlier Palazzo Thiene (fig. 12) and reconstructed from the tetrastyle hall of the ancient Roman house.

Bibliography:

I Quattro libri, II, pp. 8–10

R. Wittkower, *Architectural principles in the age of Humanism* (London 1949; 3rd ed., 1967), pp. 78–9

J. S. Ackerman, *Palladio* (Harmondsworth, 1966), pp. 103–7

H. Burns, L. Fairbairn and B. Boucher, *Andrea Palladio 1508–1580; the portico and the farmyard* (London, Arts Council of Great Britain, 1975), pp. 232–4

D. Lewis, *The Drawings of Palladio* (Washington D.C., International Exhibitions Foundation, 1981), pp. 114–5

12 Andrea Palladio. Left half of final façade design for the Palazzo Chiericati, Vicenza

Late 1560s

Pen and brown ink with grey wash over faint scorelines

286 × 395 mm. Single sheet of very thin paper with two vertical folds down centre. Spots of brown discoloration over whole sheet

Watermark: anchor in circle surmounted by crossed bar motif; countermark: AC (?)

Inscribed by Orazio Palladio in pen and brown ink at top of sheet: *Fronte della casa de i Chierecati*; and by Andrea Palladio with dimensions in Vicentine *piedi* within elevation. *Verso* is inscribed by John Talman in pen and brown ink: *150:* ⊢:

Scale: 10 ft = 44.5 mm ($1\frac{1}{2}$ Vicentine inches)

RIBA Palladio XVII/5*r*.

This is a preliminary drawing for the woodcut plate of the Palazzo Chiericati in *I Quattro libri* (Book II, p. 7), published in 1570. It illustrates Palladio's economical late graphic style, which rendered the moulding-courses in short, inset lines at the profiles rather than in continuous horizontals. Jones imitated this technique for his own preliminary designs between 1616 and 1619 (cat. nos 14, 34), and as a preparatory method when setting out the moulding-courses on presentation designs in the same period (resulting in an untidy overlap of ruled and freehand lines at the moulding profiles, e.g. cat. nos 21, 22). Palladio's technique, however, is much cleaner than Jones's before about 1620. Scorelines are marked with a rounded ebony or ivory stylus and are followed precisely by the pen lines.

The drawing shows half the eleven-bay façade of the Palazzo Chiericati, more or less as built from 1551, but does not make clear that some of the columns are engaged and some free-standing. In fact all but the central five bays of the upper floor of the palace are recessed behind the columns, forming deep loggias looking on to a large open space called the Isola, at the east end of the main Corso in Vicenza. As Wittkower has noted, Palladio probably visualized the façade in terms of the porticoed frontages of a Roman forum, employing superimposed colonnades of a type he was to reconstruct in *I Quattro libri* for the walkways surrounding Roman public spaces (Book III, pp. 33–4). The ground-floor colonnaded passageway, however, was a traditional north-Italian form, and occurs on the earlier Palazzo Civena in Vicenza (1538–9).

The lower order of the façade reproduces Palladio's own recommended proportions for the Doric order exactly, and contrasts with Jones's much freer handling of the same order in his designs for gateways (cat. nos 17, 40, 41, 42). It has a frieze exactly $1\frac{1}{2}$ modules (i.e. half-column diameters) high, with triglyphs 1 module wide. The columns are 17 modules high and the entablature is a quarter the column height.

Bibliography:

R. Wittkower, *Architectural principles in the age of Humanism* (London 1949; 3rd ed., 1967), pp. 81–2

R. Cevese (ed.) *Mostra del Palladio; Vicenza, Basilica palladiana* (Milan/Venice, 1973), pp. 100–1

H. Burns, L. Fairbairn and B. Boucher, *Andrea Palladio 1508–1580; the portico and the farmyard* (London, Arts Council of Great Britain, 1975), p. 40

D. Lewis. *The drawings of Palladio* (Washington D.C., International Exhibitions Foundation, 1981), pp. 161–2

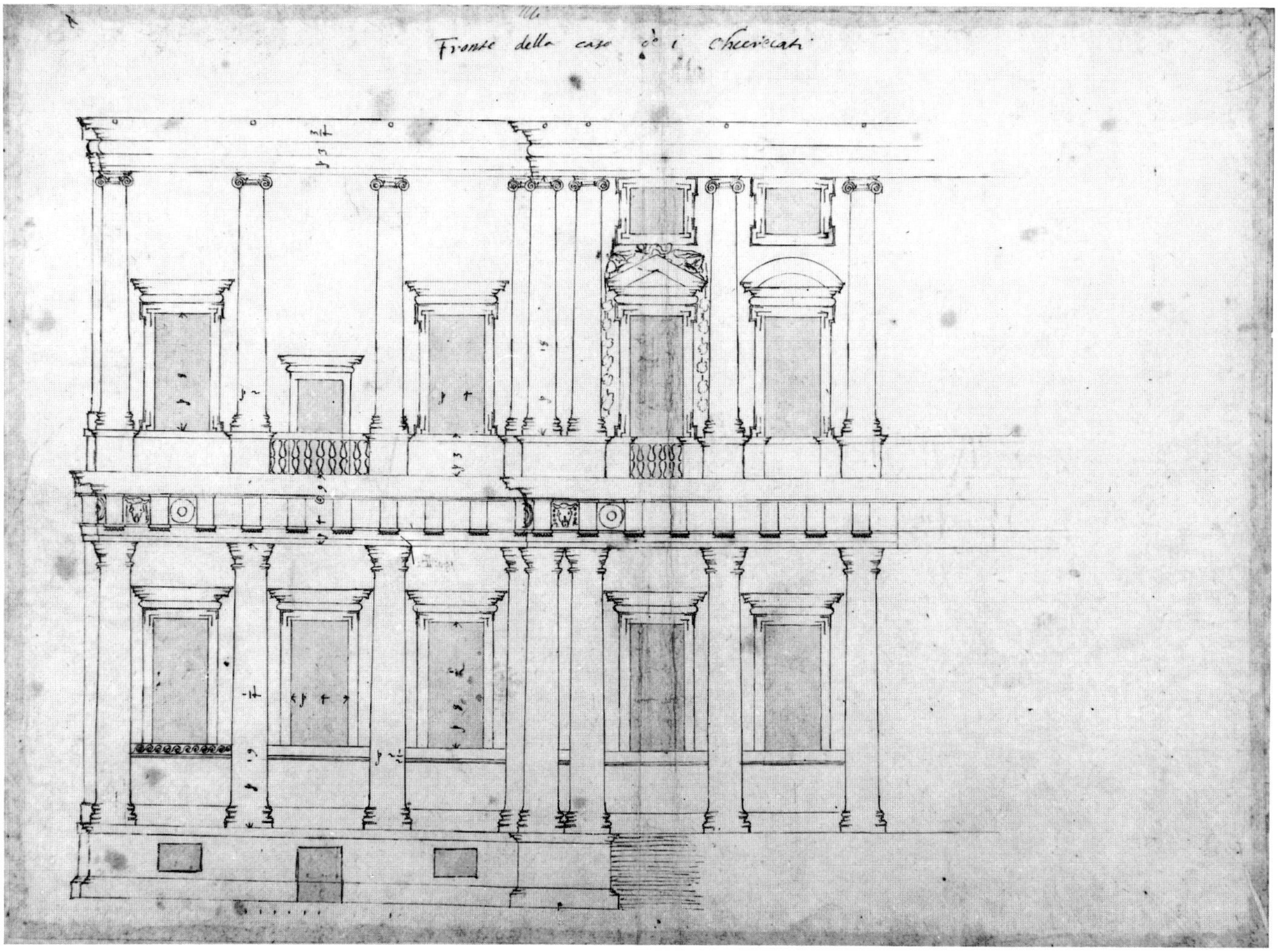

Surveyor to James I and Queen Anne of Denmark, 1615–25

Jones was quite unlike any previous Surveyor. In the words of his faithful assistant John Webb, he was the 'supream officer'. To compare the operations of the King's Works before and after 1615, is to recognize a transformation in the style of royal building and in the method of design and administrative command. A writer reflecting from 1667 over the previous thirty or so years could comment that 'there was [. . .] scarcely any one office in his Ma^{ts} Court of greater reputation both for able officers, good conduct, frugality of expence, and sure payment, then [*sic*] the office of his Works'.

Jones was in total control, and he laid down a personal code of design law. Under Simon Basil and previous Royal Surveyors there had been a great deal of delegation of responsibility, and even important buildings could be designed empirically, and often by several architects. This stopped under Jones, and what came from his drawing-board he saw executed with fidelity. It is astonishing that he was the sole master of royal design from 1615 to 1638, as well as the Court masque designer. It is not often in European architecture that one chief architect so tightly controls the whole. Of course, he was a Renaissance supremo, the autodidact of royal architecture. By 1615 he was not an ordinary servile officer, but a courtier, a friend of the most powerful in the land, and certainly a confidant of kings and queens. It is in this light that his remarkable Surveyorship must be judged.

It is a tragedy that the royal purse was so small, and that Jones was never given the opportunity to design palaces and great suites of royal apartments of truly regal scale. During the ten years of his Surveyorship under James I, annual expenditure never exceeded that during the first ten years of the King's reign. On the other hand, if Jones was constrained by frugality, it was often to his advantage. Like Sir William Chambers in the following century, Jones was the master of the small-scale unit of design, and this ability shines forth in the works for James I and Queen Anne of Denmark. Small works enabled him to concentrate his attention upon a unit of comprehensible and managable design, such as the Oatlands Palace Vineyard gateway to the park, 1617 (cat. no. 17), or a ceiling for the House of Lords, 1623–4 (fig. 52). Even the Newmarket Lodging and the Banqueting House are small exquisite essays, perfected and jewel-like, as was his very last work (and one of his greatest) for James I, that monarch's catafalque in 1625 (cat. nos 53, 54). Nevertheless, despite financial constraints, the Newmarket Lodging, the Queen's House (admittedly incomplete), the Banqueting House, the Queen's Chapel at St James's, and the revamped House of Lords, comprise a distinguished *œuvre*. The manner in which Jones used Palladio's Book IV on Roman antiquity to compile a grammar of ornamental architecture must also be stressed. It is not often observed that this was neither Palladio's way, nor indeed that of any other European architect before Lord Burlington in the early eighteenth century.

Jones might have possessed grander visions if he had been trained to architectural competence in a professional office or studio, and been compelled, as had many Renaissance architects before him, and John Webb under his own surveillance, to go through the mill of producing academic designs based upon building types. As we know from the evidence of theoretical drawings, Webb had these academic visions for palaces (Whitehall), cathedrals and public buildings, but not Jones. It is possible to sense in Jones the attitude of the artist-courtier, who could judge percipiently what was and what was not possible. Leave it to Webb to be the paper visionary. By 1625 Jones could rest assured that he alone had carried off single-handedly Edmund Bolton's prophesy in 1606 that he would bring 'the elegant arts of the ancients [. . .] across the Alps into our England'.

J.H.

Bibliography:

King's Works, iii, pp. 129–42

The Queen's House, Greenwich, 1616

As one of Queen Anne of Denmark's great works, her royal residence intended to have been built *de novo*, the Queen's House has been recognized as the fount of the classical tradition in Britain. Yet, its architectural history is undocumented and its origins obscure. The building accounts are incomplete because it was paid for out of the Queen's privy purse. The account closed on 30 April 1618, for reasons that may have been due to the ill health of the Queen, who had to cancel a *Masque of Ladies* early in 1618. She died 2 March 1619.

If one is tempted to speculate that the Queen desired a small pleasure pavilion near the royal palace, it is reasonable to ask why she had it built over the public highway for pedestrians and coaches with large windows, inconveniently looking onto noisy traffic.

There was, however, nothing surprising in building across the road, for there was already a Tudor gatehouse linking the palace precincts on the north or river side to the hunting park across the road.

What really matters is not whether it was a glorified bridge or a pleasure pavilion, but that right from the start Jones was exploring other solutions. Two designs may be associated with the need for a small palace untrammelled by the road. One (cat. no. 13), of Villa Aldobrandini derivation, is for a long 188 ft front (the Queen's House as built was a 115 ft square), 50 ft wide. Fenestrated 5-4-5 bays, it was to have a six-column portico on one front and a pilaster one on the other. In plan, parts of the Queen's House as built are adumbrated: the oval stair adjacent to a 40 ft square hall. However this hall was

Fig. 14
Adriaen Van Stalbemt and Jan Van Belcamp. Charles I and his Court at Greenwich, *c.* 1632

Fig. 15
Detail of Inigo Jones (left) and Endymion Porter from Van Stalbemt and Van Belcamp, fig. 14

Fig. 16
Detail of Queen's House from Van Stalbemt and Van Belcamp, fig. 14

Fig. 17
Detail of the ground elevation of the Queen's House, probably as built from 1616 to 1618. From Van Stalbemt and Van Belcamp, fig 14

to be vaulted, i.e. not a cube, and the stair was to have a grander 20 ft diameter, compared to the executed 15 ft one.

Two further surviving designs may relate to a second payment for an executed design on 8 October 1616. One lacks a scale (cat. no. 15), and as it is a side elevation of the H astride the road, it is possible to ascertain that the wings (or ends of the H) are only about 25 ft wide, of 'cabinet' size, and the whole is of about 125 ft width. Projections on the north and south fronts imply full pedimented Corinthian porticoes. Both can be seen to relate to a plan copied by Webb for an H-shaped building across a 'highway' (fig. 19). One façade of this is of 'villa' proportions that would fit the other surviving design (cat. no. 14), a magisterial one for a villa façade with loggia. This is pregnant for eighteenth-century Palladianism, because Lord Burlington, having found it among Palladio's drawings, assumed it to be by Palladio and used it as authority for villa designs in the 1720s.

Notwithstanding these surviving designs, all that can be said about the Queen's House in 1616–18 is that it was H-shaped. There is one other crucial document that needs to be discussed, suggesting that the elevation of the ground floor was quite different to that completed by 1635. In about 1632 Adriaen Van Stalbemt and Jan Van Belcamp painted a hunting picture with the King and Queen standing on the slopes of Greenwich Hill with a group of courtiers, among whom is no less than our Inigo (figs 14, 15). Down below in the middle ground is the incomplete Queen's House. Now, compared to earlier topographical views, all the details of the old royal palace and environs are correctly drawn. If the Queen's House is examined closely, it will be seen that the façade is carefully delineated and has voids with a tall arched central doorway and four arched windows each side, set rather high up in the wall (figs 16, 17). There are similar, almost square, arched basement windows in the town house façades in the 'Cupid's Palace' masque design (cat. no. 94).

All that one can suggest from this evidence is that the building was first of much smaller extent. It could have had a 40 ft vaulted hall on the palace side, but it is possible that the main reception room was to be placed over the bridge. From about 1632 Jones was operating in a different idiom elevationally, and must have demolished the 1616 walls to the foundations so as to extend his building.

J.H.

13 Preliminary ground-plan for the Queen's House, Greenwich

1616

Pen and brown ink with brown wash, over scorelines and slight graphite under-drawing

200 × 404 mm. Central vertical fold

Watermark: fleur-de-lys within shield surmounted by coronet (bottom cut off)

Inscribed by Jones in pen and brown ink, with dimensions in ft: *60, 40, 29, 20, 8*; and on *verso* by John Talman in pen and brown ink: *54:* [illegible]*:*

RIBA Jones & Webb 18

This is one the earliest surviving designs by Jones after he was created Surveyor of the King's Works on 1 October 1615. James I had assigned Greenwich Palace to his Queen in February 1614, and soon after this she engaged Simon Basil to improve her lodgings in the garden. When Basil died, Anne turned to the new Surveyor, fresh from his Italian journey, to design a self-contained villa in the grounds of the palace which would serve her as a retreat from Court life in her years of declining health.

By 8 October 1616 Jones had received payments for two designs for the new building: £10 for the first and £16 for the second (executed) design. This drawing can be associated with the Queen's House by virtue of the large spiral staircase and 40 ft square entrance hall, two distinguished features of the finished building in the 1630s. Since drawings cat. nos 14 and 15 approximate to what we know was begun at Greenwich between 1616 and 1618, the present sheet is possibly the first, rejected design for which Jones was paid £10. It is for a much larger building than the other two, with a front some 188 ft long. At this stage Jones seems to have been trying to reconcile three types: the traditional English country-house with its imposing entrance hall, ceremonial staircase and long gallery; the rationally planned Palladian palace with a classical front and atrium hall; and the compact Palladian villa. His ultimate model was the larger type of Palladian villa, with two floors of equal height and a vaulted entrance hall, as at the Villa Pisani at Montagnana and the Villa Cornaro at Piombino (*I Quattro libri*, II, 52, 53).

In technique, the drawing is closely modelled on plans by Palladio in Jones's collection. It introduces the discipline of the ruler and Palladio's conventions for door and window openings, vaulting and staircases, and dimensional notation.

Bibliography:
King's Works, iv, pp. 114–15

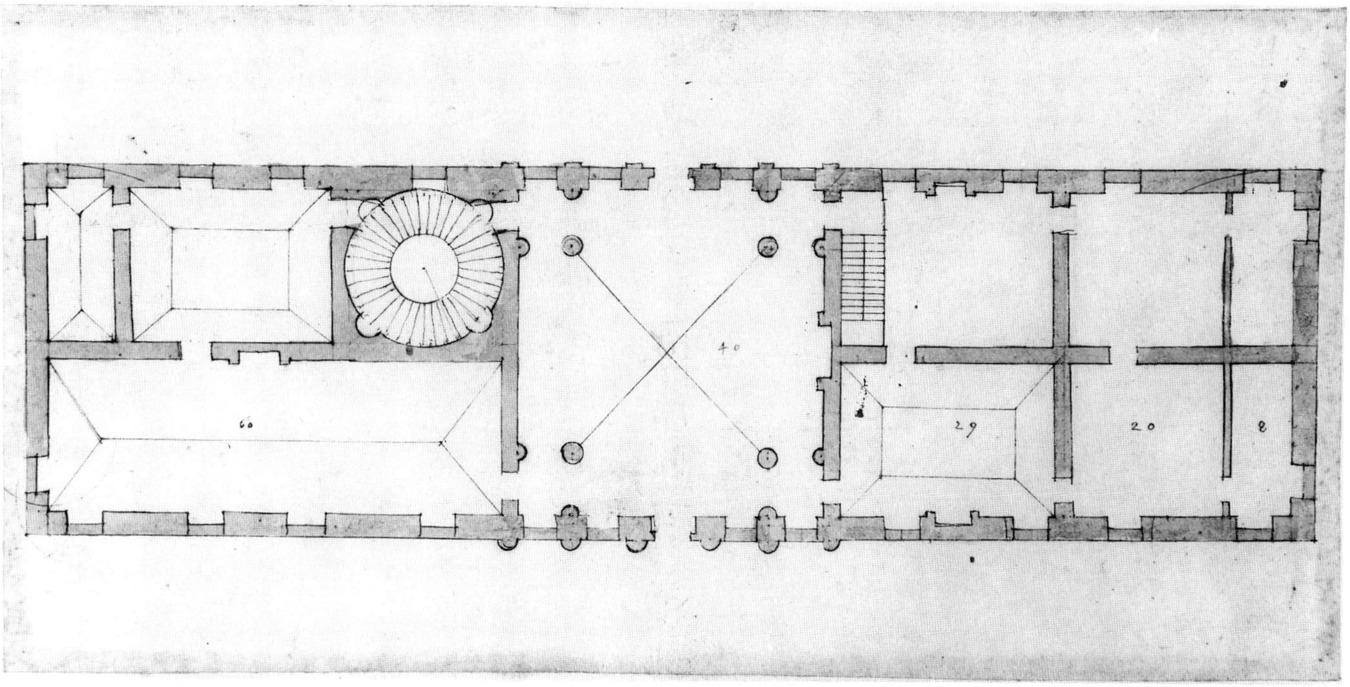
40
60
29
20
8

14 Preliminary design for the north or south façade of the Queen's House, Greenwich

1616

Pen and dark brown ink over scorelines, with graphite and black chalk under-drawing and additions

315 × 465 mm. Laid down on 18th-c. paper and trimmed. Thick cream-coloured paper with heavy vertical fold in centre, split and repaired in places. Tear and grey stain near bottom left-hand corner

RIBA Jones & Webb 19

Until published by Dr Margaret Whinney in 1970, this drawing had been assigned to Palladio, and bound in the volumes of his drawings at the RIBA (vol. XIV/8). Dr Whinney compared the technique to Jones's designs in the second decade of the seventeenth century and tentatively ascribed the elevation to the early Queen's House of 1616. Her conclusions have since been doubted but are reaffirmed here. The heavy under-scoring, the blotting and fading of the ink outlines, and the wavy-lined profiles of the rustication in the central basement find exact parallels in Jones's drawings of 1616–17 (cat. nos 17, 19, 21). Typical of the period before 1620 is his use of the scorer for experimentation in the under-drawing.

As Dr Whinney observed, the design can be matched with Jones's side elevation of the Queen's House at Worcester College (cat. no. 15). Not only are there two floors of almost equal height, a ground floor treated as a rusticated basement and an upper floor with shared features such as pulvinated friezes and a blocking-course above the entablature, but each elevation has quoins at the first-floor angles and a provision for statuary on the pediments. The porticoes on the two designs are also consistent, since the paired end-columns on the RIBA design would be the natural termination for the side walls shown on the Worcester College drawing. This type of portico, shown on John Webb's plan of a villa presumed to be the Queen's House (fig. 19), is found on several of Palladio's villa designs in *I Quattro libri* (e.g. Villa Pisani at Bagnolo and Villa Trissino at Meledo, Book II, pp. 47, 60).

The rich articulation of Jones's façade is typical of the 1616–19 period and contrasts sharply with the executed building at Greenwich (fig. 68). By the 1630s Jones had moved away from direct dependence on Palladian or Scamozzian models to a more severe type of elevation, with windows isolated in broad stretches of plain, unarticulated wall surface.

Although Jones's design did not rise far from the ground at Greenwich, it had a somewhat distorted after-life in the eighteenth century, thanks to a copy drawing by Henry Flitcroft which rendered Jones's projecting (or recessed) portico as an applied order (fig. 18). Flitcroft's version was apparently copied by Colen Campbell for Lord Pembroke's house in Whitehall (finished 1724), and for Roger Morris's Marble Hill House at Twickenham (*c.* 1724–30).

See colour illustration on p. 149

Fig. 18
Henry Flitcroft. Redrawing for Lord Burlington of cat. no. 14, 1720s

Bibliography:
M. Whinney, 'An unknown design for a villa by Inigo Jones' in H. M. Colvin and J. Harris (eds), *The Country Seat* (London, 1970), pp. 33–5
King's Arcadia, p. 148
D. Lewis, *The Drawings of Andrea Palladio* (Washington D.C., 1981), pp. 217–18 [attributing the drawing to Palladio's studio]
King's Works, iv, p. 159 [ascribing the drawing to Hyde Park Lodge, 1634–5]

15 Preliminary elevation for the east or west sides of the Queen's House, Greenwich

1616

Pen and dark brown ink, shaded in black chalk or charcoal, over graphite under-drawing and heavy scorelines

330 × 432 mm. Thick whitish paper

Very faint watermark

Worcester College H & T 12

The essence of the early Queen's House is contained in this diminutive drawing for an H-shaped villa straddling a road. For many years the authorship and dating were questioned, but they can be established by comparison with Jones's 1616 design for an entrance bay to an unidentified house, which has a similar style of freehand pen drawing in the quoins and running mouldings (cat. no. 21).

Queen Anne of Denmark's reasons for wanting a building with the main living-room spanning a public road between Deptford and Woolwich have not been recorded, but we know that the villa replaced a Tudor gatehouse on the same site which provided a bridge between the palace gardens on the south side of the road and the royal park on the north. By placing the villa over the road Jones ensured that the public way did not intrude on the prospects from the porticoes on each side of the villa and at the same time created access between the two royal properties.

In the finished building of the 1630s the H-shaped plan is retained but the frontages on each side of the road are much larger than the one-bay projections envisaged here (figs 67–70). That the building began on this small scale is confirmed by references in the Works accounts of 1617–18 to a single main room heated by a 'stove', and two or three separate rooms, apparently unheated. It is therefore reasonable to assume that a substantial rebuilding on larger foundations took place in the 1630s and that the villa begun by Anne of Denmark was very different in character to the one eventually occupied by Henrietta Maria.

Stylistically, this design is wholly consistent with the period soon after Jones had returned from Italy and was working in the idiom of Palladio's villa and palace designs. The tall rusticated basement and enriched main floor reflect the Vicentine palace type, in particular an early Palladio design in Jones's collection for the Palazzo Civena at Vicenza (*c.* 1539–40) which has similar round-arch voussoired openings on the ground floor (RIBA Palladio XVII/14). That Jones was thinking of a small-scale rural villa of the type illustrated in Book II of *I Quattro libri* is apparent from his imitation of Palladio's conventions of over-sized pediment statues and a combination of diagonal and vertical shading lines (cf. the Villa Maser, Book II, p. 51). The projecting porticoes with arched openings in the side walls are a feature of Palladio's Villa Rotunda at Vicenza (*I Quattro libri*, II, pp. 18–19) and Scamozzi's Villa Molin, near Padua, two buildings which Jones personally inspected in the course of his travels.

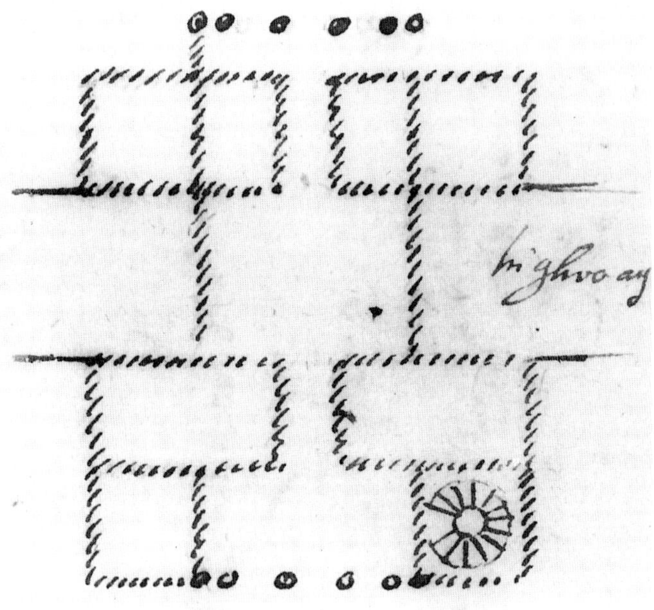

Fig. 19
John Webb. Record of a plan for a building set across a 'highway', a copy of a lost plan for the Queen's House by Inigo Jones, 1640s(?)

The drawing can be linked with a thumbnail sketch by John Webb on a sheet of his copy plans at the RIBA showing an H-shaped villa spanning a 'highway' (fig. 19). It was probably copied from a lost plan of the Queen's House corresponding with Jones's elevation on the present sheet, although it is surprising that Webb did not acknowledge the design as 'Mr Surveyor's', as he did on several other thumbnail drawings including Jones's design for Sir Peter Killigrew's house in Blackfriars (figs 109, 110).

Bibliography:

J. Charlton, *The Queen's House Greenwich* (London, 1976)

D. Lewis, *The Drawings of Andrea Palladio* (Washington D.C., 1981), pp. 25–6

King's Works, iv, p. 115

16 Ideal plan for a centralized villa

c. 1617

Pen and brown ink with brown wash over graphite, heavy underscoring and compass marks. Later red ink ruled border lines around edges of sheet

337 × 323 mm. Horizontal fold through centre of plan

Inscribed by Jones with feet dimensions (as *piedi*) within plan, and below with cardinal points of compass: *N, E, S, W.* Numbered by an 18th-c. hand in top right-hand corner: *28*; inscribed on *verso* by John Talman in pen and brown ink: *54:*⊩*:*

Scale: 10 ft = approx. $\frac{29}{32}$ in.

RIBA Jones & Webb 60

This would seem to be a preliminary idealized scheme for a centralized villa rather than a project intended to be put in hand, as it is based directly on plans and instructions by Scamozzi for the layout of suburban villas in his *L'Idea*. Jones acquired his copy of this treatise (now at Worcester College) on 25 March 1617 and was soon annotating the chapters on villa design in Part I, Book III. The plan depends on Scamozzi's woodcut of the Villa Pisani at Lonigo (1576–9) and the Villa Bardelini at Monfumo (1594–1600), both of which have central circular halls adjoining a recessed portico (*L'Idea*, Part I, pp. 273, 279). For the curved loggias Jones turned to Palladio's illustration of the Villa Trissino at Meledo in *I Quattro libri* (Book II, p. 60). This brought the plan closer to the requirements in Scamozzi's text, which states that porticoes of suburban villas should face due south and have covered walkways on each side (*L'Idea*, Part I, pp. 271–2).

That the design was prepared with the practicalities of an English setting in mind is shown by Jones's introduction of chimney-pieces in two of the niches of the rotunda and in the angles of the four corner rooms. In technique, the drawing cannot be much later than the Queen's House designs of 1616 and this has given rise to a suggestion that the villa was conceived for the hill at Greenwich Park (now occupied by Wren's Royal Observatory). But though it is tempting to imagine this villa on a hill top, like Palladio's Villa Rotunda in Vicenza, there is no evidence for such a project in 1616, and the strong connections with Scamozzi indicate that the drawing was prepared at least six months after work had begun on the Queen's House.

Bibliography:

J. Harris, *The Palladians* (London, 1981), p. 45

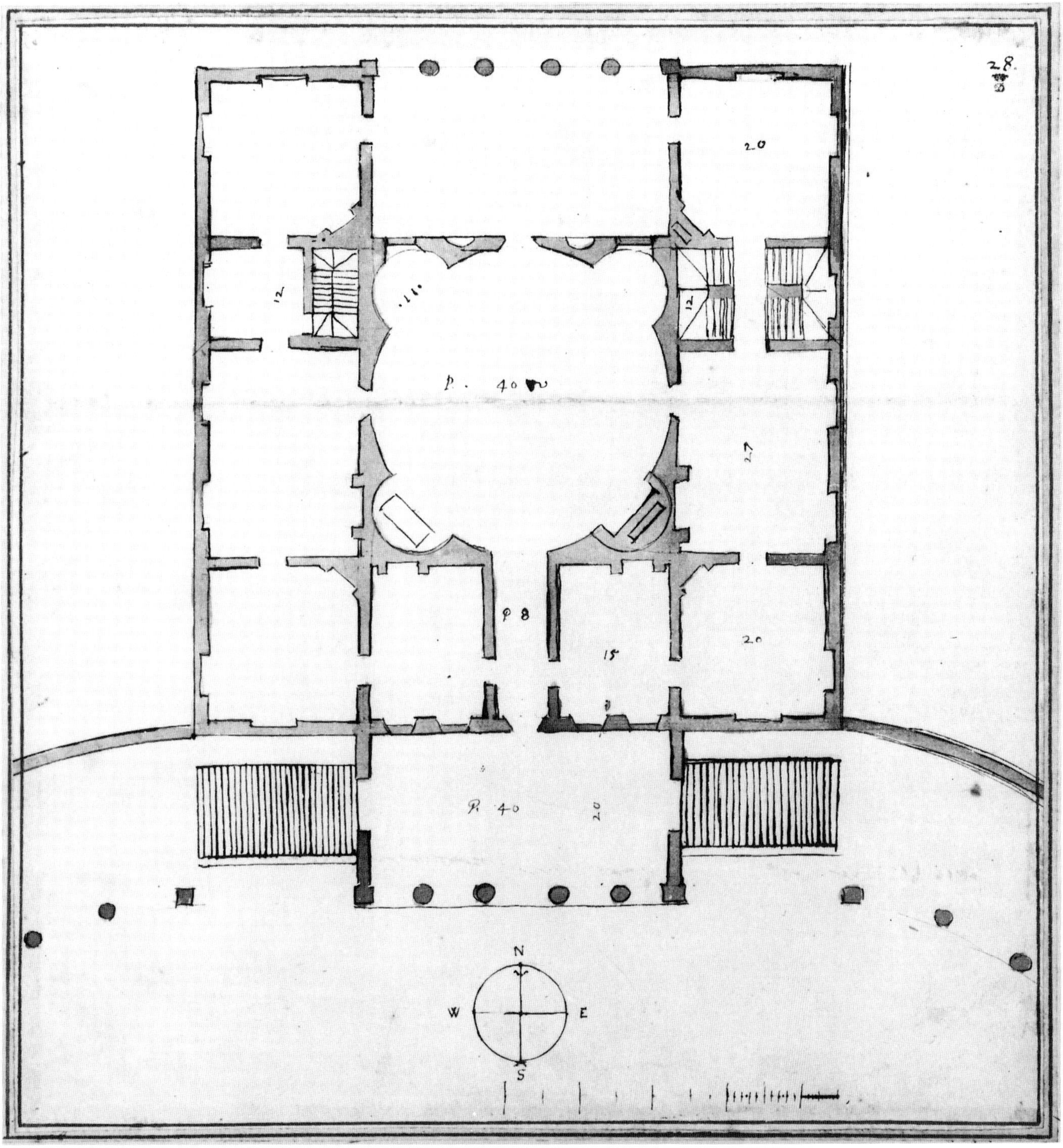
28.
20
12
12
P. 40
27
φ 8
20
15
P. 40
20
N
W
E
S

Oatlands Palace, Surrey, 1617

Oatlands became a royal palace in 1537 when Henry VIII acquired it by exchange. Although the existing house was a large one, by 1544 a huge Middle Court had been added in the style of Hampton Court, preserved for us in the valuable sketches made by Wyngaerde in 1555. As with most of her palaces, Queen Elizabeth's alterations or additions were minimal, as indeed were those by Queen Anne of Denmark, who was granted the palace in August 1611. In 1616–18 Jones designed the 'greate gate' to the Vineyard, two other gates, and various minor improvements to the Privy Garden which occupied a group of eight plots or *parterres* in an area bounded on two sides by the old mansion, and on one by Henry VIII's addition. South of this garden was the Vineyard enclosed by a massive 11 ft high wall, nearly 700 ft long. Here was the gateway seen in the background of Van Somer's portrait of the Queen (fig. 20).

Fig. 20
Paul Van Somer. Queen Anne of Denmark, with Oatlands Palace and the Vineyard gateway in the background, 1617

After the Queen's death there were minor alterations, but even when granted to Queen Henrietta Maria in March 1627 little of consequence was done, although one would like to know if Jones designed the timber stable in 1629–30 and the 'Archt Arbor of Tymber' 263 ft long, 14 ft high and 14 ft wide built in the Little Garden 1631–2. Between 1635 and 1638 occur the interior improvements effected by Jones and for which some designs exist (cat. nos 69–71). All this was destroyed by the Parliamentarians and a modern housing estate occupies the site, but fragments of Jones's Vineyard gateway survive at Weybridge Museum as a sad reminder of what must have been a great Tudor palace.

J.H.

Bibliography

King's Works, iv, pp. 205–17

17 Elevation for the front (outer) side of the Vineyard gateway, Oatlands Palace, Surrey

1617

Pen and brown ink over scorelines and with additions in graphite

387 × 294 mm. Comprises main sheet, 328 × 293 mm, and upper sheet, 87 × 294 mm, pasted across pediment with 27 mm overlap. Modern repair over diagonal tear on left side of elevation

Watermark: scrolled cartouche containing Crozier of Basle and bugle motif, surmounted by fleur-de-lys

Signed: *Inigo Jones* in pen and brown ink in bottom right-hand corner

No scale (but same as on cat. no. 18)

RIBA Jones & Webb 62

Detail of fig. 20, by Van Somer, showing Oatlands Palace with the Vineyard gateway in the foreground

This gateway is shown at the entrance from the park to the Vineyard in the background of Paul Van Somer's portrait of Anne of Denmark at Oatlands in 1617 (fig. 20). Works accounts record the erection of a 'greate gate' in June and July 1617, and refer to 'doricke Columns cutt rusticke with a frontispeece and square table of marble sett over the same'. The gateway was re-erected in 1735 for the 9th Earl of Lincoln in his park at Oatlands, but was subsequently demolished. Some fragments of rusticated walling and a piece of cornice survive at Weybridge Museum, Surrey.

The rough-cut rustication of this gateway was entirely novel in England in the second decade of the seventeenth century, for although Serlio's designs for rusticated Doric and Tuscan entrances in the *Regole generali di architettura* (Venice, 1537) and the *Extraordinario libro di architettura* (Venice, 1558) were widely available, no Englishman before Jones had studied original examples in Italy. His design is based on two examples in the *Extraordinario libro*, but the inspiration comes from what Lord Burlington described in a note in his copy of *I Quattro libri* as 'the best school that ever was for rusticks': Palladio's Palazzo Thiene in Vicenza. The two types of rustication echo those of the entrance-hall columns and exterior ground floor at the Palazzo Thiene (figs 11, 12). Jones noted of the entrance hall, next to his sketches in his copy of *I Quattro libri* (fig. 13), that there was 'an admirable discretion in thes Bozzi [rusticated blocks] for ye Scapi [shafts] Q being sllender answearth to ye heayght of the Placce and the adiuncte of ye Bozzi to ye strength and rustick of the reste' – in other words, he saw an agreement of effect between the slenderness of the columns and the height of the hall, as contrasted with the heaviness of the rustication on the columns and walls. Similar contrasts are at work on this design and explain its ennervating combination of mass and upward movement. Jones has deliberately cramped the proportions so that the bulging columns are in relatively narrow jambs, the pediment is unusually steep, and the triglyphs are closer together than the usual $\frac{3}{4}$ column-diameter proportion (or $1\frac{1}{2}$ modules). The cornice is very deep, with a large top moulding, and the pediment is stretched up with a tall central pedestal. Mass and verticality compete with one another in a tension of opposites, expressed in the draftsmanship by the upward lift in the diagonal shading.

Bibliography:

W. G. Keith, 'The Palace of Oatlands', *Architectural Review*, xxxix (1916), pp. 76–7

King's Works, iv, pp. 213–14

18 Elevation and plan for the rear (inner) side of the Vineyard gateway, Oatlands Palace, Surrey

1617

Pen and brown ink over scorelines and graphite

423 × 335 mm. Single sheet with flap, 64 × 335 mm, across top of arch. Central horizontal fold. Top right-hand corner torn away and repaired with later paper

Watermark: shield surmounted by crown

Signed near lower right-hand corner in pen and brown ink: *Inigo Jones*; and inscribed by Jones with scale of inches vertically in centre of gate: *12, 14* [*sic*], *36*. *Verso* is inscribed by Jones in pen and brown ink in lower right: *Horscombe quarry in* [*sic*] *10 myles of bristow*; and below with calculations: *64/72/36/24/20/*[=] *216*; and to right *12/6/*[=] *72*; and above, near centre right of sheet, by John Webb in pen and brown ink: *The Gate of y*[e] *vineyard at/Oatelands*; and in bottom right-hand corner by an 18th-c. hand: *Door. 7.*

Scale: 1 ft $=\frac{9}{14}$ in.

RIBA Jones & Webb 64

This elevation faced into the Vineyard at Oatlands Palace. It illustrates Jones's fascination with rough-cut surfaces soon after his return from Italy, for not only is the arch surround in chamfered rusticated blocks but the brick frieze below the pediment is cut in similar fashion. The blocks in the two courses above the arch are progressively wider towards the centre, as if to emphasize the expanding profile of the arch. Below the flap across the arch head is an alternative treatment with five instead of four voussoirs each side of the keyblock. The flap design is more satisfactory as the voussoirs are nearly the same depth as the other blocks. This drawing gives us a close-up view of wall treatment envisaged by Jones for the Queen's House, Greenwich in 1616, the designs for which show similar rough-cut stone surfaces offset by brick (cat. nos 14, 15).

19 Elevation for the park gateway, Oatlands Palace, Surrey

1617

Pen and dark brown ink over scorelines

394 × 280 mm. Two sheets joined near the top, 330 × 280 mm and 67 × 280 mm, with modern strip on back

Watermark: elaborate coat of arms surmounted by crown and with golden fleece below

Inscribed by Jones in pen and brown ink at top right: *The Gaate that goith into the Parke.*; and below arch: *The scall of the 2 gaates in to the vineyard and the Parke*; and on *verso* by an 18th-c. hand in pen and brown ink: *Door* (number indecipherable); the *verso* has a pen and brown ink outline of the reveals of the rear side of the gateway drawn over the imprint of the *recto* design

Scale: 1 ft = approx. $\frac{29}{32}$ in.

RIBA Jones & Webb 66

This classical stone arch probably gave access to the park at Oatlands from a walled garden adjoining the Vineyard on the south side of the Tudor palace. Although inscribed as having the same scale as the Vineyard gateway (cat. no. 17), this is not the case; nor can we be certain that this is one of two 'smaller gates being both of one propocon' mentioned in the Vineyard gateway account: there is no companion for this drawing and it is larger than suggested by the relative costs of timber for the three pairs of doors (£6. 8s. for the Vineyard gate and £4 for the two smaller gates).

The elevation is based on a design from Palladio's studio for a rusticated arch with a ball-finial decoration which was later copied by John Webb (RIBA Palladio XV/3; Worcester College H & T 182E, Plate 118). A similar formula but with flat channelled rustication rather than ashlar masonry was used for the garden gateway at New Hall, Essex, in 1623 (cat. no. 43).

Bibliography:

PRO Declared Accounts (Audit Office), Bundle 2487, Roll 356

King's Works, iv, pp. 213–14

20 Elevation for a rusticated doorway, ascribed to Oatlands Palace, Surrey

c. 1617

Pen and brown ink over heavy scorelines and graphite

302 × 247 mm

Watermark: water-pot surmounted by a coronet with five quatrefoils and a quatrefoil above

Scale: 1 ft = just under $\frac{5}{8}$ in.

RIBA Jones & Webb 85

This powerful design must date within a year of the drawings for gateways at Oatlands even though the paper – thin, and with a water-pot watermark – is a type found only after 1620 among Jones's securely dated drawings. The roughly handled pen and ink lines, the heavily marked and untidy scorelines, and the loosely scribbled surfaces of the rusticated blocks are all characteristic of Jones's drawings in 1616 and 1617 (e.g. cat. nos 14, 17–19). It was probably for a gate at Oatlands, one of which, located at the 'lower end' of the Privy Walk adjacent to the Vineyard, is described in the account as 'a rusticke dore cutt in bricke and finished over' (i.e. rendered). This suggests the type of rendered-brick rustication used by Palladio on the ground floor of the Palazzo Thiene in Vicenza (fig. 11). Brick rustication of this kind occurs on the rear elevation of the Oatlands Vineyard gateway (cat. no. 18) and is implied by a similar drafting technique on the present design. The drawing should be compared with another elevation by Jones for a square-headed doorway dating from this period which shows a similar preoccupation with the alignment of the voussoirs (cat. no. 115).

Bibliography:

King's Works, iv, pp. 213–14

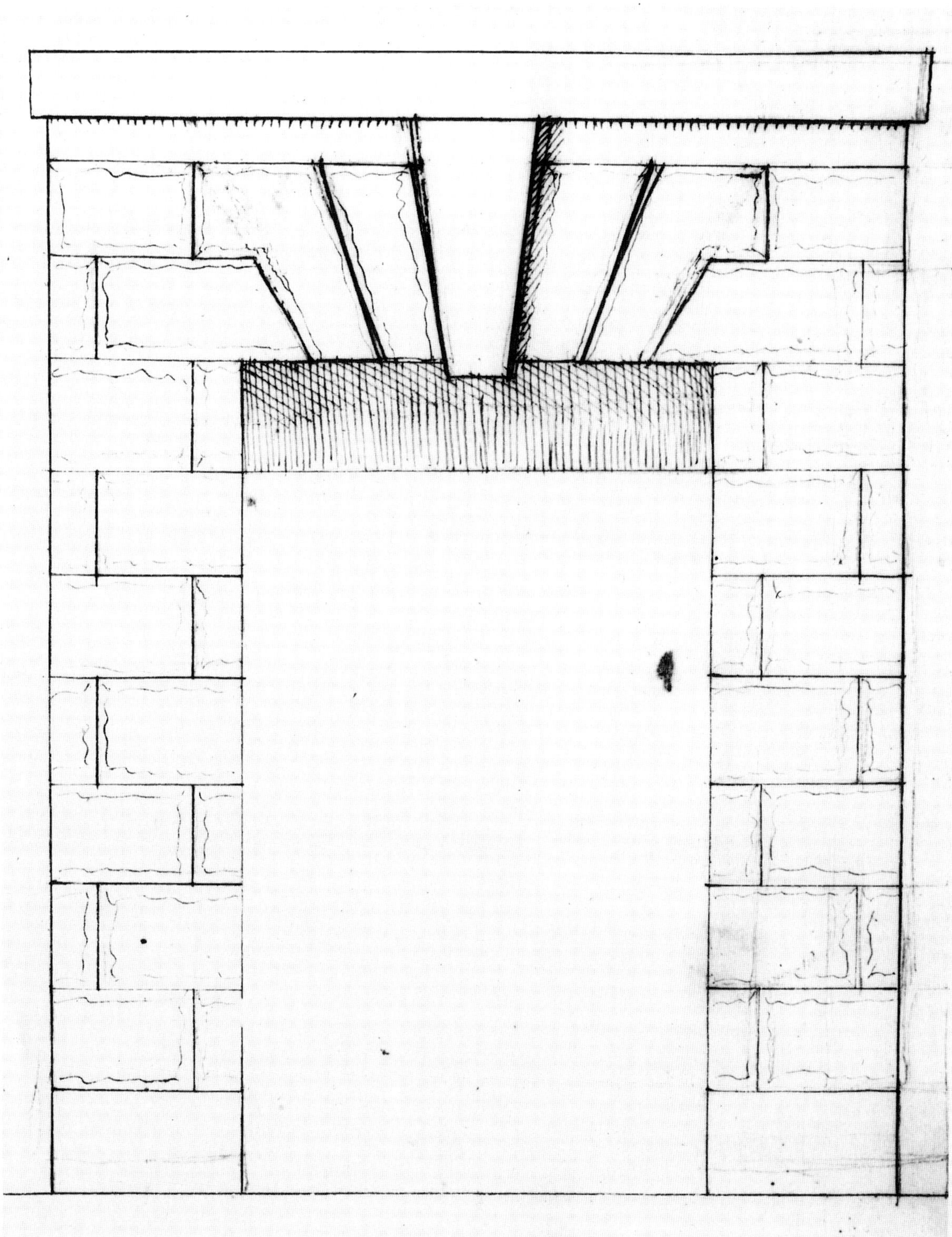

Inigo Jones and Courtier Designs 1616–19

Jones did not return from Italy in 1615 ready to be the fully-fledged British Palladio or Vitruvius. There was a need to settle in, and to assess his new role as Surveyor of the King's Works – a huge challenge. Also, at that time, expenditure on royal buildings was not high. Therefore Jones had time to devote to designing for his courtier friends. Once demands were made upon him by James I and Queen Anne of Denmark, they came first in priority. In any case, one senses that Jones was not keen to encourage a courtier practice.

A few courtiers were special, and of these Lord Arundel stands out. At Arundel House Jones probably built the gallery wing, as well as a gateway, entrance door, a small house with blocked cornice on the courtyard, and laid out the garden with gates. There were also works at Arundel's houses at Greenwich (alas burned down) and Highgate. The gallery was a substantial job, built of brick with stone dressings, and with a pair of windows joined by an iron pergola to the River Thames. There was a door or porch for Lionel Cranfield (later Earl of Middlesex, of Beaufort House, Chelsea) at Pishiobury, Hertfordshire, for which an account dated June 1615 was in the Cranfield papers, but is now missing. Fulke Greville's house with its pedimented and scrolled gable, and Sir Edward Cecil's pergola entrance are datable 1617–18.

The most tantalizing and grand commission of these early years is Houghton Conquest, Bedfordshire (figs 21–3), possibly begun just before Jones returned from Italy, in traditional Jacobean Court style (the style of say John Thorpe, or even Simon Basil). The patron was Mary, Dowager Countess of Pembroke, the mother of the 3rd and 4th Earls of Pembroke, a close friend of Lord and Lady Arundel, and one who danced in Jones's masques. It is possible that in the building process she was persuaded to provide modernity to the house by inserting

Fig. 21
Houghton Conquest, Bedfordshire. North front in 1785. Watercolour by W. Kimpton

Fig. 22
Houghton Conquest, Bedfordshire. The west front colonnade, *c*. 1900, before restoration

Fig. 23
Detail of the north front entrance of Houghton Conquest, *c*. 1900, showing Dudley and Pembroke crests in frieze

classical frontispieces into the north and west fronts. These could only be by Jones, so classical are they in Jacobean England. As such, they are precious relics of his designing skills in this early period, probably in mid-1615 and certainly before 1621 when the countess died. The north front (fig. 21) echoes the Convento della Carità in Venice, and both the arched system of this front and the remarkable superimposed colonnades of the west front, remind us strongly of the two-storey portico that was probably added to Byfleet Palace, Surrey, for Queen Anne of Denmark, a lost and undocumented work, but recorded in a drawing by John Aubrey.

What is fascinating about this early period in Jones's career, is that his sources can be as much in Palladio's book as in north European Classicism. If this was all he did for courtiers between 1615 and 1618 (and there must have been more), it constituted a body of work that struck a new note in the London street scene. There is a sympathetic link between Fulke Greville's house (cat. no. 22) and façades in, say, Augsburg; indeed Fulke Greville's house may be seen as the root source of London Street architecture around Covent Garden and Lincoln's Inn Fields of the type described in 1631 as 'with the like Balcony wyndowes and Gable ends'. One senses that Jones's subordinates could better understand these somewhat eclectic earlier works than the mature intellectual designs of the great upland period of Jones's life beginning with the Prince's Lodging at Newmarket Palace in 1619.

J.H.

Bibliography:

Greater London Council, Survey of London, xxxxvi: *The Parish of St Paul's Covent Garden* (London, 1970), p. 30

John Harris, 'Inigo Jones and the courtier style', *Architectural Review*, clix (July, 1973), pp. 17–24

King's Arcadia, pp. 109–10

21 Elevation for the entrance bay to an unidentified house

1616

Pen and brown ink with grey wash over scorelines

358 × 310 mm. Central horizontal fold

Watermark: shield containing fleur-de-lys surmounted by a coronet and with a 4WR monogram below (Wendelin Riehel's mill, Strasbourg)

Signed in bottom right-hand corner: *Inigo: Jones: fecit. 1616*; and on *verso* by John Talman in pen and brown ink: *54:* [illegible]:

RIBA Jones & Webb 73

This is perhaps one of the most tantalizing of Jones's unidentified designs because it is both signed and dated, and is the date of the Queen's House. Just how seriously intended it was is demonstrated by the related design (cat. no. 114) for the doorway with quoin and voussoir surround which shows the fragment of a similar signature. For 1616 it is tempting to associate this with one of Lord Arundel's commissions. The exclusion of the adjacent elevations suggests that this was an addition to an existing earlier house, with a height 44 ft from ground to balustrade. If anything, the architecture could be described as a compromise between Palladio and the Jacobean tradition, and is in a style that might have developed in England if Jones had never existed. Characteristically Jacobean are the stone quoins, pierced balustrade and Serlian wooden door; Palladio's influence is registered in the hierarchy of a rusticated ground floor and *piano-nobile*-style first floor enriched with classical mouldings.

See colour illustration on p. 150

Bibliography:
King's Arcadia, pp. 106–7

22 Presentation design for a town-house façade, ascribed to Sir Fulke Greville's house (Brooke House), Holborn, London

c. 1617

Pen and brown ink with grey-brown wash over scorelines, with black chalk and graphite under-drawing

420 × 257 mm. Trimmed sheet, laid down on mount within frame of double red ink ruled border lines

Inscribed by Jones in pen and brown ink with numbered scales at foot of sheet

Scale: 1 ft = just under $\frac{1}{5}$ in.

Chatsworth (unnumbered)

The ascription to Sir Fulke Greville's house, Holborn, has been made from a comparison with John Smythson's drawing of *Sur foulke gryvelles: in houlbourne/1619* (fig. 24), showing a three-bay façade, a central pergola or balcony, and a strong three-part entablature crowned by an attic and a scrolled gable with pediment. The house as built, sometime before 1619, was an extension to Greville's older Bath House (renamed Brooke House when he was created Lord Brooke in 1620).

In technique, the drawing dates to the 1616–19 period, as there is much over-inking and uncertainty in the ruled and freehand lines. The competent handling of quoins and voussoirs suggests it is slightly later than the entrance-bay elevation of 1616 (cat. no. 21); but there is a trace of the rounded stylus used on designs from 1619, and the freehand drawing is less fluent than on the Banqueting House elevations of that year (cat. nos 33, 34). Thus a date in the middle of the 1616–19 period seems the most likely.

What is important about Sir Fulke Greville's house in the context of urban street patterns is the early appearance of the northern gable in its classical form (seen by Jones in Augsburg and Heidelberg in Germany, and possibly in the Low Countries), and the incorporation of the pergola, a form of balconied window, derived from sixteenth-century examples in Venice and Rome. The pergola became enormously fashionable in the middle decades of the seventeenth century in England following its use by such subordinate Court architects as Nicholas Stone and a host of lesser artisans. A painting by an unidentified Frenchman of James Street, one of the exit streets from Covent Garden, laid out by Isaac de Caus as executant architect to Jones from *c.* 1630, shows sequences of gabled façades with projecting first-floor balconies (fig. 91), as does Hollar's view of the estate.

Although the narrow proportions of the façade are typical of the early seventeenth-century London town house, the composition and detailing of the elevation (excluding the gable) are based on Palladio's designs for Vicentine palaces (e.g. cat. no. 11). The ground floor is treated as a semi-rusticated basement and the first floor like a true Italian *piano nobile*, with enriched window surrounds, continuous balcony rail and enlarged central opening. The proportions of the windows, the main entablature and eaves cornice come from Book I of *I Quattro libri*, and have been carefully marked out in the under-drawing with points of the dividers (e.g. the main entablature is $\frac{1}{5}$ the wall space below).

Fig. 24
John Smythson. Record drawing of Sir Fulke Greville's house, Holborn, London, 1619

See colour illustration on p. 151

Bibliography:

J. Harris, 'Inigo Jones and the Prince's Lodging at Newmarket', *Architectural History*, ii (1959), p. 40

—, 'Inigo Jones and the courtier style', *Architectural Review*, clix (July 1973), pp. 17, 19

H. J. Louw, 'Anglo-Netherlandish architectural interchange *c.* 1600–*c.* 1660', *Architectural History*, xxxiv (1981), pp. 10–11

23 Elevation for a pergola entrance to Sir Edward Cecil's house, Strand, London

c. 1617

Pen and brown ink with grey-brown wash over scorelines and slight graphite under-drawing. Later red ink ruled border lines on edges of sheet

486 × 360 mm. Horizontal fold through centre of sheet and vertical fold near right edge

Watermark: same as cat. no. 21

Scale: 1 ft $= \frac{29}{32}$ in.

RIBA Jones & Webb 11

Once again John Smythson comes to our rescue by recording, in 1618–19, *The Pergular at Coronall: Sissell's House in the Strande*, showing a rusticated arched entrance and iron-railed balcony which nicely match Jones's design (fig. 25). Smythson's drawing also makes the link between this design and another at the RIBA for an internal doorway with a flat cornice and pulvinated frieze (cat. no. 24).

Mid-sixteenth-century examples of this type of entrance occur on Via Giulia in Rome, but Jones's more immediate source was probably an engraving in Francart's *Premier livre d'architecture* (Brussels, 1616) (fig. 26). He purged the Flemish original of fussy Mannerist details and used a step height of 6 in. as a module for simple proportions, such as the equivalence of the arch height (9 ft) with the width of the arch and piers (5 ft and 2 ft each).

Sir Edward Cecil (1572–1638) was related to both Sir Fulke Greville and Robert Cecil, 1st Earl of Salisbury. With Jones and Lord Arundel he witnessed the Deed of Foundation of Dulwich College in 1618.

See colour illustration on p. 152

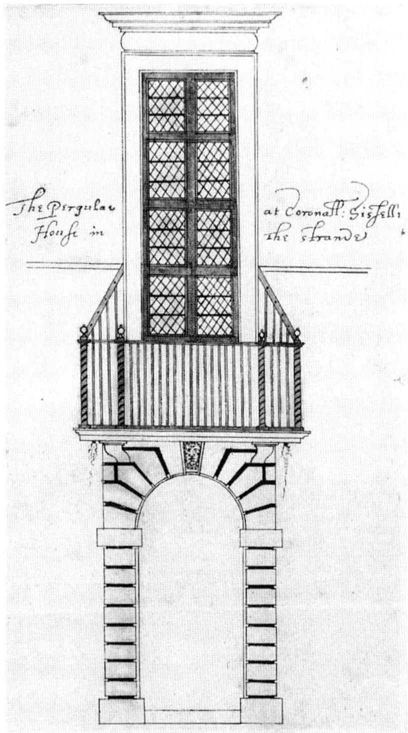

Fig. 25
John Smythson. Record drawing of Sir Edward Cecil's pergola entrance, Strand, London, 1619

Fig. 26
Engraved doorway from Francart's *Premier livre d'architecture* (Brussels, 1616)

24 Elevation of internal doorway, probably for the pergola at Sir Edward Cecil's house, Strand, London

c. 1617

Pen and dark-brown ink with grey wash over scorelines, graphite and black chalk on *verso*

322 × 410 mm. Two vertical folds on centre left

Watermark: shield containing horn surmounted by coronet, with 4WR monogram below (Wendelin Riehel's mill, Strasbourg)

Verso: inscribed by Jones in graphite to left of a graphite sketch drawn sideways on left side of sheet, showing a three-bay house with pergola: *y^e holl breadth of y^e / wale is 37*^{fo}; and below sketch to right: *y^e Pergola must be 14*$^{fo}\frac{1}{2}$. Superimposed on whole *verso* is a black chalk sketch of an arched entrance flanked by columns and pilasters, with niches in the outer bays

RIBA Jones & Webb 75

Fig. 27
Verso of cat. no. 24, showing rough study for an arched entrance flanked by columns and niches, and (upper left-hand side of sheet) a sketch for a house elevation, probably Sir Edward Cecil's house, Strand, London

Fig. 28
Reconstruction by Gordon Higgott of Jones's sketch for a house elevation on the *verso* of cat. no. 24

It can be shown that this drawing and cat. no. 23 represent the outside and inside of the same architectural feature. In style the drawing belongs firmly in the 1616–19 period, as there is a patchy quality in the ink outlines and pen shading akin to that of the Arundel House 'Italian' gateway of 1618 (cat. no. 40). On the *verso* of the sheet is a rough sketch in graphite drawn sideways on the left half, which shows a house façade with central first-floor pergola above a door, flanked by canted bay windows (figs 27, 28). The pergola railing is carried on heavy consoles and a keyblock, and the walls each side are blank. Jones has written below the sketch that the pergola 'must be 14$^{fo}\frac{1}{2}$'. Fourteen and a half feet is exactly the height from the ground to the balcony floor on Jones's design for Sir Edward Cecil's pergola (cat. no. 22), and if we compare Smythson's drawing of the first-floor opening (fig. 25) with this one there are corresponding features, such as the flat cornice with pulvinated frieze and the string-course at a 'leaning height' each side of the doorway, which link the two elevations conclusively.

The door-frame derives from flat-headed window openings on Palladio's Palazzo Chiericati in Vicenza (cat. no. 12) and is a leitmotif of Jones's domestic style in the period from 1616–19 (e.g. cat nos 14, 15, 22, 30, 31). In the hands of Lord Burlington and William Kent it became an essential component of the eighteenth-century Palladian interior.

Superimposed on the graphite sketch of the pergola is a rough black chalk sketch, which uses the shadow image of the front design to create a three-bay monumental entrance, with an arched opening, niches and groups of Corinthian columns or pilasters carrying an entablature. The arrangement is similar to that of the entrance on St Paul's north transept front of *c.* 1634 (cat. no. 80). Jones uses black chalk more frequently in the 1630s, and was fond of exploiting shadow images on the backs of his sketches in the Roman Sketchbook at the same period (cat. no. 99).

25 Elevation for an arched doorway surmounted by a pedimented attic containing a barred oval window

c. 1620

Pen and brown ink with grey-brown wash over black chalk, scorelines and compass marks

408 × 302 mm. Torn and repaired across centre and on right

Watermark: shield containing turret above rampant lion on left and eagle above rampant lion on right. Coronet above and golden fleece below. Similar to cat. nos 19 and 39

Inscribed on *verso* in pen and brown ink by an 18th-c. hand: *Door.6.*

Scale: 1 ft = 1 in.

RIBA Jones & Webb 81

Like cat. 23 this entrance design is a classicized version of a plate in Francart's *Premier livre d'architecture*. The pedimented attic is based on a similar feature in Serlio's *Extraordinario libro*, plate XIII.

At first sight the layered wash technique and virtual absence of ruled lines suggest comparisons with very early drawings such as the Cotton monument design of *c.* 1610 (cat. no. 6). But in fact the technique is more mature than almost any drawing by Jones before about 1620. The wash is smoother and more accurately applied, and the freehand lines are firmer than on similar large-scale drawings of 1617 or 1618 (cat. nos 23, 24, 40). Even so, the drawing cannot be as late as the meticulous gateway designs of 1622–3 with their fully ruled outlines and precise under-scoring (cat. nos 43–5). A date around 1620 seems the most likely, and there is some confirmation of this in the similarity between freehand pen style on this drawing and on the design for a rusticated Ionic doorway of about 1619 associated here with the Banqueting House, Whitehall, and drawn on identically watermarked paper (cat. no. 39).

The doorway is 4 ft wide, as in the Francart source. It has no steps and has a downward-sloping tunnel light in the barred oval window. This would imply an entrance to a ground-floor hall or corridor. Clues for purpose may reside in the Neptune-like head on the keystone and the strap-work motif in the pediment resembling an anchor, both of which suggest that the entrance was near water. One possibility, given the *c.* 1620 date, is the Lodging which Jones had built for the Marquis of Buckingham on King Street, next to Whitehall Palace, between 1619 and 1621. It was brick-built, with sizeable first-floor rooms above ground-floor accommodation, and had, according to a Parliamentary survey of 1650, a 'Large Entry or Passage paved wth brick Tyle made like a Cloyster'. This passage could have been the same as that 'leading to the Marquis of Buckingham's new Lodgings' which was paved (with ragstone) in 1620–1. The iconography of the design would be entirely appropriate for Buckingham, who was created Lord High Admiral in January 1619.

See colour illustration on p. 152

Bibliography:
King's Works, iv, pp. 326–7

26 Study of a voussoired window, after Serlio

1618

Graphite over scorelines, partly reinforced in pen and brown ink with brown wash

167 × 165 mm. Cut from a larger sheet

Watermark: small scrolled cartouche, cut off at top, containing a tiny Crozier of Basle

Inscribed by Jones in pen and brown ink to left of window: *the exampell of / this wth bottzi / on ye sydes and / risuolti on y^e / head is in Serlio / Li.7.fo.63.*; and: *I think that yf / ye Bottzi on ye sides / be as longe as / ye midell Keysto⁻ / yt will do well / but longer the⁻ / the risuolti doth / well*

On same mount as cat. nos 27 and 28

RIBA Jones & Webb 76

27 Two studies of square voussoired windows

1618

Graphite (left window), pen and brown ink (right window), with brown wash, over scorelines

82 × 198 mm. Cut from larger sheet

On same mount as cat. nos 26 and 28

RIBA Jones & Webb 77

28 Two studies of voussoired windows, after Serlio, with studies of sill mouldings

1618

Graphite, partly reinforced with pen and brown ink, with brown wash, over scorelines

280 × 191 mm

Inscribed by Jones in pen and brown ink to left of windows: *In thes kynd of / windowes rusticke / or dowres whear / thear ar but 3/bottzi thus seperated / the midel most is / bigger then thos / of the sydes by* $\frac{1}{4}$ */ Serlio of gaates fo.5. / and fo.14*; and: *noat that in Serlio / y^e· Spaces ar more large / the⁻ y^e bottzi arr and / the[y] hange doune lower / the⁻ y^e head of y^e window*; and: *but whear thear is / 4 botzi thear theay / bee all of a lyke breadth / and the 2 outermost /Com to y^e corner of / the head of y^e window / or dowre se. Serlio / of gates fo 8 and fo / 16.*; and below: *y^e* [numeral missing] *of Aprill / 1618*

Fig. 29
Sebastiano Serlio. Detail of entrance to a palace from *Tutte l'opere d'architettura et prospettiva* (Venice, 1619), Book VII, fol. 63

On same mount as cat. nos 26 and 27

RIBA Jones & Webb 78

Although cat. nos 26–8 appear to be studies of a theoretical nature, the presence of a string-course and the precise dating to April 1618 would suggest that Jones had a particular project in mind, and obviously some façade with voussoired windows. He is consulting his Serlio (fig. 29), but is not slavish in imitation, rather critical, and is applying his mind with vigorous intellect to improve Serlio's design by making the spaces between the voussoirs equal to the width of the two narrower (outer) ones, and the opening of the windows a double square. Possibly these excercises are for one of the courtier commissions, such as Fulke Greville's design (cat. no. 22) which has somewhat less prominent triple voussoirs to the head. In 1618 Jones's first works at Newmarket were beyond the design stage, and the Prince's Lodging not yet begun. However, it is worth observing that keystones identical to cat. no. 27 appear on the south front of Raynham Hall, a house composed from elements culled from Jones's designs, possibly seen by Sir Roger Townshend when he visited Newmarket Palace.

Bibliography:

R. Wittkower, 'Inigo Jones, architect and man of letters', *RIBA Journal*, lx (1953), pp. 83–4 (Repr. 1974)

J. Harris, 'Inigo Jones and the Prince's Lodging at Newmarket', *Architectural History*, ii (1959), pp. 37–40

—, 'Raynham Hall, Norfolk', *Archaeological Journal*, cxviii (1961), pp. 180–7

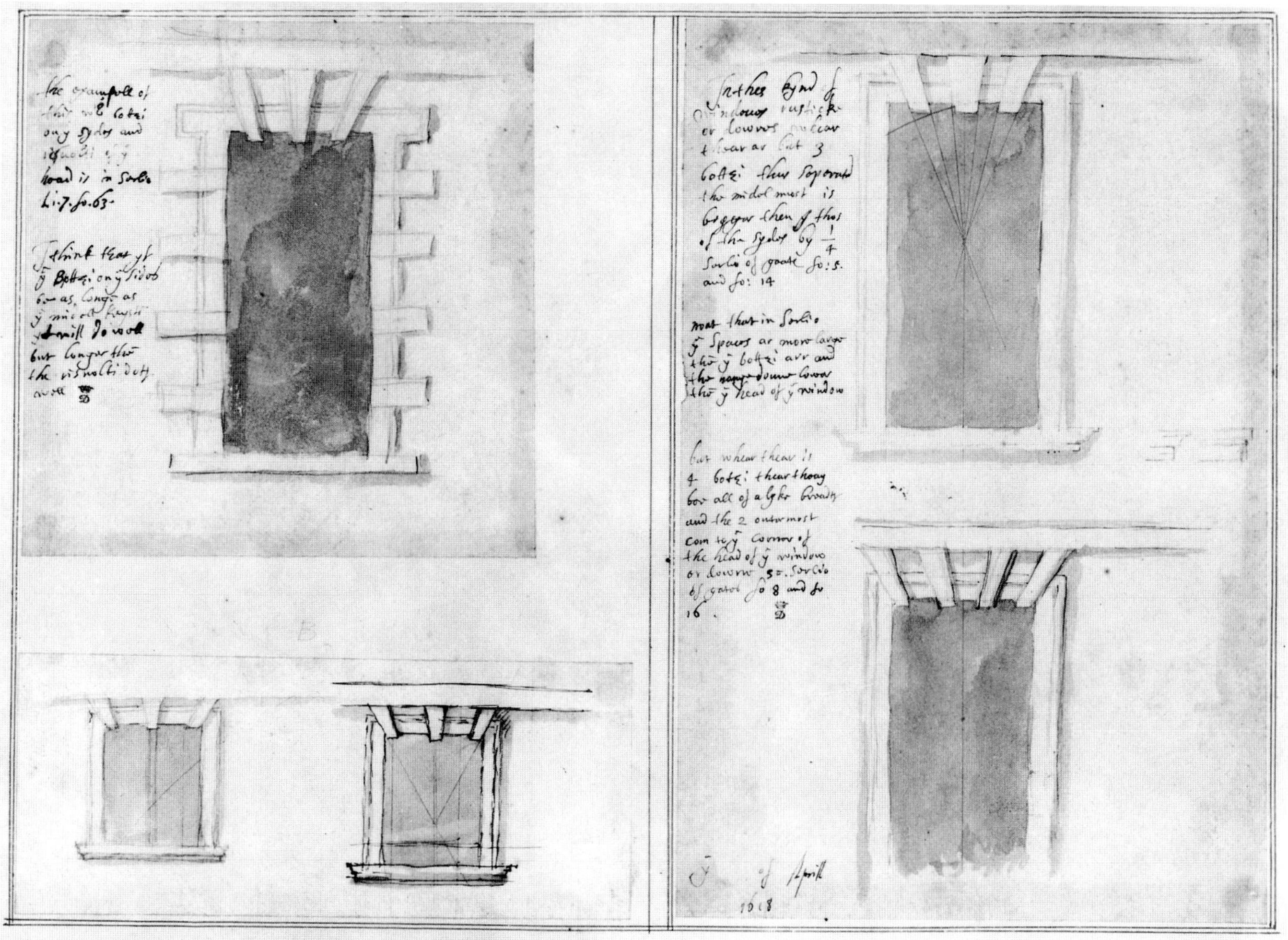

The Star Chamber, Palace of Westminster, London, 1617

29 Plan for a new Star Chamber

1617

Pen and brown ink over scorelines, divider and compass marks, and some graphite under-drawing. Faint black chalk additions on ceiling and niche

530 × 844 mm. In two pasted sheets, recently rejoined, with 25 mm overlap. The left (niche-end) sheet is 530 × 430 mm and the right (vestibule-end) sheet is 526 × 439 mm. Central horizontal fold

Watermarks (same on each sheet): bunch of grapes surmounted by fleur-de-lys crossed with diagonal bar

Inscribed by Jones in pen and brown ink: *1, 2, 3, 4, 5* consecutively near the lower and upper central openings, the right-hand internal doorway, and the lower upper left-hand corners flanking the niche; and in graphite across the left-hand sheet near the centre: *55*; and along right-hand sheet near lower central entrance: *67½*; and modern pen and black ink circled numbers *1* and *2* at tops of sheets. *Verso* by Jones in pen and brown ink on left-hand sheet: *for the Modell of the / Starr chamber / 1617 /*.

Scale: unmarked, but approx. 1 ft = $5\frac{5}{32}$ in.

Worcester College H & T 20, 21

The Star Chamber was where the committee of the Privy Council met to enact legislation presided over by the monarch, and was so named because the roof was adorned with a gilded star of spectacular size. There are references to mending the Star Chamber within Westminster Palace in 1500–2, when it was located somewhere in the north-east corner of what is now called New Palace Yard. It was lengthened in 1517 and re-tiled in 1535, and altered and decorated in 1565–70. In 1579–80 it was again enlarged, and a new roof built in 1588–9, when a 'verie large starre', gilded with fine gold and fixed in the ceiling, is mentioned. The walls and furnishings were richly decorated. There survives, however, no view of the chamber, nor even a plan. When James I came to the throne in 1603 the Star Chamber soon became a powerful symbol of royal authority and determination, a place where the King could process royal policy independent of Parliament. It was in here that Charles I took many of the decisions that led him to the scaffold.

This large drawing on two sheets of paper has now been reunited perhaps for the first time since it left Jones's office. The only reference to this unexecuted project appears on 21 June 1617 when John Chamberlain wrote to Sir Dudley Carleton that 'the King wold faine have' built such a Star Chamber 'yf we could find monie'. The design needs to be put in the context of Jones's employment as Royal Surveyor in mid-1617, with only ancillary buildings at Newmarket Palace, minor works at Somerset House, and the beginnings of the Queen's House at Greenwich to his credit. Even if this was a passing whim of the King's, Jones was given the opportunity to design a major royal building and aspire to the role of a British Palladio or Vitruvius.

Jones naturally turned to Palladio's description of ancient basilicas 'where the judges attended to do justice [. . .]', and where a great niche is recommended for 'the tribunal of the *praetor*, or of the judges, if there are many' (*I Quattro libri*, II, pp. 38–9). His niche follows Palladio's in measuring half the internal width of the hall, but in plan it has eight instead of twelve encircling columns. This arrangement is found in Palladio's plan of the 'Temple of Jupiter the Thunderer' (Temple of Vespasian) in Rome (*I Quattro libri*, IV, p. 71). Moreover, the shape of the hall and articulation of its internal walls recall another Roman religious building in Palladio, that of the 'Temple of the Sun and Moon' (Temple of Venus and Rome; IV, pp. 36–8). Such associations with Roman sacred architecture prompted Per Palme to conjecture that Jones saw the building as a symbol of James I's divine authority, the gods of Sun and Jupiter being 'two deities which in the Stuart age were time and again cited as allegorical personifications of the sovereign, the crowned image of God, the very source of Justice'.

There is no denying the grandeur of Jones's design. His main façade has an applied order of giant columns, whose diameters of 4¾ ft presupposes a height (assuming a Corinthian order) of some 47½ ft. They would have been taller than the columns of Jones's St Paul's west front. Free-standing porticoes with 40 ft Corinthian orders occur on Palladio's Villa Thiene at Cicogna and Villa Mocenigo (*I Quattro libri*, II, pp. 62, 78) but there is no obvious precedent for an applied order on this scale. Internally, we can detect the incised outlines of a large circular central ceiling panel which would presumably have contained the gilded star. It would seem from the absence of articulation on three of the external walls that the chamber was to be confined by existing buildings on all but the porticoed façade, but lacking a site plan, it is uncertain if Jones's Star Chamber was intended to have been located where the old one was.

Our understanding of Jones's design has been clouded by the existence of modified copies by John Webb (figs 30–2). These have been accepted as literal reconstructions of Jones's design, but comparison between the two sets of drawings reveals many inconsistencies, notably a façade with three-quarter columns on a projecting central section instead of half columns on a straight wall, and a main chamber 76 ft long as against 67½ ft inscribed on Jones's plan. It would seem that Webb reworked Jones's drawings in a more Baroque manner, giving more depth to the modelling of the façade, a stronger longitudinal axis on the plan, and using columns almost exactly the same size as those proposed by Jones (4 ft 6½ in. in diameter by 46 ft high).

Of particular interest is the fact that Webb's rustication closely follows that on the Palazzo Thiene in Vicenza (fig. 11), a

Fig. 30
John Webb. Revised main-floor and ceiling plan (1660s) from Jones's design for the Star Chamber in the Palace of Westminster, London, 1617

building which strongly affected Jones's architectural style in the years around 1617 (e.g. cat. nos 14, 17). A more pronounced handling of the same rustication motifs can be discerned on Webb's King Charles Block at Greenwich, together with four-column applied porticoes of the Star Chamber type (1662–9). Thus Jones's lost elevation for the Star Chamber may have given Webb the essential elements for his composition and influenced the course of English Baroque architecture in the later seventeenth century.

Fig. 31
John Webb. Revised elevation (1660s) from Jones's design for the Star Chamber in the Palace of Westminster, London, 1617

Fig. 32
John Webb. Revised section (1660s) from Jones's design for the Star Chamber in the Palace of Westminster, London, 1617

Bibliography:

Per Palme, *Triumph of peace* (Stockholm, 1956) pp. 183–91
J. Summerson, *Inigo Jones* (Harmondsworth, 1966), pp. 48–9
King's Arcadia, pp. 114–15
King's Works, iv, pp. 296–300

Newmarket Palace, Cambridgeshire, 1615–21

As today, so in the early seventeenth century, Newmarket was for racing and hunting, sometimes used in conjunction with the Royal Lodge at Royston, on the London Road to or from Newmarket. James I first visited Newmarket in February 1605. In 1606–9 'new privy lodgings' were built, in 1609–10 various additions, and in 1614–15 a substantial 'pyle' of new lodgings 'with greate chamber, presence etc', three storeys high of brick with stone dressings. There was an adjoining gallery, and a covered tennis court which measured 100 by 40 ft. All this was conducted by the Royal Surveyor, Simon Basil, but after his death in September 1615, Jones was in charge, and we can assume that the Court Style of Jacobean Classicism gave way to a more Italianate one. The new Jonesian buildings first mentioned in the accounts are a stable, brew-house and dog-house from 1616 to 1617. Descriptions that include 'freeze and corniche', stone 'facias' and a 'great window' with a stone cornice, are new to the Works' vocabulary and imply classical buildings. It was so for the brew-house with its two great stone door-cases, and for the dog-house with 'freeze and cornish'. A timber riding-house 108 by 36 ft was built which had galleries raised upon columns. In 1617–18 there were stables for Sir Thomas Compton and for Mr Dupper the brewer. So far all these buildings are ancillary ones, and they must include the office for the architects and masons built 1619–20. Alas, apart from the last, accurately recorded in a drawing by John Webb (fig. 34), no visual record survives of these royal buildings at this critical early stage in the career of Jones the Royal Surveyor. We can only regret that we do not possess the eyes of Sir Roger Townshend who poked around the Office of Works on a visit from Raynham. He might have told us much about the Prince's Lodging built from 1619, for it was a royal lodging of country-house size that may well have exerted a profound effect upon those many architects who must have seen it. Happily two elevations survive as evidence of Jones's prowess at a moment just before the Banqueting House in Whitehall burned to the ground (cat. nos 30, 31).

It must first be admitted that the designs do not match the descriptions culled from the accounts of the Office of Works or the Parliamentary Survey. This latter describes a front of 70 ft and a depth of 44 ft of brick and stone, three storeys high, and a 'longe gallery' to the rear connecting to the King's Lodging. The main front seems to have had five windows on the *piano nobile* with 'swelling frieze' and there were ground-floor windows with keystones. Apart from the mention of dormers in the roof, a 'winding' staircase with an open newel, Presence, Withdrawing and Privy Chambers with coved ceilings (Jones introduced the coved ceiling to England from Italy), little else is recorded, and the building was probably utilitarian compared to Jones's two noble designs. However, a precious record drawing

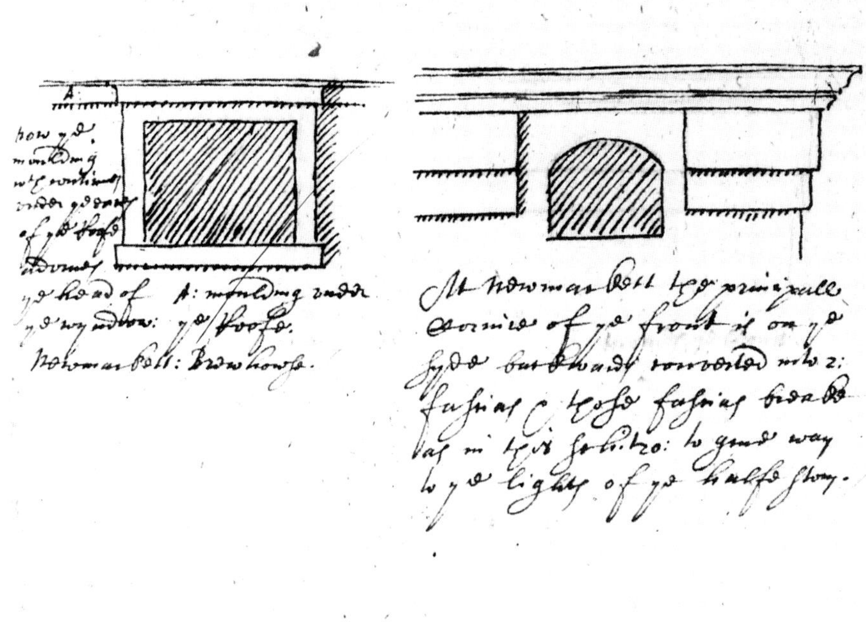

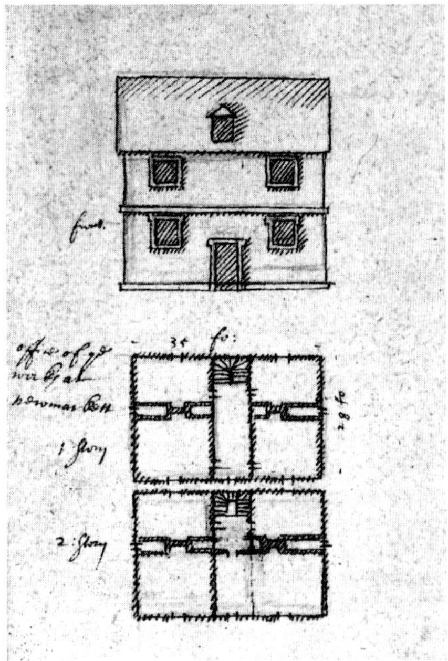

(fig. 33) by Webb survives of 'the principall cornice of ye front' which suggests that in execution the upper windows of cat. no. 31 were changed from oblongs to openings with a flattish curved head, and pushed up into the cornice.

Newmarket had a short life, for the Parliamentarians demolished much of it about 1650, and the town only came to royal favour again when William Samwell built the King's House for Charles II in 1668. As belonging to a Northamptonshire family, it is likely that Samwell by the age of forty would have seen Jones's Prince's Lodging before demolition, for there are Newmarket traits in some of his houses. There is also Townshend's Raynham Hall in Norfolk remaining as a precious evidence of the influence of Jones's designs, and the only building in brick and stone that conveys something of the nobility of his astylar elevation.

J.H.

Fig. 33
John Webb. Record drawings of windows on the brew-house (left) and on the side elevation of the Prince's Lodging (right), Newmarket Palace, Cambridgeshire, 1640s(?)

Fig. 34
John Webb. Record drawing of the Office of Works building (1619–20) at Newmarket Palace, Cambridgeshire, 1640s(?)

Bibliography:
King's Works, iv, pp. 175–9; v, pp. 214–7

30 First elevation for the Prince's Lodging at Newmarket Palace, Cambridgeshire

1618–19

Pen and brown ink with grey wash, over compass lines and scorelines and some graphite under-drawing

195 × 276 mm

Inscribed by an 18th-c. hand in pen and brown ink in top right-hand corner: *30.*; and on *verso* by John Talman in pen and brown ink: *54:* ⊑ :

RIBA Jones & Webb 61 (1)

31 Astylar elevation for the Prince's Lodging at Newmarket Palace, Cambridgeshire

1618–19

Pen and brown ink with brown wash, over compass and scorelines

190 × 274 mm

Inscribed by Jones in pen and brown ink with feet-and-inch dimensions on the left-hand side of the elevation, some on the extreme left struck through; and on *verso* by John Talman in pen and brown ink: *54:* ⊑ :

RIBA Jones & Webb 61 (2)

The drafting style of these two elevations places them in the 1618–19 period, just before the unexpected Banqueting House commission. Although the outlines have over-inked and faded passages typical of the period just after Jones had returned from Italy, the handling is tidier, with column shafts more carefully drawn and freehand lines that are both fluent and confident. Jones can now control his pen on the sheet for longer lines, as for example on the window surrounds of cat. no. 31 (which should be compared with those on the first Banqueting House façade, cat. no. 33). Attribution of the drawings to the Lodging begun for Prince Charles in 1619 is confirmed by the fact that both frontages are roughly the 70 ft width described in a Parliamentary Survey of the building in 1649, and by the use of the Prince of Wales feathers on the crests in the pediments. We may safely assume that cat. no. 30 was superseded by cat. no. 31, for not only is the latter inscribed with working dimensions but it is without applied order and has a dormered roof, as described in the Declared Accounts.

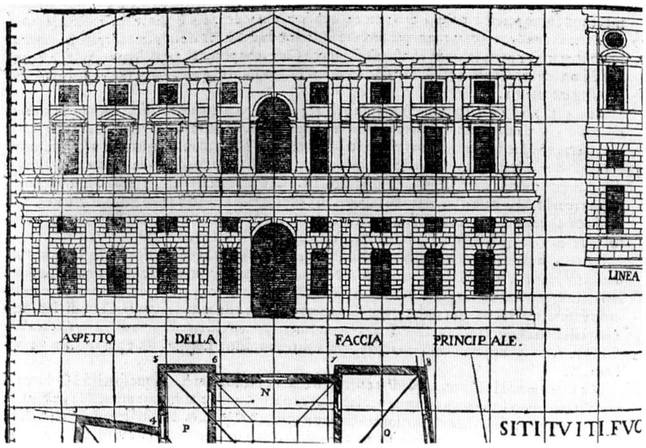

Fig. 35
Vincenzo Scamozzi. Palazzo Trissino, Vicenza, 1576–9. Woodcut from *L'Idea della architettura universale* (Venice, 1615)

If there is advance in drafting, so too Jones can be seen to advance in invention, releasing himself from the academic restraint of reliance upon Palladio and Scamozzi. This is less true of the first elevation (cat. no. 30), for which Jones has turned to Scamozzi's Palazzo Trissino in Vicenza from *L'Idea* (fig. 35), and then transformed the source by lowering the basement and eliding its mezzanine, rustication and applied order, leaving the *piano nobile* framed only by a single column at the extremities and a four-column attached portico. The result is but a shadow of the original, and already typical of Jones in the harmonic relationship between solids and voids, and in the emphasis on plain wall surface at the expense of applied orders and mouldings.

In the second, or astylar, design (cat. no. 31) Jones rises to majesty, almost leaping forward in his development as a designer. The proportions remain, but the orders are eliminated, and the roof is heightened to take four very tall pedimented dormer-windows lined up with the tiers of openings below. As these dormers are shown on the sides also, there may have been a gallery up here, for the house would have risen above the town of Newmarket giving views of the racing grounds. This was certainly the case with the palace for Charles II which dominated the landscape in the 1670s.

In eliminating the orders, Jones has replaced them with a system of quoins which run up the sides and frame the centrepiece, all subtly modulated and giving an effect of brio to the façade. Compared to the Scamozzian elevation, this is something quite different: patterned, modulated, ornamental, and sculptural, and this can best be appreciated in the attractive arrangement of the three bays of the ground-floor centre: rusticated pilasters with block capitals, niches containing statues, and the architraved door with its triple keystone.

It would be fascinating to know how much of this was transferred to the Newmarket Lodging as built. It was of brick, quoined, and had tall dormers. What remains so potent is that here, in 1618, Jones had prophesied in detail the forms of the English country-house, as it developed and became quintessentially English, after 1680. Indeed, if the astylar design had been executed by William Talman in the 1690s his authorship would hardly be doubted.

See colour illustrations on p. 153

Bibliography:

J. Harris, 'Inigo Jones and the Prince's Lodging at Newmarket', *Architectural History*, ii (1959), pp. 26–40

J. Summerson, *Inigo Jones* (Harmondsworth, 1966), pp. 59–60

King's Works, iv, pp. 177–8

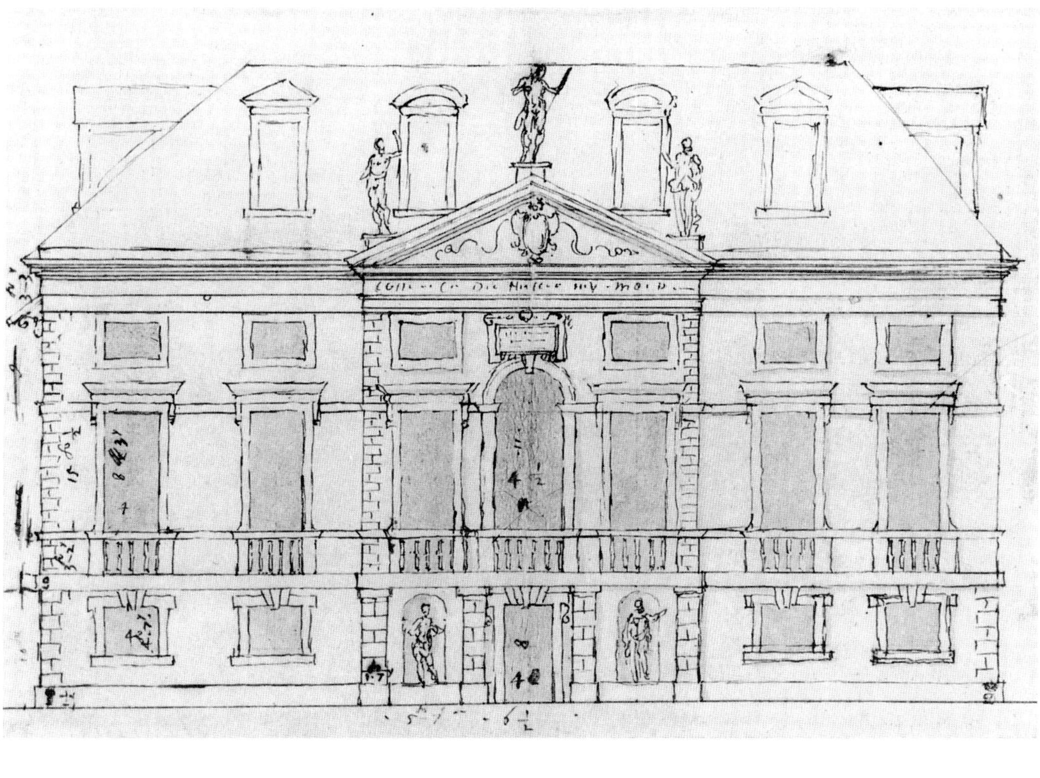

32 Plan-perspective of a beamed ceiling in nineteen compartments, ascribed to the Prince's Lodging at Newmarket Palace, Cambridgeshire

c. 1618–19

Pen and dark brown ink over scorelines and graphite under-drawing

490 × 317 mm. Very thick, dark paper (Basle or Strasbourg?)

Scale: 1 ft = ¾ in.

RIBA Jones & Webb 89

Compartmented beamed ceilings with classically moulded frames were unknown in England before Jones's Banqueting House of 1619–22, where the ceiling consists of two longitudinal and two transverse beams of great depth framing nine rectangular panels (fig. 39). This more complex plan of nineteen panels in varying sizes, some with *trompe l'œil* decoration and others in simple relief, probably derives from a late sixteenth-century Italian example, like the ceiling of the Teatro Olimpico in Vicenza, although no precise source has yet been identified.

The drawing dates stylistically towards the end of the 1616–19 period, and may be tentatively assigned to the Prince's Lodging. The loosely handled pen shading, with uneven line spacing and much hooking and scribbling, should be compared with the Oatlands Palace Vineyard gateway of 1617, or the Banqueting House Great Door of 1619 (cat. nos 17, 38). The ruled pen drawing, however, is more cleanly handled than on plans at the beginning of the period (e.g. cat. nos 13, 29).

A connection with the Prince's Lodging at Newmarket Palace is implied by the motifs in the *trompe l'œil* panel near the bottom of the design. Putti support a crest surmounted by loosely sketched Prince of Wales feathers, while the vases each side also have triple feathers (the right one, in addition, is inscribed with a 'P', possibly signifying Prince or *Principio*). The Newmarket Lodging had a royal apartment on the first floor with Presence Chamber, Withdrawing Chamber, Privy Chamber and Bedchamber. All but the Bedchamber ceiling are recorded as being coved ('haunst') rather than beamed, and were apparently quite plain. This design may belong with one of the two elevations which were themselves superseded by a plainer façade, and was probably set aside for reasons of cost. The ceiling would have measured 25 ft 6 in. by 16 ft 1 in. A room this size would fit behind the first elevation (cat. no. 30), either across the pedimented centre, where an internal length of about 27 ft can be estimated on the assumption of a 4 ft window opening, or transversely across the outer bays, where the room width would have been about 17 ft. The ceiling would not have fitted as easily behind the astylar façade (cat. no. 31), for here the central section is narrower, giving about 20 ft internal length, and the outer sections broader, about 22 ft inside.

Bibliography:
King's Works, iv, pp. 177–8

The Banqueting House, Whitehall Palace, London, 1619–22

The first Banqueting House in Whitehall was designed by Thomas Graves in 1581. Built of timber with canvas walls painted to look like rusticated stone, it served a function that concerned eating fruit as much as theatric entertainment. It was different with the second Banqueting House begun in 1606. Robert Smythson's plan made in 1609 (fig. 36) and various descriptions evoke a rather advanced plan for Jacobean England: an interior measuring 120 by 53 ft with surrounding galleries of Ionic columns, with balustrades between the columns, over Doric which must acknowledge a Vitruvian basilica plan, suggestively from an engraving by Vredeman de Vries dated 1606 and inscribed 'Ionica Super Dorica'. A reference in 1607 to the designer as the 'ld Architect' has been interpreted to mean Sir David Conyngham, King's Master of the Works in Scotland, although it is unclear as to why Conyngham and not Simon Basil, the King's Surveyor, should have designed this royal building. It has been suggested that Jones, as prince of masque designers, may have been consulted, and this is possible. However, if the interior did pay lip-service to some ancient Roman source, the exterior was thoroughly Jacobean to judge from the bay-windowed projections on the fronts drawn by Smythson (fig. 36).

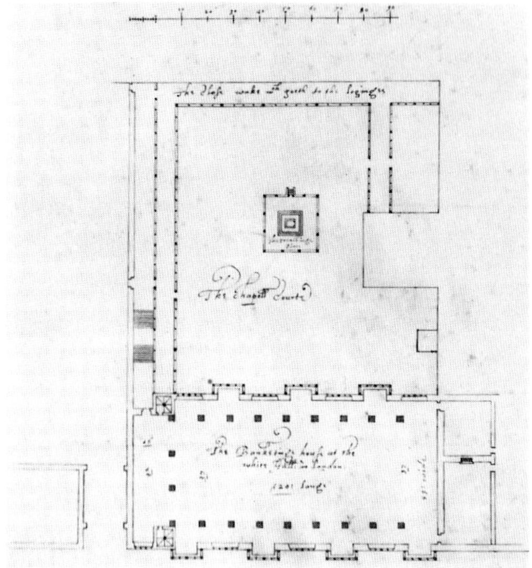

Fig. 36
Robert Smythson. Plan of the old Banqueting House, Whitehall, London, *c.* 1609

When this building was destroyed by fire in 1619 Jones was firmly in control. He built the first public structure in the Palladian style, and what became the first government building in a street eventually given over to the offices of government (fig. 37). This most celebrated building ought to be so fully researched that little is left to discover; yet, like the Queen's House, any account of its building is fraught with problems. Was it ever conceived as a Banqueting House or was it meant eventually to form part of a new royal palace of Whitehall?

We can say that by April 1619, when Jones had produced designs and estimates, he was probably concerned with a replacement Banqueting House, that is a building meant as a place for the masque. By 31 March 1622, when the accounts closed and the new building was complete, Jones had certainly designed a hall, but it is likely that by then a traumatic transformation had taken place, for during the preceding year Rubens had been first approached to paint the ceiling. In other words, a year before the Banqueting House was complete Jones had taken the step to render its use as a masquing chamber obsolete. He knew perfectly well that torch-lit masques could not be performed in a room with a painted ceiling. Indeed, once the Rubens paintings were installed in 1638, a temporary masquing chamber had to be built in the courtyard next to the Banqueting House.

As we experience the interior today, the balustraded galleries appear to form part of a homogeneous concept (fig. 38). Yet their origin is mysterious, for so far no precedents have been found in the Renaissance for a room or hall surrounded by a cantilevered gallery. It is possible, but not likely, that Jones was translating the balustraded gallery from around the central hall of Palladio's Villa Rotonda. There is also the possibility that in studying the section of an Egyptian Hall from Palladio's Book II he was prompted to transfer the balustraded outer roof terrace around the clerestory, inside. Neither of these suggestions seems the right one. Considering that the gallery idea in the Banqueting House was transferred to a cube in the Hall of the Queen's House in the 1630s, and thus became a plan form of profound and lasting influence, its origin ought to be known.

Fig. 37
The Banqueting House, Whitehall, 1619–22. Street front

It is not clear if the gallery has anything to do with the lack of access. This matter has always been disputed. As there was no internal stair, how did Jones intend to solve this problem? As can be seen in the drawing for *Time Vindicated to Himself and to His Honours* (cat. no. 36), from the very first stairs were contained in a temporary external lean-to, one that although frequently rebuilt, has survived as an obvious appendange to the present day. From the royal palace on the Privy Gallery side, access was only on the ground floor, a link that may have been designed by Jones. Somehow one feels that the gallery is related to a change of use. With Rubens's ceiling in place, the Banqueting House had been transformed into a throne room or hall of state. Even so, there are no precedents for balustraded galleries in such halls.

Fig. 38
The Banqueting House, interior looking south

If we consider the 'finished' designs with wings or outer vestibules (cat. no. 33), and if we omit a gallery from our considerations at this point, no access at a higher level would be needed. After all, in antiquity and Renaissance treatises, basilicas, Egyptian halls, or halls of assembly do not have balustraded galleries. This option at the beginning of Jones's evolving designs would account for the Great Door that would not fit into a balustraded room, but rightly answers the Great Niche at the opposite end.

Despite these fascinating problems, the transference of a design with a strong frontal and axial elevation, to one of almost passive equilibrium, and the decision almost from the first to build a throne room with a painted ceiling, suggests that Jones did reasonably look into the future, in the hope that his fragment might one day be incorporated into an all-embracing design for a new palace of Whitehall. Nevertheless, they were dreams, and it was left to Webb to put these on paper, probably after Jones's death.

J.H.

Bibliography:

Per Palme, *Triumph of peace* (Stockholm, 1956)
J. Charlton, *The Banqueting House* (London, 1964)
J. Summerson, *Inigo Jones* (Harmondsworth, 1966), pp. 50–9
J. J. Terwen, 'Di platte gronden voor het Banqueting House in Whitehall', *Opstellen voor H. van de Waal* (Amsterdam/Leiden, 1970), pp. 203–13
R. Strong, *Britannia Triumphans* (London, 1980)
King's Works, iv, pp. 322–34
J. Summerson, *Architecture in Britain, 1530–1830* (Harmondsworth. 1983), pp. 122–6

33 Plan and elevation of the first scheme for the Banqueting House, Whitehall, London

1619

Pen and brown ink with brown wash, over scorelines, those on elevation with a rounded point. 18th-c. red ink ruled border lines around edges of sheet

574 × 438 mm. In two main sheets, pasted together at centre (probably by Jones), with a 7 mm overlap. The upper sheet, 292 × 438 mm, includes a pasted strip at top, 49 × 438 mm, bearing an inked scale. The lower sheet, 291 × 430 mm, includes narrow paper strips on left (4 mm) and right (2 mm) to make it equal in width to upper sheet. Both sheets have central vertical folds and some foxing

Watermark (same on each sheet): Crozier of Basle, ending in three spheres at the bottom, showing the initial D: the mark of the Düring family mill, Basle

Inscribed by an 18th-c. hand in pen and brown ink near top right-hand corner of upper sheet: *52*; and on *verso* of each sheet by John Talman in pen and brown ink: *54:* ⊩:

Scales (same on each sheet, and marked in pen and brown ink over divider points, at bottom and top of entire sheet): 10 ft = $\frac{29}{32}$ in.

Chatsworth (unnumbered)

The design shows the east façade to the palace, with low outer wings at each end. The Great Niche which was to accommodate the throne on state occasions is at the south end, behind which is a heated vestibule adjoining the Privy Gallery of the palace (next to Holbein's gate, shown on the right of the *Time Vindicated* drawing, cat. no. 36). The main entrance to the hall would have been at the opposite end, where the vestibule would have been connected with the Court Gate ('Whitehall Gate', on cat. no. 36). Although Jones has rendered the Banqueting House as a free-standing building, we must assume that there would have been access from the ground to the raised main floor of the hall from the existing Tudor buildings on the north and south. Certainly, no internal access from ground to main floor is shown on the plan, which depicts the main floor in washed outline and the basement as a separate outline around the edges.

In the Star Chamber design (cat. no. 29) the vestibules are contained within the body of the building, but here, on the outside and only one storey high, they surely proclaim a single internal space. The walls are unarticulated, apparently without galleries, and enclose a rectangle 119 ft 6 in. by 54 ft 6 in.: longer than the double cube of the finished building (110 by 55 ft), but similar to the internal dimensions on Smythson's plan (120 by 53 ft).

Jones based his elevation on Scamozzi's Palazzo Trissino in Vicenza (fig. 35) and two palace designs by Palladio in *I Quattro libri* (Book II, pp. 71–2). As on his Newmarket Lodging façade (cat. no. 30), he has refined and reproportioned the Vicentine sources, using broader bays and fewer running mouldings. He seems poised between the solution, demanded by the fire, of a replacement Banqueting House, and something rather different: a *sala grande* for the King.

See colour illustration on p. 154

34 Elevation of the penultimate design for the Banqueting House, Whitehall, London

1619

Pen and brown ink with grey wash over scorelines and some graphite. Additions in graphite and orange chalk. 18th-c. red ink ruled border lines around edges of sheet

366 × 437 mm. Including narrow (18th-c.?) strips backing the edges all around. Original sheet is 333 × 429 mm. Central vertical fold, split in places. Horizontal fold through top of plinth in basement

Watermark: same as cat. no. 33

Inscribed by an 18th-c. hand in pen and brown ink in top right-hand corner: *53.*; and on *verso* by John Talman in pen and brown ink: *54:* ⊑ *:*

Chatsworth (unnumbered)

What is so compelling and fascinating about this design is that we are almost a witness to Jones's innermost thoughts on the matter of the final form of the Banqueting House façade. He has taken the frontal elevation with wings (cat. no. 33), reversed the sequence of segmental and triangular pediments to the lower range of *piano-nobile* windows, and proceeded rapidly to ornamentalize the whole front. The basement is now rusticated, emphasis is placed upon the three lower middle windows with figures resting upon their pediments, as in Palladio's Palazzo Barbarano in Vicenza (*I Quattro libri*, II, pp. 22–3), and a whole new episode of ornamental effect is added to the upper windows with delicate bunches of fruit dependent from the consoled brackets (cat. no. 37). Above these windows there are hints, in graphite and orange chalk, of the masks and swags that were applied between the upper capitals on the executed front (fig. 37).

And yet, almost simultaneously, Jones is intent on destroying much of the character of the first elevation. He has narrowed the length of the façade, and consequently the bay widths, from the 128 ft 6 in. on cat. no. 33 to about 117 ft at main-floor level on this elevation (calculating from the 5 ft 2 in. inscribed dimension of the central opening). In so doing he returned, momentarily, to the compactness of the Vicentine palace façade. But then he sketched a straight balustraded termination of the roof that would eliminate the pediment in the finished building. After raising the upper floor by two rusticated courses above the windows he created a continuous enrichment along the roof-line which led to the abandonment of the ornamental pendants and pediment figures. In other words, he reduced the central accent and when he covered the main floors with channelled rustication, he achieved even greater repose and equilibrium. Whether he had Rubens's ceiling in mind at this stage is unclear, but the moment that ceiling was contemplated the life of the traditional Banqueting House for the masque and theatre was cut short. Jones then achieved a *sala grande* or throne room that might take its place in a palace of the future.

See colour illustration on p. 155

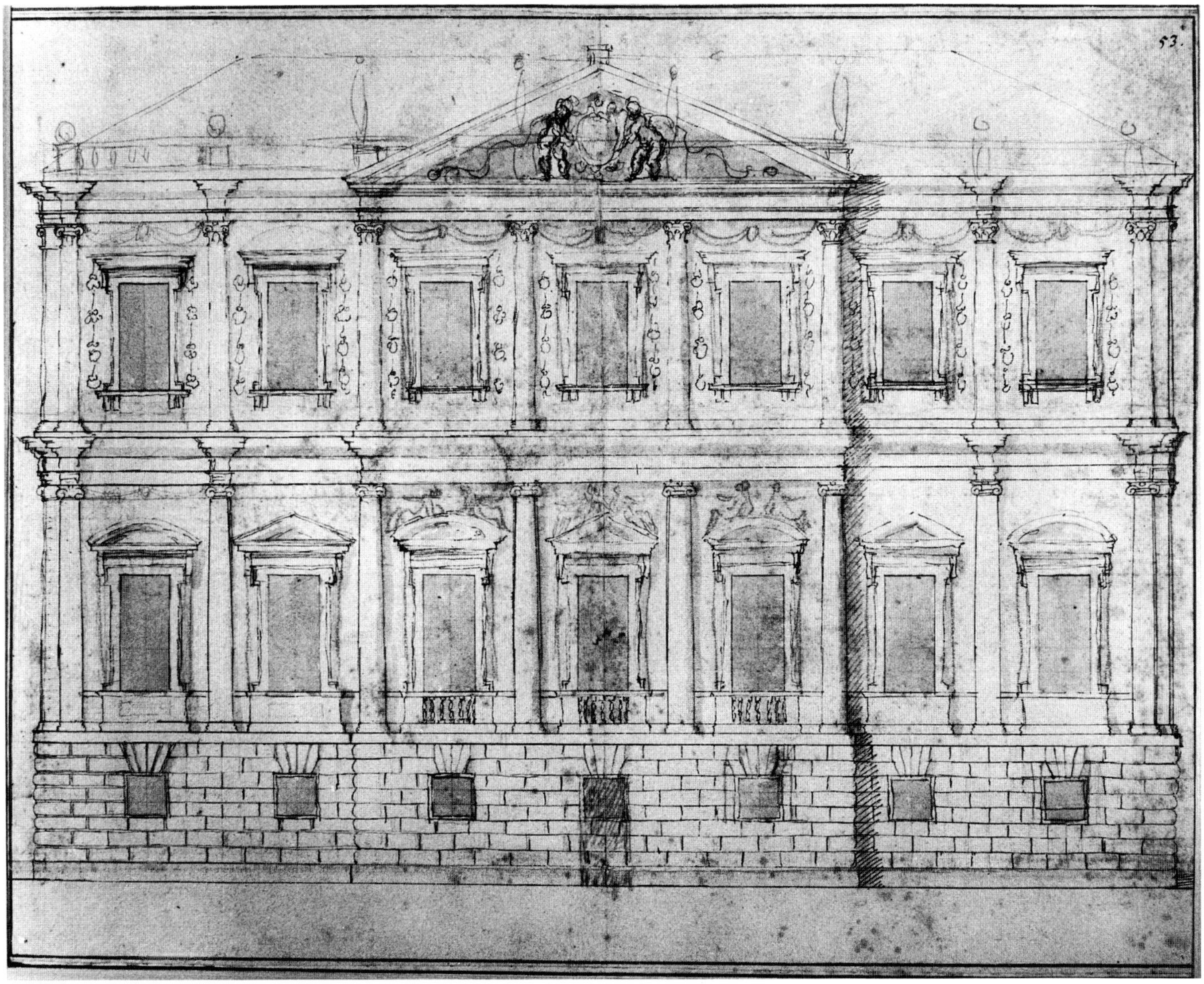

35 Main floor and basement plan for the Banqueting House, Whitehall, London

1619

Pen and brown ink with brown wash over scorelines and graphite under-drawing

334 × 574 mm. Single sheet (originally two?) laid down on card and framed later with pairs of red ink ruled border lines, crossing sheet on left and right. Central vertical fold

RIBA Jones & Webb 4

This plan was found among the Palladio drawings at the RIBA in the 1960s (XIV/17), having become detached from the other Banqueting House designs some time after the dispersal of Jones's collection in the late seventeenth century. It is directly related to the Chatsworth plan and elevation (cat. no. 33), with single-storey vestibules and probably predates the 'penultimate' design (cat. no. 34) where no vestibules are shown. Like cat. no. 33 the plan shows basement and main floor in a single drawing. The basement is drawn in outline circumscribing the shaded main-floor plan and has twenty-one groined compartments in two rows of six piers, as in the undercroft of the Banqueting House today. In this basement Isaac de Caus would construct a 'rocke' or grotto with 'shell worke' between 1623 and 1626.

The essential difference from cat. no. 33 is in the articulation of the main floor by a system of pilasters, paired at the ends and four in the centre. This establishes a connection with the double pilasters on the Banqueting House as built. Moreover, the hall itself is exactly two squares long (189 × 377 mm). In the executed plan, copied by John Webb on a sheet at Chatsworth (fig. 39), the lower stage of the hall is articulated with half columns instead of pilasters and the central portion of each façade projects. Jones removed the Great Niche and dispensed with vestibules, but left the doorways to the hall exactly as shown in this RIBA plan.

Fig. 39
John Webb. Record drawings of the main-floor plan (below) and upper-level plan with ceiling, of the Banqueting House, Whitehall

36 Drawing for the scene of the Whitehall Banqueting House for *Time Vindicated to Himself and to His Honours*

1623

Pen and brown ink over graphite and scorelines, the paper squared with graphite for enlargement

381 × 638 mm. Irregular sheet, torn away on left-hand and top right-hand sides. Central vertical fold

Inscribed by Jones in pen and brown ink: *Whitehall Gate* and *Bancquet House* above the respective buildings

Scale: 10 ft = $\frac{3}{4}$ in.

Pierpont Morgan Library, New York (O & S 122)

The masque was performed on 19 January 1623, appropriately in the Banqueting House. The poet was Ben Jonson, the masquers Prince Charles and the Lords. The Banqueting House scene is mentioned in the Office Book of the Master of the Revels, Sir John Astley, who writes of the three scenes designed by Jones, 'the first that was discovered was a prospective of Whitehall, with the Banqueting House'. As a document elucidating the Banqueting House itself, little can be said, for the façade lacks any ornamental attachments, and as the building was complete externally by the middle of 1622, this drawing is obviously incomplete. It is far more interesting for the depiction of the old Tudor Court Gate ('Whitehall Gate'), and for the earliest view of the (at first) temporary stair attachment that provided access from ground level to the main hall and gallery in the Banqueting House.

See colour illustration on p. 156

Bibliography:

J. Harris, 'A Prospect of Whitehall by Inigo Jones', *Burlington Magazine*, cix (1967), pp. 89–90

O & S, i, pp. 348–60

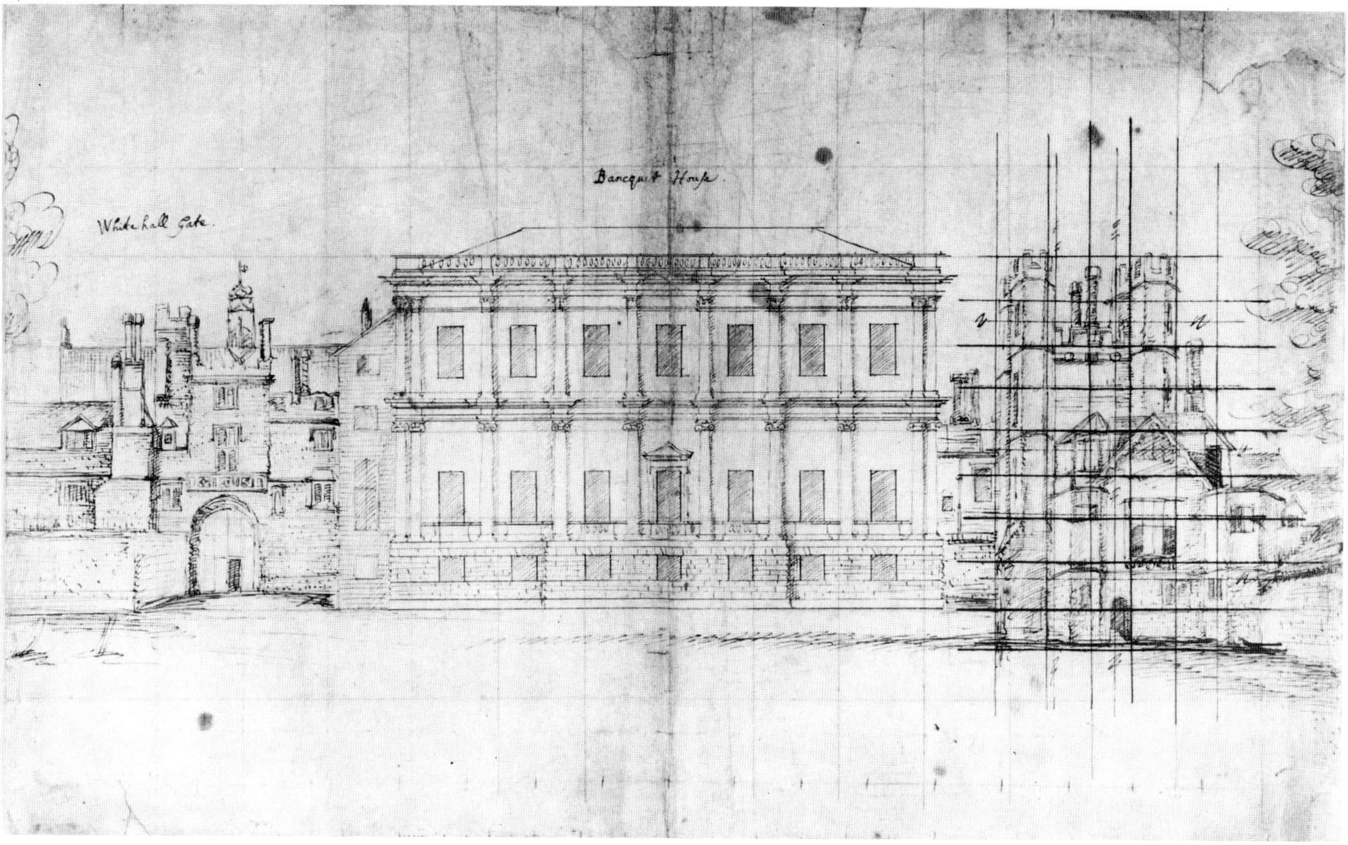
Whitehall Gate
Banquet House

37 Front and side elevation, with plan, of upper windows for the Banqueting House, Whitehall, London

1619

Pen and brown ink over scorelines and graphite under-drawing. Trace of red ink ruled border line on right edge of sheet

242 × 152 mm. Trimmed sheet

Inscribed by Jones in pen and brown ink at top of sheet: *The upper windows of yᵉ Modell*; and on *verso* by an 18th-c. hand in pen and brown ink: *window 3*

RIBA Jones & Webb 5

This working drawing is a refinement of the upper-floor windows on the 'penultimate' façade design (cat. no. 34). It presumably accompanied the final 'modell', or set of finished drawings, which Jones presented, together with an estimate amounting to £9,850 on 19 April 1619. On Palladio's Palazzo Chiericati and Palazzo Iseppo Porto (*I Quattro libri*, II, pp. 7 and 9; see cat. no. 12), and on cat. no. 34, the fruit swags hang from the cornices and fill the spaces between the windows and the applied orders, but here they depend from the consoles alongside the jambs, allowing more clear wall space each side of the windows. On the elevation as built Jones replaced the swags with *pilastrelli* like those on the lower-floor windows of cat. no. 34, and he eliminated the lower projections of the architrave frame, giving a still plainer effect. The motif of dependent clusters of fruit occurs in John Webb's post-1647 state rooms at Wilton House and may well have been used by Jones in earlier but unrecorded interior wall decoration.

38 Sketch elevation and half plan for the Great Door within the Banqueting House, Whitehall, London

1619

Pen and brown ink over black chalk and scorelines, with black chalk additions

550 × 358 mm. Roughly trimmed sheet. Horizontal folds in centre and near bottom of sheet; vertical fold near right

Watermark: elaborate coat of arms incorporating rampant lion, surmounted by coronet and with disc motif below

Inscribed by Jones in pen and brown ink in top right-hand corner: *Scitzo of the / Great Doure Ban. Ho / 1619*; and near right-hand column base: *the high of* y^{e} *Ba[se] / of* y^{e} *great Pillors*; and in plaque: *I.R.M.B.*; and with measurements: $5^{fo}\,\frac{1}{2}$, $11\frac{1}{2}$, $12^{fo}\,\frac{1}{2}$; and on *verso* by Jones in pen and brown ink at top right-hand side: *Great Doure and Mouldings / for* y^{e} *Ban Ho /Not taken 1619*; and by an 18th-c. hand, in pen and brown ink in bottom left-hand corner: *Door.4.*

RIBA Jones & Webb 6

This design was doubtless intended for the central door at main level, which on the final plan (fig. 39) has an internal opening of 5 ft 6 in. The executed door is much simpler, with only a moulded frame, consoles and a broken pediment. As no outline of a door with columns is shown on either of the preliminary main-floor plans (cat. nos 33, 35), it seems that this proposal was never taken beyond the initial sketch. This is confirmed by Jones's note 'Not taken' on the *verso* of the sheet. The door may have been conceived at the same time as the RIBA plan (cat. no. 35) to answer the Great Niche and then discarded when the niche was abandoned. With a sculptural display above the pediment it is hard to imagine this doorway fitting comfortably beneath the present gallery, and this tends to support the view that Jones added his galleries at the final stage.

Bibliography:

Per Palme, *Triumph of peace* (Stockholm, 1956), pp. 227–8

39 Elevation for a rusticated Ionic doorway with a broken segmental pediment, possibly for the Banqueting House, Whitehall, London

c. 1619

Pen and dark brown ink with some graphite and with additions in black chalk; heavy under-scoring and divider markings

448 × 348 mm. Two sheets joined at top of door opening, the lower sheet 304 × 348 mm and the upper sheet 170 × 345 mm, with 22 mm overlap. Three horizontal folds across sheet, the upper one (near join) partly cracked on left side. Trimmed at top

Watermark (on upper sheet); shield containing turret above rampant lion on left and eagle above rampant lion on right, surmounted by coronet, and with golden fleece below. Very similar to cat. no. 25

RIBA Jones & Webb 82

The style and technique of this lavish design are consistent with a date around 1619, when Jones's outline drawing was becoming more fluent, although he continued to rely on the scorer for testing ideas in the under-drawing. The penmanship and style of rustication compare closely with those on the 'penultimate' Banqueting House façade design (cat. no. 34). Like the Great Door design (cat. no. 38), it is an Ionic entrance with a broken segmental pediment, surmounted (in faint black chalk) by reclining figures and a cartouche. It also has applied columns set on tall plinths. The plinths on the Great Door design were to align their bases with those of the main Ionic order and these would seem to have a similar purpose. This design might be for the same internal door, or more likely for an external door on the same upper ground-floor level.

Gateway and Entrance Designs

Fig. 40
Tuscan gateway, demolished *c.* 1890, formerly flanking St Paul's Church, Covent Garden, *c.* 1631

Nearly a quarter of Jones's surviving drawings are for gateways and doorways. These classical entrances were a speciality which Jones furnished to his royal and courtier patrons for two decades after his return from Italy in 1614 and include some of his most pleasing architectural compositions.

There are three main types of entrance. The most elaborate is the rusticated courtyard or garden gate, articulated with columns or pilasters and surmounted by an entablature and pediment. Appearing first at Oatlands Palace in 1617 (cat. no. 17), it derived from town-house and city gates in Italy, especially Genoa (fig. 43), and from printed examples and designs for the orders in Serlio (1537, 1558), Vignola (1562), Palladio (1570) and Scamozzi (1615). The Oatlands gate was followed by three further Doric gates of a similar pattern between 1618 and 1623 (cat. nos 40–2), and by several grandiose renderings of the same theme in the Tuscan order from 1622 to about 1631 (cat. nos 44–8; fig. 40). The second type of gate is a simple arch in rusticated or ashlar masonry, topped with coping and sometimes ball finials. Much imitated by Lord Burlington in the eighteenth century, this type was used for subsidiary entrances at Oatlands Palace (cat. nos 19, 20, and possibly cat. nos 115 and 122), Arundel House (cat. no. 116) and New Hall (cat. no. 43). Jones's third form of entrance was the most widely influential, even though only one design survives. This was the pergola doorway, or balconied entrance, exemplified by the design for Sir Edward Cecil's pergola in the Strand of *c.* 1617 (cat. no. 23), but also seen on the elevation for Sir Fulke Greville's house (cat. no. 22). It soon appeared on houses by subordinate architects and became a commonplace of the London street scene in the later seventeenth century (fig. 91).

The designs for rusticated courtyard and garden gates are of particular interest because they give us a close-up view of Jones's handling of the classical orders. In these designs Jones explored the expressive range of the Doric and Tuscan orders, selecting details and proportions which accorded with his preference for a 'masculine and unaffected' style of architecture. This preference is implicit in the change from Doric to the more rudimentary Tuscan order in about 1623, but is also apparent in Jones's handling of detail. He often eliminated mouldings for the sake of a bolder and more ponderous effect; he simplified the Doric capital on three of the designs (cat. nos 17, 41, 42), introduced a new type of Doric base (fig. 45) and modified the triglyph and guttae (cat. no. 42). One of the Tuscan designs has a capital treated like an architrave (cat. no. 47); another has an entablature with over-sized mouldings taken from door and window dressings intended by Palladio for use at a much smaller scale (cat. no. 45).

The proportioning of the gates exhibits the same flexibility of mind. Jones set out his Doric designs using the module of a half column diameter at the base of the shaft, but rather than seeking an abstract, mathematical harmony of ratios, he was motivated by a quest for unity in the visual sense. Thus he did not feel bound to Vitruvius' prescriptions, copied by the Renaissance theorists, which required the triglyphs and metopes in the frieze to be 1 module and $1\frac{1}{2}$ modules wide respectively, but expanded or contracted these features to generate a visually coherent proportional scheme, be it narrow and attenuated on the Oatlands Vineyard gateway design, where the metopes are only $1\frac{5}{12}$ modules wide, or broad on the Beaufort House design, where the triglyphs are nearly $1\frac{1}{12}$ modules across and the frieze is only $1\frac{5}{12}$ modules high.

After 1620 there is an increasing emphasis in the gateway designs on breadth and plainness. Wall surfaces widen and the horizontal courses of masonry become the dominant motif (cat. nos 45, 47). On the lost pair of gateways which flanked St Paul's Church, Covent Garden from *c.* 1631 (fig. 40), the walls and Tuscan pilaster are fused by the horizontal banding which runs without interruption by pedestals and imposts from the ground to the entablature, a solution inspired by the walling of the Roman amphitheatre at Verona.

Underlying Jones's creative handling of the Doric and Tuscan orders is a belief in the necessity of variation from the standard forms of classical ornament derived from Vitruvius. Jones was guided by Daniele Barbaro's commentaries on Vitruvius in his copy of the 1567 edition of *I Dieci libri dell'architettura di M. Vitruvio Pollio*, now at Chatsworth. In his notes Jones drew attention to passages of text and commentary concerning the freedom permitted to an architect to vary from the rules. Barbaro cites Roman remains as evidence of the licence possible within the Vitruvian framework, and Jones concludes with him that 'it is alloud between the greater and lesser exses [excesses] to varry ye mean jiudgment' (Book IV, chap. i, p. 165). Expanding on this theme in one of his longest detached notes on variety in architectural design, Jones observed in his copy of *I Quattro libri* how Roman pedestals illustrated in Book IV had cornice mouldings more greatly varied from their bases than those in Palladio's orders in Book I. The striking fact about the Roman examples was that the mouldings were 'of on[e] nature of Strength of Slendernes for hearin Concistes ye art of Composing thes mouldings'. Jones concluded that such variety was only possible if 'the liberty of Composing wth reason is not Taken a waye', although whoever 'follows ye best of ye ansientes can not much earr' (*I Quattro libri*, IV, p. 98).

G.H.

40 Elevation for the 'Italian' gate at Arundel House, Strand, London

1618

Pen and brown ink with dark brown wash over scorelines and slight graphite under-drawing; some additions in graphite

438 × 368 mm. Vertical fold near left edge of elevation

Inscribed on *verso* by an 18th-c. hand in pen and brown ink: *Door.1.*

John Smythson's plan of the garden at Arundel House shows the 'newe Italyan gate' in the centre of the right-hand wall, on the western side of the terrace which overlooked the Thames (fig. 41). Unlike the Oatlands Vineyard gateway which faced outwards to the royal park (cat. no. 17), this gate looked inwards along the main axis of the walled garden towards a simpler rusticated arch at the opposite end. The second gate is shown in a separate drawing by Smythson and can be identified with another design by Jones at the RIBA (cf. cat. no. 116).

As with the Oatlands Vineyard gateway, the startling novelty of Jones's design lay in its richly textured rustication and the purity of its classical detail. The scheme of voussoired arch and bossed columns seems to derive from Galeazzo Alessi's Porta del Molo (Porta Siberia) in Genoa of 1553 (fig. 43), but with the important difference that the bosses on Jones's columns are smooth rather than rough-cut, so that the order as a whole is set off by the rusticated walling rather than the columns by the bosses. This more decorative handling of the bossed rusticated order probably comes from the woodcut illustration in *I Quattro libri* of the façade of Palladio's Palazzo Thiene in Vicenza (Book II, p. 14), where the rusticated bossed columns of the first-floor windows are shown smooth, although on the building itself they are rough-cut (fig. 11). When studying the woodcut, Jones noted that the bosses were flush with the bases, and repeated the detail on his design. The solution had far-reaching influence on English Palladianism. John Webb used the smooth-bossed order in designs for Whitehall Palace from about 1638 (published by William Kent in 1727), and it was taken up in various guises by Colen Campbell, James Gibbs and Roger Morris from the 1720s.

The order of the gateway is a rendering of Vignola's Doric (fig. 42). Jones marked Vignola's scale of 12 parts to the half-column diameter with dividers on the right half of the right column shaft, and marked a further scale of modules on a vertical scoreline near the right edge of the sheet. Using these scales he extemporized on Vignola's simple Doric ornaments, stripping away the fine details to give the columns and entablature a severity in tune with the heavy, plain bosses. He adjusted the projections of the order to align with the bosses, narrowing Vignola's bases and capitals by 5 parts each, so that the bases are a mere 2 modules

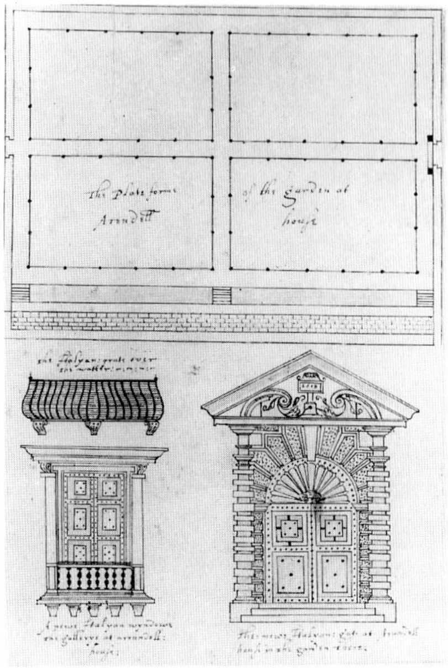

Fig. 41
John Smythson. Record drawings of the garden platform, Italian balcony, Italian window and the Italian garden gate at Arundel House, Strand, London, 1619

Fig. 42
Giacomo Barozzi da Vignola. Engraving of Doric base, pedestal and impost in *Regola delli cinque ordini d'architettura* (Rome, 1607) (Inigo Jones's annotated copy)

Fig. 43
Galeazzo Alessi. Porta del Molo, Genoa, 1553

5 parts wide and the capitals 2 modules 2 parts. The pedestals are allowed to project from the verticals by a single part, and the verticals of the bosses to align with the faces of the blocks in the scrolled half pediments, and with the projections of the ovolo mouldings beneath these blocks. In this way the upper and lower elements of the façade are brought together by shared outlines and similar surface treatment. The elaborate pediment comes from an engraving of Michelangelo's Porta Pia in Rome (1561) published in an appendix to the 1607 edition of Vignola's *Regola delli cinque ordini d'architettura*, known to Jones from his own copy of the treatise now in the library of Worcester College, Oxford.

See colour illustration on p. 157

Bibliography:

R. Wittkower, 'Pseudo-Palladian elements in English Neo-classical architecture', *Journal of the Warburg and Courtauld Institutes*, vi (1943), pp. 154–64 (repr. 1974)

R. Strong, *The Renaissance garden in England* (London, 1979), pp. 170–4

41 Elevation for a Doric gateway at Beaufort House, Chelsea, London

1621

Pen and brown ink with grey-brown wash over scorelines and with additions in black chalk

425 × 272 mm

Inscribed by Jones in pen and brown ink at the top left-hand corner: *for the M: of the Wardes/at Chelsey./1621*; and numbered *1* to *11* over scale beneath elevation; inscribed on *verso* by an 18th-c. hand in pen and brown ink: *Door.12.*

Scale: 9ft $=\frac{9}{14}$ in.

RIBA Jones & Webb 8

Jones designed this gateway for Sir Lionel Cranfield, James I's Master of the Court of Wards (and from 1621 to 1624 his Lord Treasurer). It is possibly the gateway shown as leading on to the King's private road in Kip and Knyff's view of Beaufort House, Chelsea, in *Britannia Illustrata* (1707). In 1738 Lord Burlington bought the gate from Sir Hans Sloane, then owner of Beaufort House, and re-erected it at Chiswick. Today it is one of only seven surviving, fully authenticated buildings by Jones, and it is the only one for which we have a final presentation drawing (cf. figs 44, 45).

The elevation is much plainer than the two earlier designs for Doric gateways (cat. nos 17, 40). The shafts of the columns are unrusticated and the entablature and pediment are not encumbered with carved ornament or rough-cut stone. This reflects a tendency towards less heavily articulated façades in Jones's architecture around 1620 and is also the outcome of a more disciplined drafting technique which places more emphasis on clean outlines, as a result of fuller use of the ruler and firmer handling of the profiles. Jones can now rule the horizontals of his moulding-courses right to the profiles, without need of freehand inset lines at the edges (still seen beneath the ruled lines on the capitals of the Arundel House design). He can also draw the curved, tapering profiles of the column shafts almost without overlap.

The clearer definition of wall surfaces and details goes hand in hand with a broader proportional scheme which gives more space to the wall in relation to the column, and stresses the horizontal over the vertical. This can be seen from the way in which the columns are set in piers that are wider (in relation to the column diameters) than those on the Oatlands Vineyard gateway (cat. no. 17). While the Oatlands columns are $16\frac{1}{2}$ modules high, heavily rusticated and set in piers just under $4\frac{1}{4}$ modules wide, the smooth-shafted Beaufort House columns are a more slender 17 modules and set in piers $4\frac{1}{2}$ modules across. The proportioning

Fig. 44
Beaufort House gateway, 1621, now at Chiswick House, London. Front elevation

Fig. 45
Beaufort House gateway, 1621. Rear elevation

of columns and piers affects the spacing of the triglyphs and metopes in the Doric frieze. In the canonical Doric order which Palladio used on his elevation for the Palazzo Chiericati (cat. no. 12), the frieze is exactly 1½ modules high (i.e. ¾ column-diameter at the base), and the triglyphs and metopes are 1 module and 1½ modules wide respectively. Jones felt no compulsion to follow such rules exactly, although he respected the detailing and general proportional scheme of the Doric order. By using slender columns on broad piers Jones created an excessively wide space, (in terms of modules) between the central axes of the columns. This meant he needed broader than usual members in the frieze if the triglyphs at each end were to align with the axes of the columns. As a result, Jones's triglyphs are nearly $\frac{1}{12}$ module more than the canonical 1 module wide. That this was a deliberate, stylistic preference for a more broadly proportioned Doric order than in the Italian treatises is shown by the fact that the height of the frieze is $\frac{1}{12}$ module less than the standard 1½ modules thus creating unusually squat triglyphs. The same logic is pursued in the upper parts of the elevation through the use of a very shallow pediment. The upper apex has been positioned on a geometrical system illustrated in Serlio's Book IV, where a segment of a circle is drawn from a radius which is the diagonal of the square formed by outer extremities of the pediment. This technique, visible in Jones's compass arc around the pediment, gives a proportion of 1:5 between the height and width of the pediment triangle (measured by the outer lines of the corona mouldings). It compares to a 1:4 proportion on the Oatlands Vineyard gateway and the 2:9 proportion recommended by Scamozzi in his discussion of pediments in Book VI of *L'Idea* (Part II, p. 42).

The proportional effects are enhanced by Jones's choice of detail. The capitals are simplified versions of the normal Doric type, without the plinth in the abacus, immediately above the ovolo moulding (cf. cat. no. 40). This is an innovation without published precedent and is found on two of Jones's other Doric gateway designs (cat. nos 17, 42). It enabled him to enlarge the remaining members of the capital, in keeping with the plain and massy character of the Doric order. The boldly detailed imposts borrowed from Vignola serve the same purpose (fig. 42).

Many characteristics of Jones's design appear on the building itself, demonstrating that his ideas on paper were indeed followed in practice (figs 44, 45). The columns of the gateway at Chiswick are 18 modules high (1 ft 4 in. by 12 ft 3½ in.) and are set in piers nearly 5 modules wide (3 ft 3½ in.). The gate opening is 6 ft, the same as on the drawing. The use of slightly narrower columns and broader piers on the gateway meant that the members of the frieze had to be even wider than on the drawing if they were to fill the space between the columns. What we see at Chiswick is, therefore, an exaggeration of the tendencies in the drawing. The triglyphs of the frieze are an average 1¼ modules across (10 in.), while the metopes are just over 1½ modules across (1 ft ½ in.). In order to accentuate the effect of breadth, however, Jones's frieze at Chiswick is a mere 1⅓ modules high (10¾ in.). Thus the frieze on the building is lower and its elements are wider than on the drawing. In fact, the proportions have been broadened to such a degree that the triglyphs, normally 1½ times higher than wide, are closer to a square proportion (10 in. by 10¾ in.) than the metopes (1 ft ½ in. by 10¾ in.), which are invariably square in the published sources. The pediment at Chiswick has the same proportion as on the drawing, and although the unusual capitals of the RIBA design are not present at Chiswick, Jones has employed the simple imposts found in Vignola.

Turning to the rear elevation at Chiswick we come across further peculiarities. This side of the gateway has pilasters instead of columns, and as a result the projections of the entablature and pedestals are shallower. As if in response to the low relief of the façade Jones flattened some of the details. Beneath the tenia of the architrave Jones substituted shallow triangular dentils for the usual wedges seen on the front elevation and the RIBA drawing. Another unprecedented variation from Doric norms is the base of the pilastered order which has two torus mouldings, one above the other, joined to a fascia. It looks like a compressed version of the Doric base; flattened, so to speak, against the pilaster shaft.

The principle behind such modifications is a harmony of the parts through shared characteristics of broadness, plainness or shallowness. Although Jones used the Doric module as a unit of proportion, he was not concerned with proportional harmony in the mathematical sense (as Wittkower has argued). His approach was largely dictated by intuitive, stylistic factors which sought balance in the general character of proportion and detail rather than in an abstract numerical scheme. The guiding principles are simple concepts such as the 'strength' or 'slenderness' which Jones perceived in the entrance hall of the Palazzo Thiene in Vicenza (see pp. 53–4), and the underlying tendencies are to emphasize the wall at the expense of the applied order and to simplify the ornaments.

See colour illustration on p. 157

Bibliography:
R. Wittkower, 'Inigo Jones, architect and man of letters', *RIBA Journal*, lx (1953), p. 84 (repr. 1974)

42 Elevation for a Doric garden gateway at New Hall, Essex

1623

Pen and ink with grey-brown wash over scorelines and graphite under-drawing

370 × 270 mm. Trimmed sheet of smooth, cream-coloured paper. The cartouche is on a separate sheet (45 × 50 mm) pasted over a plaque on the pediment

Watermark: elaborate shield with ball motifs on the handles surmounted by a crown and finial

Inscribed by Jones in pen and brown ink and struck out at lower right (partly cut off): *for East B[ ] / for M[ ]*; and on *verso* in pen and brown ink by an 18th-c. hand: *Door.3.*

Scale: 1 ft = $\frac{3}{4}$ in.

RIBA Jones & Webb 56

43 Elevation for a garden gateway at New Hall, Essex

1623

Pen and brown ink with grey-brown wash over scorelines

352 × 306 mm

Inscribed by Jones in pen and brown ink in lower right-hand corner: *for the garden gate at East Bauly. 1623*; and on *verso* in pen and brown ink by an 18th-c. hand: *Door.11.*

RIBA Jones & Webb 55

These two drawings belong to a campaign of work at the Essex estate of the royal favourite, George Villiers, Marquis of Buckingham, referred to in a memorandum by Jones of 25 September 1622 on the *verso* of cat. no. 44 (cf. also cat. no. 49). It was natural that Buckingham, then at the apogee of his political career, should employ the King's Surveyor to modernize his Tudor mansion at New Hall (also known as East Beaulieu, or 'East Bauly' in Jones's phonetic spelling on cat. no. 43). The two gateways were probably for complementary entrances to a walled garden, like those for Arundel House (cat. nos 40, 116). We do not know if they were built, and it is possible that the Doric gateway design was reused elsewhere, for Jones has pasted a cartouche over a plaque in the pediment and struck out his annotation on the drawing.

The Doric design is one of the most skilfully contrived of all Jones's classical elevations. It employs a similar vocabulary of forms to the Arundel House and Beaufort House gateway designs but the penmanship is more precise and every feature now tends towards an effect of monumentality which belies the smaller size of this gate. In the columns, for example, Jones followed Scamozzi's fluted Doric order, but he made the column broader (16 modules instead of 17), the flutes wider, and the fillets bigger in relation to the spaces between them (a third the width of the channels rather than Scamozzi's quarter proportion in *L'Idea*, Part II, p. 84). The imposts are a simplification of those in Vignola (fig. 42) and the capitals are bolder versions of the innovative type already seen on the Oatlands and Beaufort House gateway elevations (cat. nos 17, 41). Complementing the massive quality of the detailing is a sense of breadth in the main lines of the gate, achieved through the use of canted rather than straight voussoirs around the arch, slightly oblong pedestals, a low frieze of only $1\frac{1}{3}$ modules and a shallow pediment.

In the architrave Jones wilfully departed from Doric norms by reducing the guttae beneath the triglyphs from the customary six to five and omitting the fillet to which they are usually attached (cf. cat. no. 12). The triglyphs themselves have the channels continued right to the top rather than stopping just below. In the same spirit of simplification and enlargement Jones contracted the lowest two mouldings of his cornice and increased the ovolo from its $\frac{1}{5}$ module proportion in Palladio's example (*I Quattro libri*, I, p. 27) to $\frac{1}{4}$ module, so that it mirrors the ovolo on the capital (also $\frac{1}{4}$ module high) and gives mass to the upper members of the cornice.

The second New Hall design (cat. no. 43) follows the pattern of the Oatlands park gateway of 1617 (cat. no. 19), but here again there is an enormous advance in technique and style. Jones increased the scale of his masonry blocks and enhanced them with channelled joints. His clearly ruled design is almost without under-scoring, in contrast with the heavy handling on the earlier drawing.

44 Elevation for a Tuscan carriage gateway incorporating two schemes for the paired order and attic, for Hatton House, Ely Place, London

1622–3

Pen and brown ink with grey-brown wash over scorelines in rounded point; some graphite under-drawings and additions. Later red ink ruled border line on left edge of sheet

362 × 291 mm. Trimmed sheet, with central horizontal fold

Watermark: water-pot inscribed DVL and surmounted by a coronet and crescent moon

Inscribed by Jones in pen and brown ink in top right-hand corner: *for my lo Stuarde / for Hatton house / 1622 / 1623*; and on plaque over arch: *IN HO:E:MAX COO TRI C:IVI/E DI: IACOBUS IMP: MAG BRIT/Quam huc extruxit exfund / amento corfera(?)*; and below right-hand pier: *scalle of feete*; and on *verso* by Jones in graphite, at bottom right-hand corner of sheet, partly cut off by trimming and partly indecipherable: *to be donn att New/hale 25 of Sept / 1622 / To make ye stabell high / eune wth the other flow[er] / To make a gallery fa[ir(?)] / or armory ouer it the [ ] / raised/to voltt ye seller and/roomes ouer the[m] / to make an estimatt[for the(?)] /chappell adorned to a[llter(?)] / the closett and in larg [ ] /lakroddes(?) allter the w[indo] / wes fitt paintinges / to put y^e Kinges wiste(?) [ ] / on[e] of the windowes in [the(?)] /chappell / (?) the estimattes of /* (rest cut off)

Scale: 1 ft = $\frac{1}{4}$ in.

RIBA Jones & Webb 14

45 Presentation elevation for a Tuscan carriage gate for Hatton House, Ely Place, London

1622–3

Pen and dark-brown ink with grey wash over scorelines and graphite under-drawing

440 × 286 mm. Comprising a main sheet, 396 × 285 mm, trimmed at top in stepped shape and overlaid on *recto* by two sheets pasted above the cornice; a lower sheet, 111 × 286 mm, also stepped up at centre, and an upper one, 77 × 286 mm, pasted between the two other sheets. The whole sheet has been trimmed close to the design and along the slopes of the pediment

Inscribed by Jones in pen and brown ink with numbers *1* to *14*, right to left, above scale at bottom of sheet

Scale: 1 ft = $1\frac{5}{16}$ in.

RIBA Jones & Webb 16

These two magnificent designs for carriage gateways at the Holborn House of Lodovic Stuart, 2nd Duke of Lennox, show Jones experimenting with a monumental Tuscan order for the first time in his career. Serlio's woodcuts of rusticated Tuscan city gates in Book IV of *Tutte l'opere d'architettura* (Venice, 1619) gave Jones a starting point for the preliminary design of 1622–3 (cat. no. 44), which displays alternative schemes for a paired order against a massive, rough-cut arch surmounted by an attic. But as with other ideas which began with Serlio (e.g. cat. nos 17, 26, 28), Jones refined the detailing and rationalized the proportions. He took the attic from a gateway by Domenico Fontana published in 1590 (fig. 46), and applied mouldings from Palladio's Tuscan order in Book I of *I Quattro libri*. Serlio was happy to leave the design of his low attics to the 'workmen's discretion', but Jones ensured that the attic was integrated with the whole proportional scheme by making its height equal to that from the ground to the top of the main arch imposts (15 ft 5 in.), and the main arch height almost exactly half the overall height of the gate to the apex of the pediment (21 ft 6 in. and 43 ft 6 in.). The arch height, in turn, is nearly the same as the combined width of the arch and one of the gate piers (12 ft and 9 ft 8 in.). Moreover, the overall width of the attic (27 ft 9 in.) is almost equal to the height from the ground to the top of the main entablature (28 ft).

Within this framework of shared dimensions and repeated ratios, Jones roughed out the details of the gate with his scorer and graphite, redrawing or erasing the pen lines as necessary. The technique recalls the Banqueting House 'penultimate, design (cat. no. 34) and carries with it the same feeling of indecision as Jones hovers between solutions. Working from left to right, as

Fig. 46
Domenico Fontana. Design for the Porta Exquilina, Rome (unexecuted). Engraving in his *Della trasportatione dell'obelisco vaticano et delle fabriche di nostro signore Papa Sisto V . . . libro primo* (Rome, 1590), fol.79*r*.

he did on most of the gateway designs, Jones thought first of a broad attic with paired pilasters, and pencilled the left attic cornice above the scored lines of the pilaster. In the ink drawing he tried a bossed order below, and used Palladio's Tuscan cornice on the attic. The preferred scheme seems to be on the right, where the columns are plain-shafted and there is a modified form of the attic cornice, redrawn to the right with even greater emphasis on the corona moulding. The stress on one moulding at the expense of others is typical of Jones's method at this period, when he was striving for an idiom in the details of his orders. Below, he has employed a very thick astragal at the top of the column shafts and a tall collar as the lower member of the capital. The accent on the lower part of the capital is matched by the use of a large cavetto at the bottom of the cornice.

The second design (cat. no. 45) is a 'presentation' drawing bearing the arms of Lodovic Stuart, 2nd Duke of Lennox, and Frances, widow of the 1st Earl of Hertford. They were married in June 1621 and the Duke died in February 1624. Although this would appear to be a final design, we do not know if it was built. The attic is a refinement of that on the 'preliminary' design, but has been pasted over the top of the lower design, concealing a simple pediment with a cartouche. This lower gateway has banded rustication across the pilasters in the manner of Fontana's gateway (fig. 46) and one of Serlio's Tuscan arches, both of which derive from the arcades of the Roman amphitheatre at Verona.

The scale of the detailing in the lower part of the design is astonishingly bold. Aiming at the utmost severity and simplicity, Jones proportioned his pilasters after Serlio's Tuscan order, and modelled the entablature on large-scale profiles in Palladio's Book I (p. 57) intended for door and window surrounds. These gave him the authority for such unprecedented Tuscan features as the enormous cymatium on the architrave ($\frac{1}{3}$ its height), the pulvinated frieze which echoes the bulging rusticated blocks, and the unusually thick fillets on all the mouldings. The whole elevation is tied together on a modular system of proportion taken from the diameter of the pilaster shaft at its base. This accounts for the harmonious treatment of the mouldings, since most of the fillets are $\frac{1}{6}$ module deep. The attic height of $4\frac{1}{4}$ modules is half that of the gateway from the ground to the top of the main entablature ($8\frac{1}{2}$ modules).

See colour illustration on p. 158

46 Elevation for a Tuscan carriage gate, possibly for Greenwich Park

c. 1622–3

Pen and brown ink with grey wash and graphite under-drawing

392 × 307 mm. Horizontal fold through centre of sheet

Watermark: same as cat. no. 21

Inscribed on *verso* in pen and brown ink by an 18th-c. hand: *Door.21.*

Scale: 1 ft = $\frac{5}{12}$ in.

RIBA Jones & Webb 80

Unusually for Inigo Jones this drawing has no under-scoring. The preparatory technique is entirely in graphite and incorporates alternative schemes for the size of the Tuscan order and spacing of the channelled blocks. The neat grey ink shading and the cleanly ruled brown ink lines place the drawing near in date to the Hatton House and New Hall gateway designs of 1622–3. A date in the early 1620s would also be consistent with the preparatory graphite technique (cf. cat. no. 52).

The design is for an exceptionally large rusticated gateway, with an arch 12 ft wide and 23 ft high. Crowned with ball finials, it would seem to be for a park gate, like two other drawings by Jones (cat. nos 19, 47). Given the stylistic dating, the only possibility is the 'greate gate' erected at the entrance to Greenwich Park, near the Queen's House, in 1623–4, and shown from its rear side in the background of Van Stalbemt and Van Belcamp's painting of Charles I and his Court at Greenwich in about 1632 (fig. 14). Another view of the same buttressed rear elevation by Hollar, in a panorama of Greenwich Palace and Park, *c.* 1637, confirms that the gate was for coach and horses, and that the arch was at least as big as in the drawing. In the Declared Accounts the gate is 'arched over with a rusticke arche and rusticke pillausters with architrave freeze and parte of the cornishe rounde about and a Perrymente over heade together with a skeame arch over the gate [. . .] with two great buttresses into the parke'. The description alludes to the continuous rusticated arch around the gate and the pilasters supporting blocks of cornice. No segmental ('skeame') arch is shown in the drawing, but this may have been intended to fit beneath the main arch, or for the rear elevation as on the Oatlands Vineyard gateway (cat. no. 17).

Jones followed Fontana's design for the Porta Exquilina in Rome (fig. 46) by carrying the channelled courses of the walling up to the keystone without interruption by imposts. This motif of arch without imposts recurs in Jones architecture in the 1630s (e.g. cat. nos 59, 80) and typifies his tendency to minimize surface ornament on late elevations. He used an almost identical treatment of channelled arch and pilasters for a pair of gateways flanking St Paul's Church, Covent Garden, *c.* 1631, tragically demolished at the end of the last century (fig. 40). Jones based his Tuscan order on Palladio's but deepened the upper two mouldings of the cornice to give maximum emphasis to the skyline.

Bibliography:

J. Charlton, *The Queen's House* (London, 1976)

King's Works, iv, pp. 118–19

47 Elevation for a park gate at St James's Palace, London

1627

Pen and dark brown ink with grey wash over graphite under-drawing and scorelines

362 × 251 mm. Thick creamy paper

Watermark: same as cat. no. 21 but 4M monogram below shield

Inscribed by Jones in pen and brown ink in top right-hand corner: *for the Parke St James/1627*; and on *verso* in pen and brown ink by an 18th-c. hand: *Door.22.*

Scale: 1 ft $= \frac{21}{64}$ in. (4 ft $= 1\frac{5}{32}$ in.)

RIBA Jones & Webb 30

Although dated 1627 this must be the design for a gateway with a cornice built into the park wall of the Privy Garden at St James's Palace in 1631–2. With characteristic economy Jones pared his Tuscan order down to the barest elements, treating the pilasters, imposts, architraves and frieze as plain fascias, scarcely distinguishable from the channelled walling, and rendering the capitals like dropped-down pieces of architrave. So minimal is the architecture on this elevation that it is surprising to discover that the gateway was to be as big as a two-storey house: 28 ft from the ground to the top of the blocking course and 24 ft across. The 20 ft pilasters were to be double the height of the wooden Tuscan columns in the colonnade of the nearby Sculpture Gallery, completed in 1630 to house King Charles's collection of antique statuary acquired from the Duke of Mantua in 1627.

Bibliography:

King's Works, iv, pp. 249–51

for the Parke St James
1627

48 Elevations for two entrance doorways

c. 1630

Pen and grey-brown ink over scorelines

235 × 387 mm. Single sheet of thin, grainy paper with central vertical fold

Watermark: water-pot inscribed with two balls and surmounted by a crescent moon

Inscribed by Jones in pen and brown ink on right-hand side: *thes pilasters ar/not deminished*

Scale: 1 ft = $\frac{3}{8}$ in.

RIBA Jones & Webb 79

This sheet bears the hallmarks of Jones's mature architectural draftsmanship: thin, grainy paper folded down the centre to prick through features of the design from one side to the other, stylus markings in a rounded point, and firm, cleanly handled shading lines. The varied slant of the shading resembles that on the Somerset House Chapel window design of 1632 (cat. no. 59); by contrast, Jones's shading on drawings from the mid- and late 1630s is more regular (e.g. cat. no. 80). The inscription is in a compact italic style of Jones's handwriting dating no earlier than about 1630.

The left design is a variation on Scamozzi's Tuscan order, and both designs display a preoccupation, found in Scamozzi's account of entrances framed by the orders in Book VI of his treatise, with the alignment between the parts of the door and the architectural frame. While the left design utilizes the open-pedimented arch of Jones's park gate elevation of *c.* 1622–3 (cat. no. 46), and aligns the door opening with the bottom of the capital, the right design has the pilasters as door jambs and aligns capitals and bases with the upper and lower rails. The inscription, 'thes pilasters ar not deminished', was to ensure that the sides of the pilasters stayed vertical, rather than tapering inwards.

The designs may be alternatives for the same entrance, probably for a London town house. There is no specific commission with which they can be associated, but it is known that the Office of Works was responsible for preparing a number of important private mansions in and around London for embassies during the reign of Charles I, for example Lord Brooke's (Sir Fulke Greville's) house in Holborn, 1628–30 (cat. no. 22), and Montague House, Aldersgate Street, 1629–31.

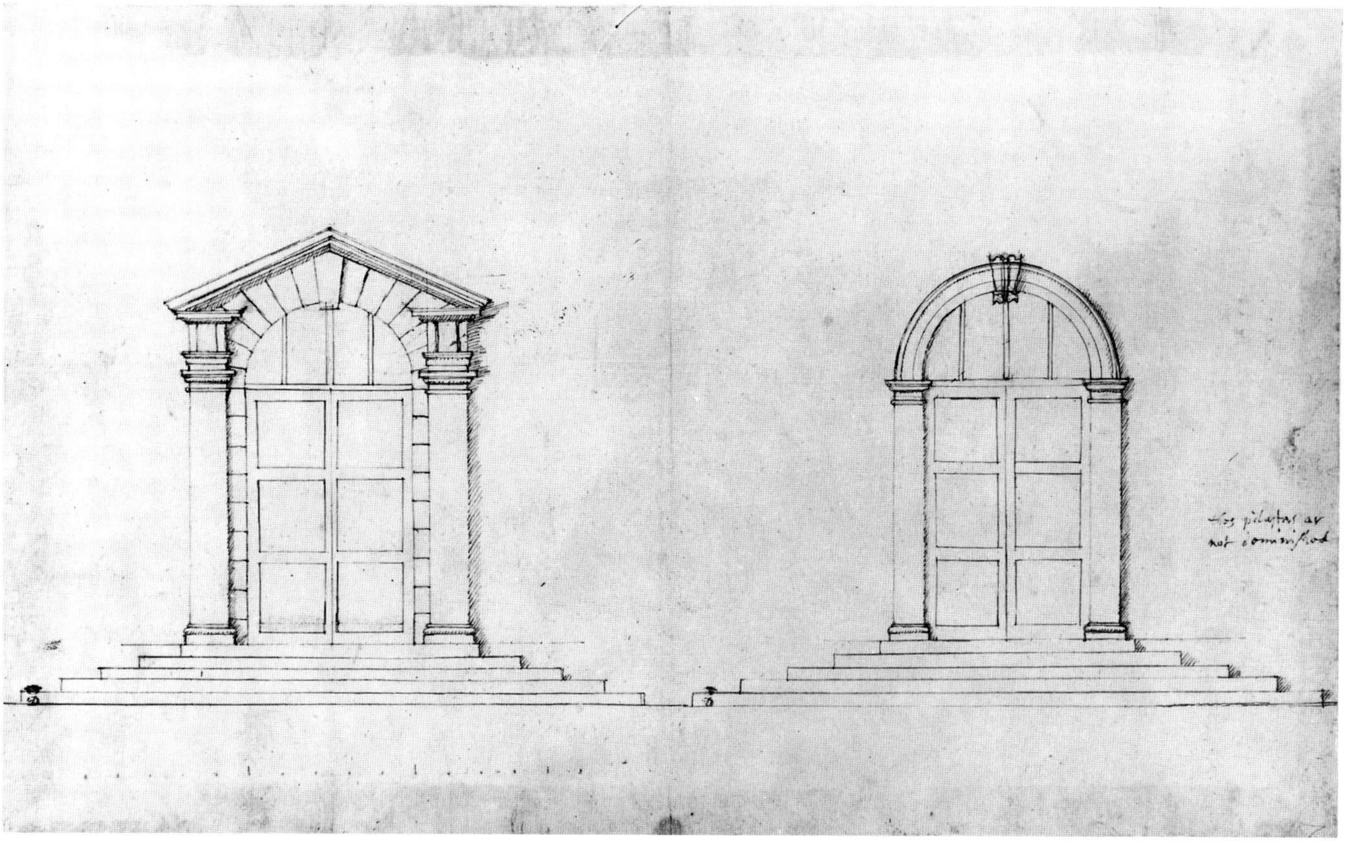

Cat. 2
Costume design for a winged masquer
Cat. 10
Costume design for a torchbearer: a fiery spirit

Cat. 3
Elevation for the New Exchange

Cat. 4
Elevation for a new termination to the tower of St Paul's Cathedral

Cat. 8
Scenery design for the masque *Oberon, The Fairy Prince*

Cat. 14
Preliminary design for the north or south façade of the Queen's House

Cat. 21
Elevation for the entrance bay to an unidentified house

Cat. 22
Presentation design for a town-house façade, ascribed to Sir Fulke Greville's house

Cat. 23
Elevation for a pergola entrance to Sir Edward Cecil's house
Cat. 25
Elevation for an arched doorway surmounted by a pedimented attic containing a barred oval window

Cat. 30
First elevation for the Prince's Lodging at Newmarket Palace
Cat. 31
Astylar elevation for the Prince's Lodging at Newmarket Palace

Cat. 33
Plan and elevation of the first scheme for the Banqueting House

Cat. 34
Elevation for the penultimate design for the Banqueting House

Cat. 36
Drawing for the scene of the Banqueting House for *Time Vindicated to Himself and to His Honours*

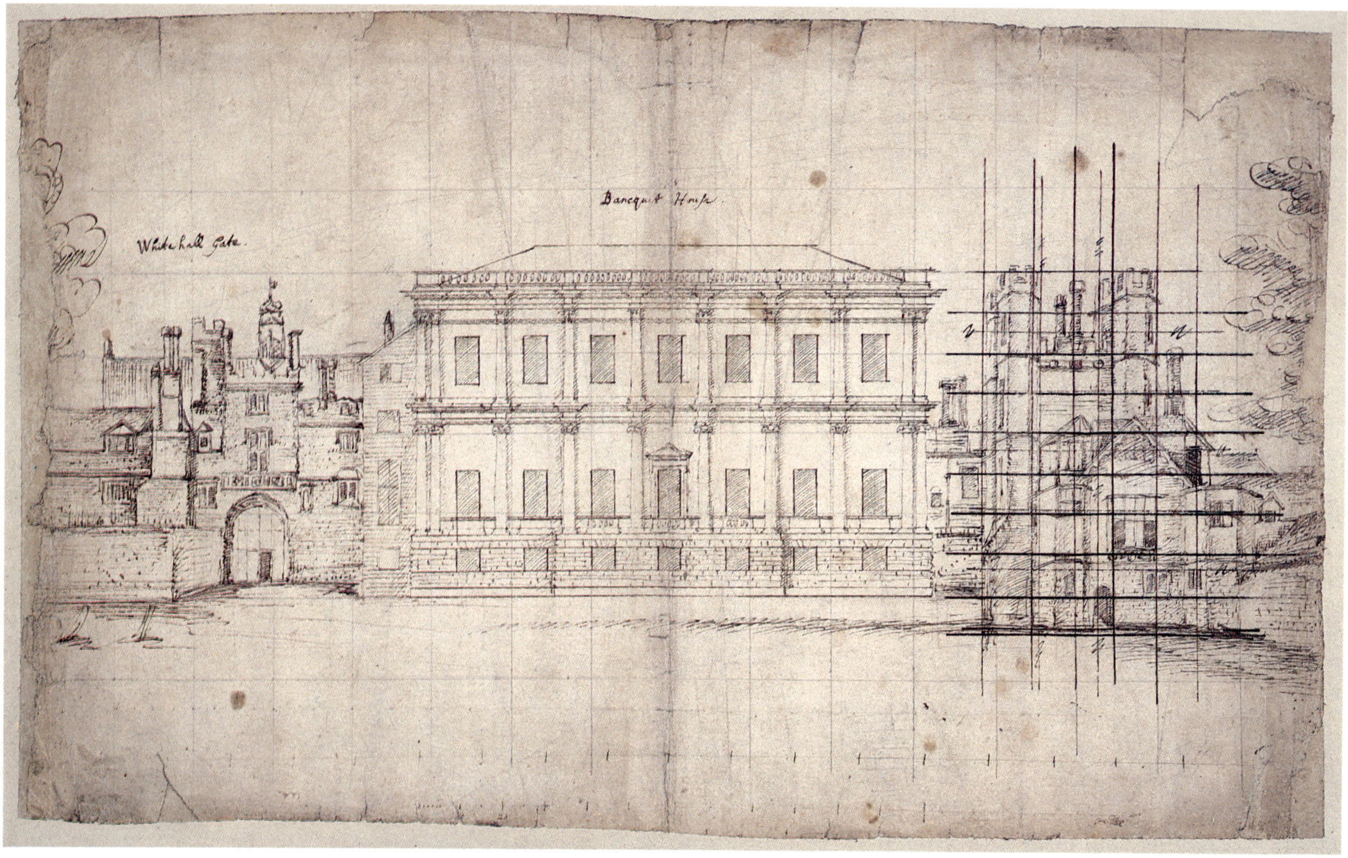

Cat. 40
Elevation for the 'Italian' gate at Arundel House
Cat. 41
Elevation for a Doric gateway at Beaufort House

Cat. 45
Presentation elevation for a Tuscan carriage gate for Hatton House

Cat. 49
Design for one bay of a coffered ceiling, ascribed to the Marquis of Buckingham's chapel closet at New Hall

Cat. 53
Finished elevation for the catafalque of James I in Westminster Abbey

Cat. 57
Design for a painted frieze with a female head in a roundel, a swag and cupids

Cat. 58
Design for a painted vertical panel with grotesque ornament and the cypher of Queen Henrietta Maria

Cat. 68
Two half elevations for a chimney overmantel ascribed to Basing House

Cat. 69
Sketch elevation for a chimney-piece with alternative overmantel designs for Oatlands Palace

Cat. 71
Design for painted frames in the lower gallery of Oatlands Palace

Cat. 75
Sketch elevation for the Cabinet Room chimney-piece and overmantel, the Queen's House

Cat. 78
Elevation for the west front of St Paul's Cathedral

Cat. 82
Sketch elevation for a triumphal arch at Temple Bar

Cat. 83

Longitudinal section for a second scheme for a triumphal arch at Temple Bar

Cat. 87
Elevation for a seven-window house with an iron pergola

Cat. 90
Plan and elevation for a brew-house ascribed to Hassenbrook Hall

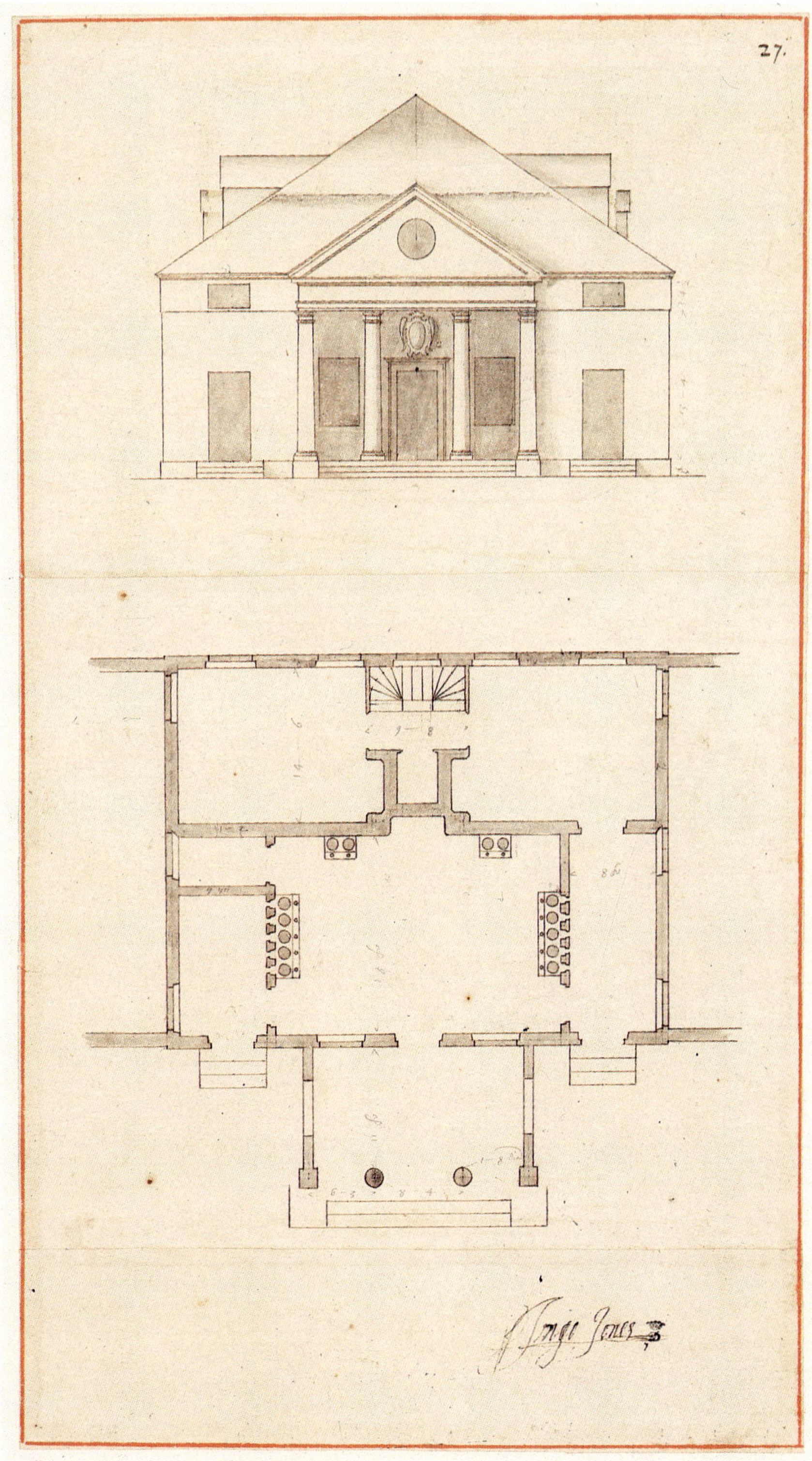

Cat. 91
Elevation and plan for a playhouse, possibly for Sir William Davenant's unexecuted theatre project

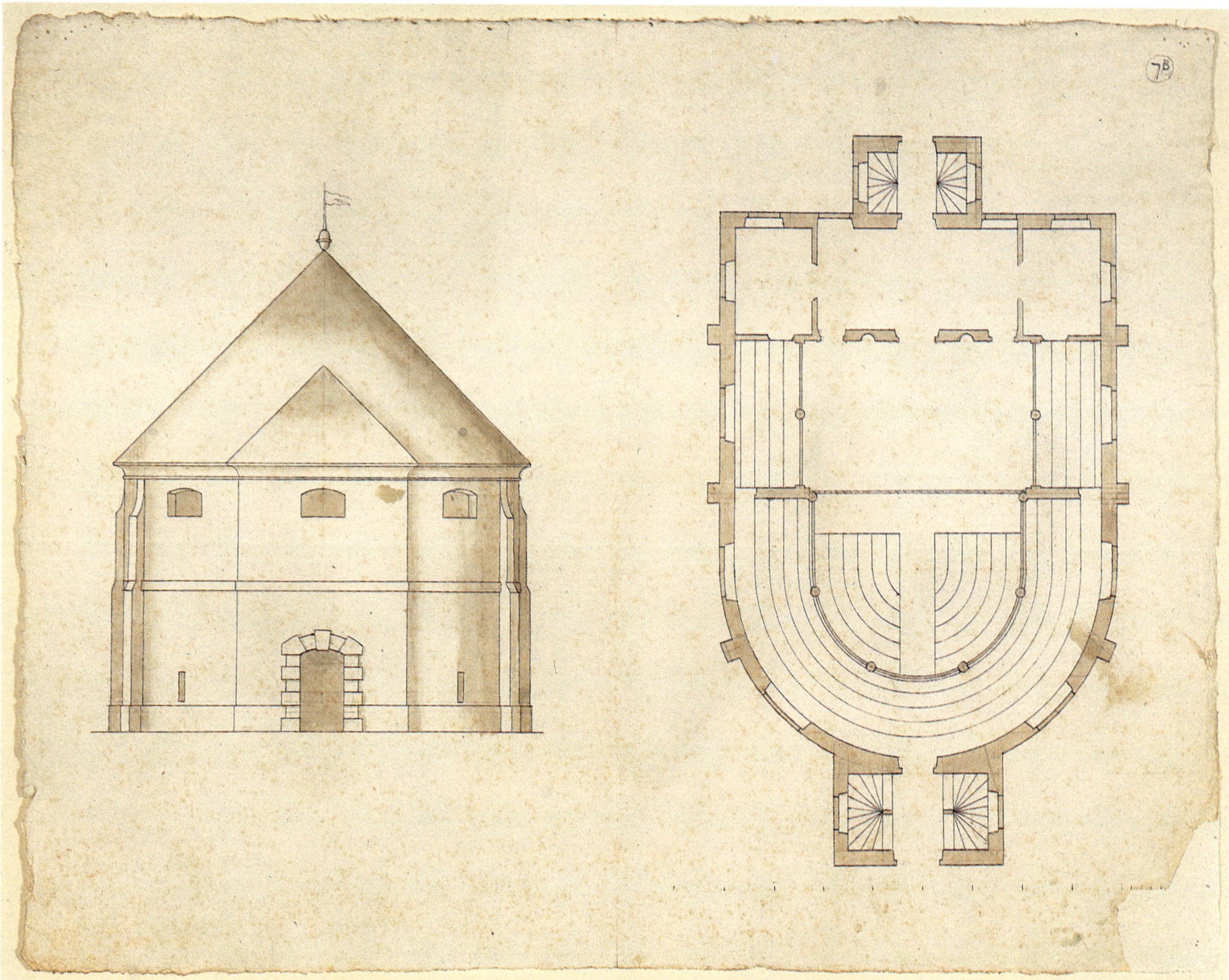

Cat. 92
Two transverse sections of the design for a playhouse, possibly for Sir William Davenant's unexecuted project

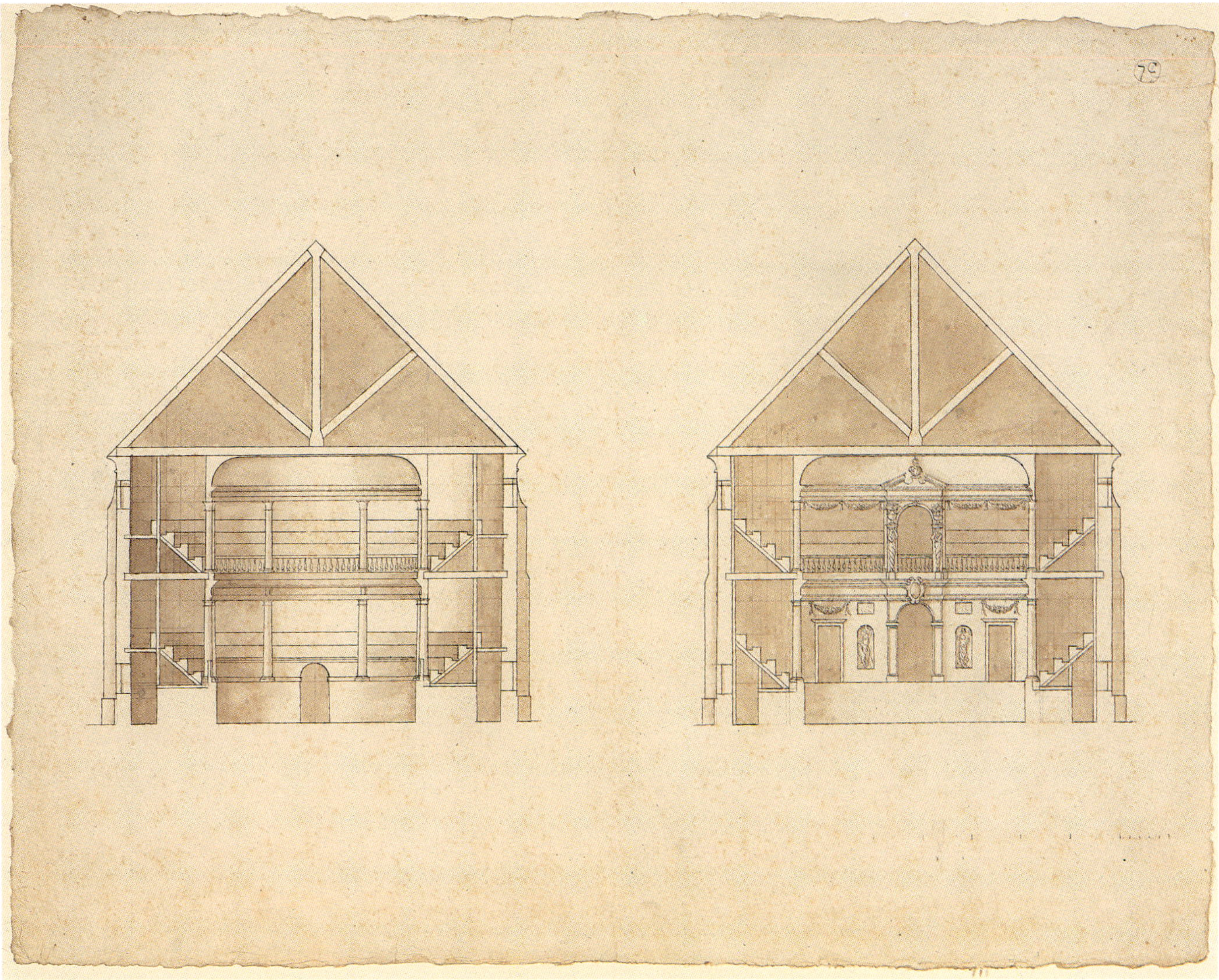

Cat. 95
Scenery design for the masque *Albion's Triumph*

Cat. 97
Scenery for the play *Florimène*

Cat. 113
Group of eight heads in various positions

Designs of the 1620s

In the 1620s Jones's perspective on the classical tradition began to widen. No longer satisfied with Palladio's interpretation of the orders in Book I of *I Quattro libri*, he sought authority in Vitruvius and in illustrations of Roman buildings in Palladio's Book IV and Serlio's Book III. A reverence for antiquity conditioned his outlook and dictated his architectural style. It led to his famous mistake when, in 1620, he was asked by King James to provide an account of the origin and purpose of Stonehenge. He concluded, in 'some few indigested notes' published by John Webb in 1655, that the megalith was a Roman temple in the Tuscan order, open to the heavens, and dedicated to Coelus, or Uranus, the oldest god of the classical pantheon. Soon Jones was himself designing in the Tuscan order or emulating its severe simplicity on his domestic façades (cat. nos 45–7, 50). He was attracted to the plain walling, boldly handled cornices and richly coffered vaults of Roman temple architecture (cat. no. 46, figs, 50, 51). Interiors became more lavish, in contrast to the austere façades. There are hints of this in the scrolls and cartouches on the catafalque for King James in 1625, borrowed from an exuberant design by Domenico Fontana (cat. nos 53, 54, fig. 53). By the end of the decade the French taste of Queen Henrietta Maria for figurative and grotesque interior ornament had asserted itself and Jones's mature architectural style was formed (cat. nos 56–8).

The more restrained exterior style of the 1620s went hand in hand with a more disciplined drafting technique. Jones used the ruler for almost all straight lines and controlled his pen far better than in the period from 1616 to 1619. Outlines are cleaner, firmer and thicker, defining the wall surfaces with greater clarity and allowing the solids and voids to speak for themselves. Through mastery of the pen and ruler Jones gained command of the details on façades, distilling them to a few essential mouldings, and in this way evolved his own distinctive idiom from a blend of Roman and Renaissance sources.

G.H.

49 Design for one bay of a coffered ceiling, ascribed to the Marquis of Buckingham's chapel closet at New Hall, Essex

c. 1622–3

Pen and brown ink with brown and grey wash shading, washed with red, gold and blue gouache. Graphite under-drawing; scoreline and compass marks

392 × 307 mm. Laid down

Inscribed by Jones in brush and brown ink with motto of George Villiers, Marquis of Buckingham, beneath the arms of Villiers impaling Manners, for Catherine Manners, his wife: *FIDEI COTICULA CRUX*

Worcester College H & T 3

This beautiful design for one bay of a wooden ceiling is modelled on Palladio's illustration of the coffering of the 'Temple of Neptune' (Venus Genetrix) in Rome (*I Quattro libri*, IV, p. 133). It is one of only two colour-washed architectural drawings by Inigo Jones (see cat. no. 83) and employs a gouache technique similar to several of his early costume designs (cat. no. 2).

The drawing dates between 20 May 1620, when George Villiers, Marquis of Buckingham, married Catherine Manners, and his elevation to Dukedom on 18 May 1623. Summerson has ascribed it to the dining-room ceiling of Buckingham's Lodging in King Street, Whitehall, built 1619–21. This was a 'large and Comely Roome', but though the Works accounts describe the painting of seventy 'great lights of windowes', they do not refer to the ceiling. More probably the design was made for the ceiling of the chapel at Buckingham's Tudor mansion of New Hall in Essex. According to a memorandum on the back of another drawing (cat. no. 44), Jones was working there from 25 September 1622. The works included designs for two gateways in the garden, dated 1623 (cat. nos 42, 43), and several tasks specified in the memorandum. The most important task was the refurbishment of the chapel. Jones was to make an estimate for work at the chapel and its closet, altering windows and fitting paintings:

> [. . .] to make an estimatt [for the (?)]
> chappell adorned to a[llter (?)]
> the closett and in large [ ]
> lakroddes (?) allter the w[indo]
> wes fitt paintings
> to put ye Kinges wiste (?) [ ]
> on[e] of the windowes in [the (?)]
> chappell [. . .]

Although a ceiling is not mentioned, it is clear that a substantial refitting was proposed. Jones's design seems to be for a *trompe l'œil* modification to an existing Tudor panelled roof, as it has a typically late-medieval moulded wall plate and Tudor-style beaded mouldings between the panels. Moreover, it is a type of Roman coffered ceiling which Jones employed on other chapel interiors at St James's Palace, 1623–5 (cat. no. 51) and Somerset House, 1630–5 (fig. 60).

See colour illustration on p. 159

Bibliography:
J. Summerson, *Inigo Jones* (Harmondsworth, 1966), pp. 57, 59, 64
King's Works, iv, pp. 326–7, 172–5

FIDEI COTICVLA CRVX

50 Elevation and (on *verso*) transverse section for an unidentified stable

Pen and brown ink with brown wash over scorelines

470 × 359 mm. Single sheet folded in half across centre. The elevation is on the upper *recto* and the section is upside-down on the lower *verso*

Watermark: same as cat. no. 21

The elevation has heavy brown ink dots and lines along the cornices, quoins and right-hand eaves, and scribbled keyhole, spyhole and hinges: all apparently the doodles of a later hand

Worcester College H & T 57

Formerly attributed to the stable at Newmarket Palace, 1616–17, this small yet imposing design can be reassigned to the early 1620s on stylistic evidence, and assumes an important place in the evolution of Jones's domestic style between the second and fourth decades of his career.

Like several of Jones's mature architectural drawings, the design is presented on two halves of a folded sheet, the elevation on the *recto* having been used to prick through the outlines of the section on the *verso*, upside down on the lower half of the sheet (fig. 47). Outlines are almost fully ruled and evenly inked, in contrast to the half-ruled, half-freehand and more tentative style of the 1616–19 period (cf. cat. nos 21, 30). Under-scoring, although with a sharp metal point, is also tidier than examples from the pre-1620 period and the wash is less patchy. The drawing must be much earlier than the precisely handled domestic designs of the late 1630s (e.g. cat. nos 84, 86), and would seem to date a few years before the Whitehall Clock House design of 1627 (cat. no. 55). The Clock House design is also on a folded sheet, but has firmer outlines and a smoother, more accurate wash technique.

The stable elevation is in the brick-and-stone idiom of the 1619 Newmarket elevations (cat. nos 30, 31) but is more restrained in the handling of quoins and mouldings. By using a single depth of quoin block across the whole front, and aligning the joints with his ruler, Jones tied together the outer and middle bays of the composition without need of running mouldings, or of a progression of enrichment from sides to centre. To emphasize the central arch Jones merely widened the blocks and raised them forward of the wall surface. A similar combination of plain, unarticulated wall and uniform quoin blocks rising the full height of the building is found on the Queen's Chapel at St James's Palace, 1623–5 (fig. 50).

The sectional drawing (fig. 47) suggests that the structure of this stable was similar to the one of *c.* 1610 (cat. no. 9). The horse boxes are in the intermediate bays, but instead of having flat, balustraded roofs the bays are under single slopes, thus providing extra loft space for the storage of fodder.

Bibliography:
J. Harris, 'Inigo Jones and the Prince's Lodging at Newmarket', *Architectural History*, ii (1959), p. 34

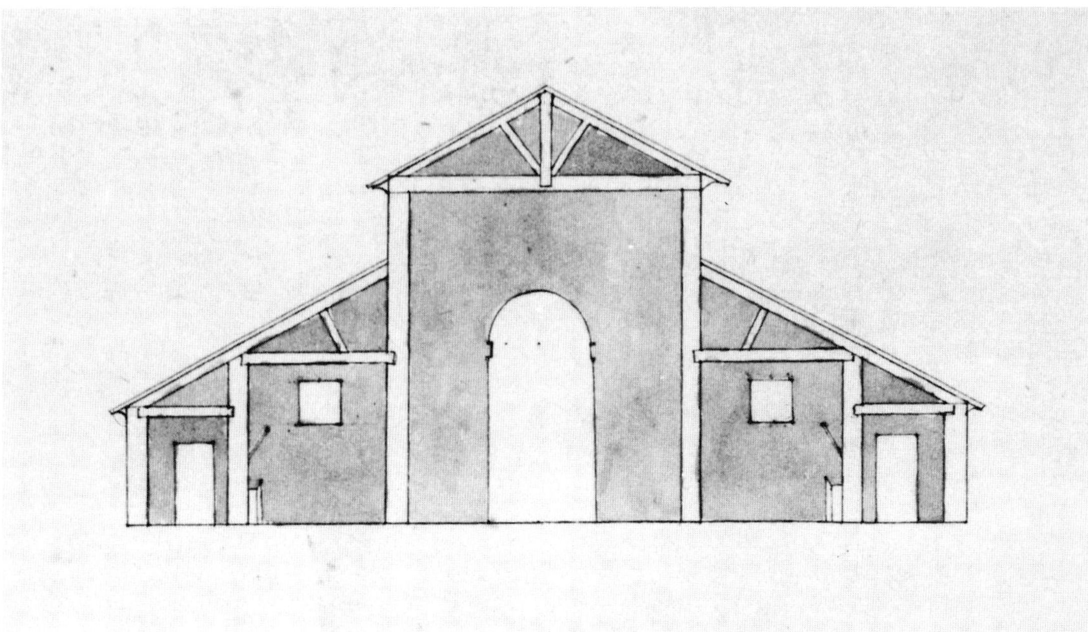

Fig. 47
Transverse section through the unidentified stable on *verso* of cat. no. 50, *c.* 1620–5

51 Henry Flitcroft. Longitudinal section through the Queen's Chapel at St James's Palace, London (1623–5)

1720s

Pen and grey ink with grey wash; black ink ruled border

322 × 526 mm. Including rectangle, 271 × 182 mm, cut out and replaced (with different paper) on left-hand side of sheet

Watermarks: main sheet has shield containing fleur-de-lys surmounted by coronet and with a 4 monogram beneath (rest cut off). Replacement sheet shows 4WR monogram (both sheets from Wendelin Riehel's mill, Strasbourg)

Inscribed by Flitcroft in pen and grey ink with numbers below scale

Scale: 10 ft = $2\frac{1}{8}$ in.

This measured drawing resulted from Lord Burlington's purchase, from John Talman, of designs by Inigo Jones in 1720. Burlington discovered paper evidence of hitherto unknown buildings by the master – the Queen's Chapel at St James's Palace, Somerset House Chapel, Winchester Cathedral Choir Screen, and many minor works – and almost immediately ordered his draftsman, Henry Flitcroft, to measure them. The two royal chapels were disguised in the early eighteenth century and for this reason had not been known to Colen Campbell, for whom the Queen's Chapel in particular would have been considered worthy of inclusion in *Vitruvius Britannicus* (1715).

The chapel was initiated in 1623 when Prince Charles was to marry the Roman Catholic Spanish Infanta. Jones was ordered to prepare designs 'wth great state and costlines', and on 16 May the first stone was laid. By the end of the 1625 the chapel was complete, at a cost of £4,027. Of course, by this time Charles had rejected the Spanish match and married Queen Henrietta Maria, but it mattered little, for it is was still a Catholic chapel.

Of all Jones's works, the Queen's Chapel at St James's Palace is probably the best preserved. Its Portland-stone masonry exterior with mortar rendering 'drawne like Ashler' is as executed, and although the fittings inside date from 1682, the whole of the ceiling and cornice are original, as is the Reigate-stone chimneypiece in the Closet (cat. no. 52). Jones also designed the two-bay annexe which served as the main entrance from the palace to the royal closet, and John Webb records one of the lower windows in a thumbnail sketch at Worcester College (figs 48, 49).

Jones conceived the chapel as a double-cube hall set between a pedimented three-bay west front and a huge Venetian window set in the east (fig. 50). Inside, the ceiling provided a majestic barrel-vaulted canopy of coffered timber adapted from

Fig. 48
The Queen's Chapel, St James's Palace, London. View of west front, showing the original adjacent wing to the south

Fig. 49
John Webb. Record drawing of ground-floor window on the south wing adjacent to the Queen's Chapel, 1640s(?)

Fig. 50
View of the exterior of the chapel from south-east

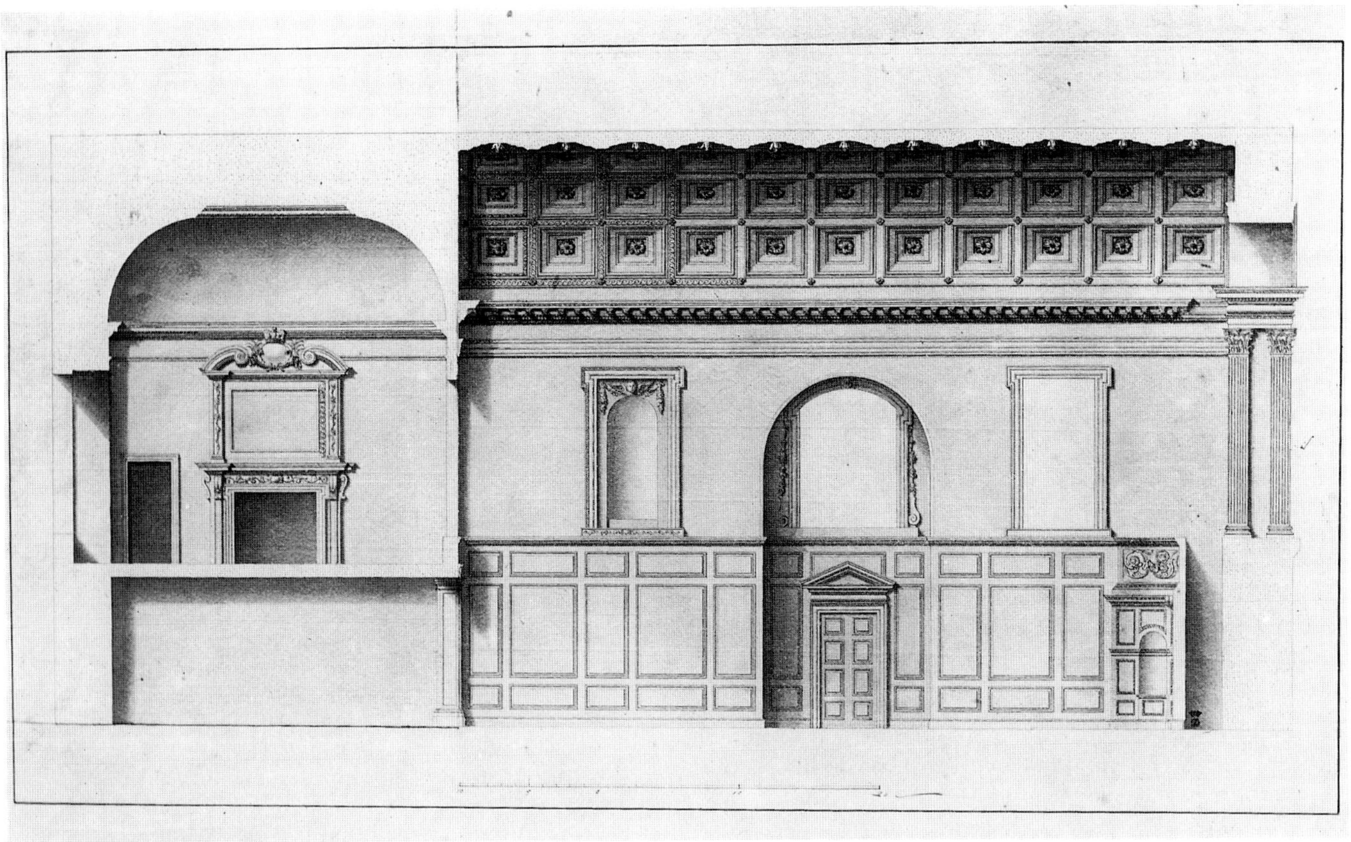

Fig. 51
Engraved view by Johannes Kip of the chapel as fitted out 1686–8 for Roman Catholic services for Mary of Modena, Queen of James II

Fig. 52
Peter Tillemans. Queen Anne in the House of Lords, painted between 1708 and 1714, showing Jones's coffered ceiling of 1623–4 and a chimney overmantel of similar date

Palladio's woodcuts of the Temple of Venus and Rome in *I Quattro libri* (IV, p. 38) (fig. 51). The formula of a single nave lit by a Venetian window at the east and served by a gallery at the west was recognized by Sir Christopher Wren as an adaptable model for his City churches, and was imitated far and wide throughout Britain and the colonies in the eighteenth century.

Bibliography:
G. H. Chettle, 'Marlborough House Chapel', *Country Life*, lxxxiv (1938), pp. 450–3
J. Summerson, *Inigo Jones* (Harmondsworth, 1966), pp. 61–6
J. Harris, *The Palladians* (London, 1981), p. 115
King's Works, iv, pp. 248–9, v, pp. 244–54

52 Elevation for the Closet chimney-piece and overmantel in the Queen's Chapel at St James's Palace, London

c. 1624–5

Graphite outline over scorelines, with some pen and brown ink with brown wash

404 × 288 mm

Watermark: bear within a shield surmounted by a crown; monogram D and three circles below: the mark of the Düring family mill, Basle

Inscribed in pen and brown ink by John Webb across chimney breast: *6fo – 10yn*, and against right-hand side of overmantel frame: *3fo – 10*; and on *verso* in pen and brown ink by an 18th-c. hand: *Chimney.4.*

RIBA Jones & Webb 27

The chimney-piece is shown, slightly modified, in Flitcroft's section of the chapel (cat. no. 51). The design is based on an engraving in Scamozzi's *L'Idea* (Part II, p. 165), and typifies the sober, Italianate phase in Jones's interior decoration before his exposure to luxuriant French sources in the 1630s. John Webb modelled several of his Greenwich Palace chimney-pieces in 1665–6 on this example rather than Jones's French-inspired designs. Indeed, he may have intended to reuse this drawing for he has inscribed two dimensions on it which are larger than those of the chimney-piece *in situ*. The ghostly, half-finished quality of the drawing is intentional: from this period onwards Jones cared less about presentation and often left his designs as graphite outlines with little or no ink over-drawing.

53 Finished elevation for the catafalque of James I in Westminster Abbey, London

1625

Pen and brown ink with grey wash over graphite and scorelines

605 × 437 mm. Laid down. Crown on apex of dome drawn on small pasted sheet. Horizontal fold across sheet through top of blocking course of drum

Scale: 1 ft = approx. $\frac{13}{16}$ in.

Worcester College H & T 25

54 Perspective of alternative dome for the catafalque of James I in Westminster Abbey, London

1625

Pen and brown ink with grey wash over graphite and scorelines; some areas in graphite only

318 × 438 mm. Thick paper. Laid down. Central vertical fold

Worcester College H & T 26

Although Bramante's Tempietto has often been cited as a source for this catafalque, John Peacock has demonstrated that Jones was familiar with the more recent tradition of tempietto-catafalques, and drew heavily on Domenico Fontana's for the 1591 obsequies of Sixtus V (fig. 53) and Sergio Venturi's for Paul V (1623). However, as in so much else of his borrowing, Jones purifies the affected and fussy Fontana design, replacing its enriched order with the 'masculine and unaffected' Doric order from Bramante's Tempietto. There are also other refinements such as the columns pressed back against their respondent pilasters from Rusconi's *Della Architettura* (Venice, 1590), and the use of a basement with steps reminiscent of the Temple of Vesta at Tivoli from Palladio's *I Quattro libri* (IV, p. 92).

James I died at Theobalds on 27 March 1625. John Chamberlain wrote that the funeral on 7 May was 'the greatest indeed that was ever known in England', and that Jones's hearse was 'the fairest and best fashioned that hath ben seen'. The entire structure was painted by John de Critz, Serjeant Painter, and it carried twelve statues of Virtues in mourning, eight around the drum and four at the angles of the podium, executed by the French sculptor Hubert Le Sueur. Bishop John Williams, in his funeral sermon *Great Britain's Salomon* preached over the hearse, described the four statues standing around it as Religion, Justice, War and Peace.

Fig. 53
Domenico Fontana. Catafalque for Pope Sixtus V, from B. Catani, *La Pompa funerale di Papa Sisto il Quinto* (1591), Pl.24

The two figures which appear in Jones's drawing represent Religion on the left and Peace or Justice on the right. As Peacock has shown, the neo-classical style of Jones's catafalque emphasizes the idea of the King as a modern monarch in whom antique virtue is reborn, a theme that was central to Williams' comparison of James to Solomon.

In his alternative design for the dome (cat. no. 54) Jones gave more prominence to two of the cartouches and simplified the scheme of 'Iacobus Rex' insignias. This represents a further departure from the Fontana source and the dome may therefore be the executed version.

See colour illustration on p. 160

Bibliography:
D. H. Willson, *King James VI & I* (London, 1956), pp. 446–7
J. Peacock, 'Inigo Jones's catafalque for James I', *Architectural History*, xxv (1982), pp. 1–5
C. Avery, 'Hubert Lesueur, the "Unworthy Praxiteles" of King Charles I', *Walpole Society*, xlviii (1982), p. 141

55 Elevation and (on *verso*) plan for the Clock House turret, Whitehall Palace, London

1627

Pen and brown ink with grey wash over graphite and scorelines; plan on *verso* without wash

305 × 405 mm. Folded sheet of thin, grainy paper. Elevation on right half, plan on *verso* of left half, pricked through from upper half of sheet

Watermark: water-pot surmounted by coronet and crescent moon

Inscribed by Jones in pen and brown ink in top right-hand corner: *June 1. 1627 / for the clockehouse whighthale*; and to the right of bell turret: *5 – 5, 4 – 8*; and in graphite within turret: *5 f°*; and by a modern hand in black ink at top of sheet: *6* in circle

Scales: three separate scales at bottom of sheet, the upper one marked in pen and brown ink over divider points, 5 ft = $1\frac{15}{16}$ in., below this in divider points, 5 ft = $1\frac{5}{8}$ in., and at bottom, also with dividers, 5 ft = $2\frac{5}{16}$ in.

Worcester College H & T 27

The Works accounts for 1626–7 refer to the erection and decoration of a 'clock-house' in the old Palace of Whitehall. Jones shows it rising above a flat roof with a battlemented Tudor parapet. A clock house was on the north side of the northernmost court of Scotland Yard.

The design is a very attractive one. Under the open cupola hangs a bell, and below this is the clock stage, three-sided, for which Robert Moore the carver provided six Ionic capitals. De Critz painted dials on 'the twoe outer sides' only, whilst on the third side 'towardes the Lodginges' he painted 'a piece of Saturne devouring his children within a round'.

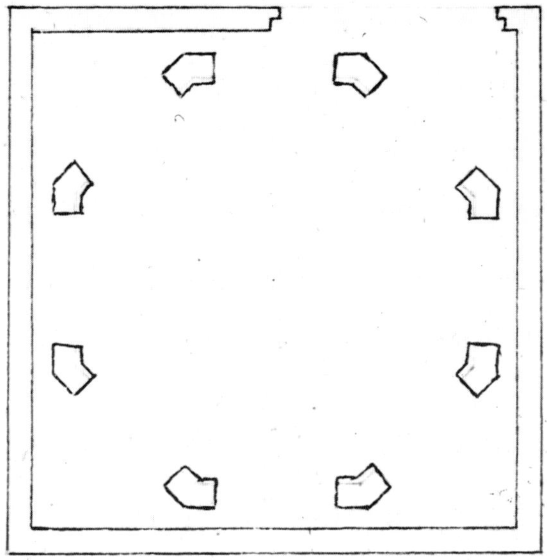

Verso drawing of cat. no. 55 showing plan of the Clock House turret, Whitehall Palace.

Bibliography:
King's Works, iv, p. 335

June 1. 1627

Jones as Surveyor to Charles I and Queen Henrietta Maria, 1625–41

James I's catafalque in 1625 was more than just a funerary tribute to a king. For Jones it marked the end of a Jacobean era that had begun with his journey to Copenhagen on what may have been his first official task as a servant, and who must even then have recognized how old-fashioned Court art and architecture were. Twenty-one years later that servant had completely renovated the Court style and the catafalque paid tribute to this.

The new reign saw no radical changes in the administration of the Office of Works. If there is a diminution in the scale of building from roughly one decade of Jones's Surveyorship (1615–25) to the other (1626–37), this is due to three 'great' works having been completed under James I: the Newmarket Palace Lodging, the Banqueting House, and the Queen's Chapel at St James's Palace. In any case, Charles's Exchequer was not up to grand projects.

A Court which was regarded as artistically one of the most brilliant in Europe, was also extrovert, and it is possible to suggest that this is reflected in royal building. For the hunting and chase Jones designed the Bagshot Lodge in 1631 and the Hyde Park Lodge in 1634. They had porticoes and although the Bagshot work was an addition to a older lodge, both may have affected to be diminutive 'villas'. It was in Charles's reign that the great Rubens ceiling was at last put in place in the Banqueting House in 1638. It was not for the pleasure of the masquers, for it necessitated the building of a new wooden masquing chamber adjacent. A double cube, 112 by 57 by 59 ft, descriptions of it are tantalizingly scarce. There was also the reconstruction of the old Whitehall Cockpit into a Court theatre in 1629. Although in planning this was in the tradition of the Elizabethan playhouse, and thus requiring the erection of a temporary proscenium when necessary, it was a most ingenious adaptation, with recollections of Palladio's Teatro Olimpico and Scamozzi's *teatro* in Sabbioneta. Webb's measured drawing of the Cockpit (made after 1660) (fig. 87) shows a curved façade with five entrances with exquisite ornamental decoration, in a language which is different from that ancient Roman one expressed in the Queen's Chapel at St James's Palace five years earlier. This new language seems to originate with Queen Henrietta Maria's works.

We know precious little about Jones's relationship with the Queen. One suspects it was a special one, for he was privately paid a pension of £20 a year as the 'Surveyor of Her Majesty's Works', although there was no establishment as such, and he received gifts from her in 1633 (gilt plate), 1634, 1638 and 1640. Although there was a pergola to her Withdrawing Chamber in St James's Palace in 1629, and some minor works at Oatlands Palace in 1631 and 1635, it was at Somerset House and the Queen's House at Greenwich that Jones attended to her wishes. In both, a new ornamental vocabulary distinguishes Jones's work from that of the preceding reign.

There is a temptation to associate the new style with the fact that the Queen was French, and there is concrete evidence for this. At Somerset House in 1636 and Greenwich in 1637, Jones was required to adapt and purify designs for chimney-pieces by an unknown French designer (cat. no. 64). Concurrently he was designing chimney-pieces based on Jean Barbet's *Livre d'architecture d'autels, et de cheminées* that had first appeared in 1633 (cat. no. 76, fig. 73). There was also the altar wall of the Somerset House Chapel as recorded by Isaac Ware in *c.* 1731 (fig. 60). Although Summerson has doubted this, and dates it to the Restoration, it may only have been modified then, for not only is it based on D. Antoine Pierretz's *Livre d'autels* (often issued with Barbet), but the vocabulary of ornament is like that of the Cockpit Theatre. Clearly, Jones was affected by French sources of design in the 1630s, but it may not be all due to the Queen, for one suspects that he was searching for a more enriched and eclectic ornamental idiom. This is particularly evident with the Closet Screen in the Somerset House Chapel (fig. 59).

The lower fluted Doric order of the screen carried a frieze with a combination of carved lion's heads and consoles, the motif taken from a Roman fragment of an entablature then in Lord Arundel's collection (next door) (fig. 61). The actual closet screen itself speaks a quite novel ornamental language, not unlike that for chimney-piece overmantels, with six term pilasters supporting a decorative acroteria arrangement of open-scrolled pediments, shells and cartouches. Even this is French, for the system was adumbrated by Jones in the designs for *Oberon* in 1610 (cat. no. 8). The term pilasters were used again in the Queen's House in about 1637 (cat. nos 72–6).

During the 1630s the Queen's House was completed. Because the Queen paid for it out of her privy purse, scant information survives as to what was actually effected, especially inside. Indeed, it is not even known how the Queen intended to use the palace. All that is certain is that the novel H-plan was laid down by Queen Anne in 1616. No doubt dispute will continue to rage, as long as there are architectural historians, as to whether the ground-floor elevation was continued in the 1630s as designed in 1616, or whether Jones, when he was painted in the hunting group by Van Stalbemt and Van Belcamp did look down upon a quite different front that he would soon drastically modify (fig. 14).

There is one further aspect of the French taste that needs consideration. From 1630 the French architect, garden and grotto expert, Isaac de Caus, was working close to Court circles. He was the executant architect for the 4th Earl of Bedford's Piazza houses in Covent Garden (fig. 54) near where he lived from 1630 to 1634, and although these houses have been attributed to Jones, there is no documentary evidence, and one must confess that they are peculiarly French! He was the architect too for the 4th Earl of Pembroke's south range at Wilton House, Wiltshire from 1636, again in the French taste. What survives today at Wilton in the state rooms is in the French Barbet taste of John Webb from 1649. De Caus's abilities should not be under-estimated,

Fig. 54
Covent Garden Piazza,
c. 1640, by an unknown
French painter

in spite of Campbell's suggestion that only Jones could have designed the Covent Garden façades.

In his work for the Stuart Court after 1626, Jones demonstrates his genius in adapting and modifying his style to suit peculiar circumstances. If the Queen wanted French chimney-pieces he would make them his own, just as he purified Serlio in the earlier years of his career. He is the evolving artist, and a Mannerist one at that. A comparison with his faithful John Webb is not out of place. With Jones one senses an immediacy in everything; with Webb the approach was plodding and academic. When invention occurs, it is the result of a long deeply considered decision. In a way it is better that Palladianism was not the style of the Restoration Court. The fire and genius belonged to a Jones who barely survived the beheading of his beloved monarch.

J.H.

Somerset House, London, 1626–38

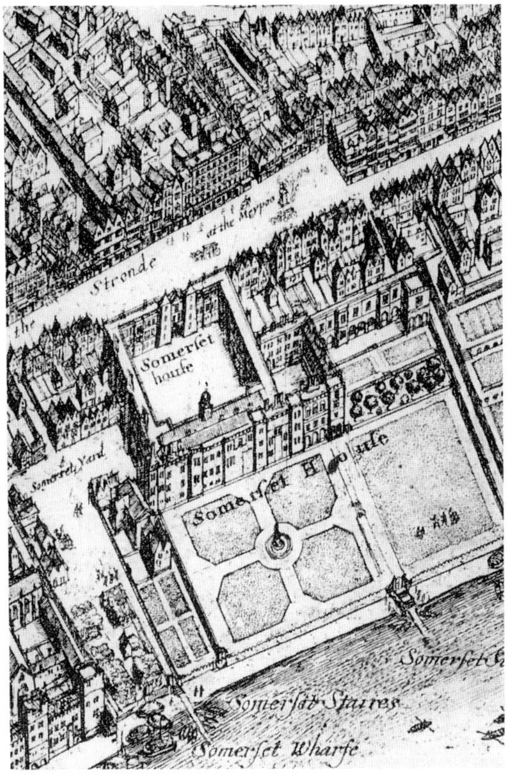

Fig. 55
Somerset House, Strand, London. Detail from bird's-eye view of London by Wenceslaus Hollar, *c.* 1658

Somerset House is so named (as is its successor in the guise of Sir William Chambers' government offices) after Edward Seymour, Duke of Somerset, executed in 1551. Here, between the Strand and the River Thames, he had built a great classical palace which was confiscated and taken into the care of the Office of Works. During most of Queen Elizabeth's reign it was never a principal royal residence, and was mostly occupied by ambassadors or embassies. It was another matter for James I, for shortly after his accession in 1603 he gave it to Queen Anne of Denmark, and from 1609 there commenced an expensive reconstruction, indeed the most expensive enterprise of the King's reign. This comprised a whole new range of apartments (Privy Gallery, Cross Gallery, Privy Lodgings etc.) to the east of the old palace, and new gardens on the river. In 1611–12 the Privy Garden was the site of Salomon de Caus's great rock fountain representing Mount Parnassus.

Queen Anne was not destined to enjoy Somerset House for long. She took up residence in 1617, the name was changed to Denmark House, and she died in March 1619. Although Jones had been Surveyor since 1615, he only effected minor works.

In September 1619 the King granted Denmark House to Prince Charles, who presented it in 1626 to Queen Henrietta Maria, thus initiating once again a period of intensive building activity that ended about 1638. Now Jones was continually employed, and it is doubtful if any part was built without his approbation and care.

His tasks are fully documented: in 1626–7 the Queen's Chapel and Closet; in 1628–30 the Queen's Cabinet Room and new water stairs; in 1630 the new Chapel; in 1632 a cistern house; and in 1635–6 the refitting of the Cross Gallery. In 1626 a pastoral *Artenice* was performed here in a theatre designed by Jones and erected at the upper end of the hall; in 1632–3 he constructed a room in the lower court for the performance of *The Shepherd's Paradise*, for which a rich group of masque designs survive, as well as a plan drawn by John Webb for this temporary theatre; and finally, in July 1638, the last entertainment performed here was *The Passionate Lovers*.

Denmark House came into its own again when it was granted to the Queen Mother Henrietta Maria as her residence in 1660. She had known John Webb, and he was her chosen architect for the handsome New Gallery built 1662–3 (fig. 56). Thereafter the palace endured vicissitudes, became lodgings in the eighteenth century, and was with some sadness demolished by Chambers in 1776.

J.H.

Bibliography:

King's Works, iv, pp. 252–71; v, pp. 254–63

J. Orrell, *The Theatres of Inigo Jones and John Webb* (Cambridge, 1985), pp. 78–79, 113–27

56 Elevation and plan for doorways in the Queen's Cabinet Room, Somerset House, London

1628–30

Pen and dark brown ink over graphite on right; graphite only on left

327 × 369 mm. Three pasted sheets, comprising main sheet, (282 × 369 mm) bottom strip (46 × 365 mm, with 4 mm overlap), and top strip, 13 mm deep with 4 mm overlap. Strongly marked central vertical fold

Watermark: water-pot surmounted by five-point coronet, quatrefoil and crescent moon

Inscribed by Jones in graphite on plan of upper doorway, on left side of sheet: *3 fo. 4, 3 fo: 3 yn* ; and on *verso* by John Webb in pen and brown ink: *ffor y^e Queens Cabinett Somersett House*

Scale: 1 ft = 1 in.

RIBA Jones & Webb 34

Following the grant of Somerset House to Queen Henrietta Maria in 1626, building activity was almost continuous until 1638. Her Cabinet Room (in effect her private office) was described as the *new* Cabinet Room so as to distinguish it from the old one situated over the south end of the Privy Gallery. This *new* room, formed and decorated between 1628 and 1630, was on the upper floor at the east end of the 1610 Cross Gallery. Indeed, its window can be seen in Knyff's engraved view (*c.* 1707) with a very large iron pergola or balcony having ninety-three upright bars (fig. 56).

This Jacobean room decorated 1613–14 retained its modified chimney-piece, but was new ceiled 'a flat round . . . wrought with foliage', and provided with a door-case carved by Zachary Taylor according to Jones's design. The painter Matthew Goodrich painted the door-case in imitation of white marble, and enriched it with gold. This was a particularly luxuriously decorated room, the walls ornamented with 218 panels of grotesque work (presumably blue, yellow, red and green etc.) on a white ground with gilded mouldings. The faces of the stone window were in gold arabesque on white with an edge of gold next to the glass. The chimney-piece was white, blue bice and gold, and this sumptuous colour scheme extended on to the balcony where the railing was painted cobalt blue, the stanchions and iron balls gilded, the soffit of the balcony stone colour, and the four cartouches supporting it, blue and gold.

The doorway, by virtue of its design in Lord Burlington's collection, exerted great influence, for his lordship used it as a model for Chiswick, and it was favoured by many other Palladians including Lord Pembroke and William Kent.

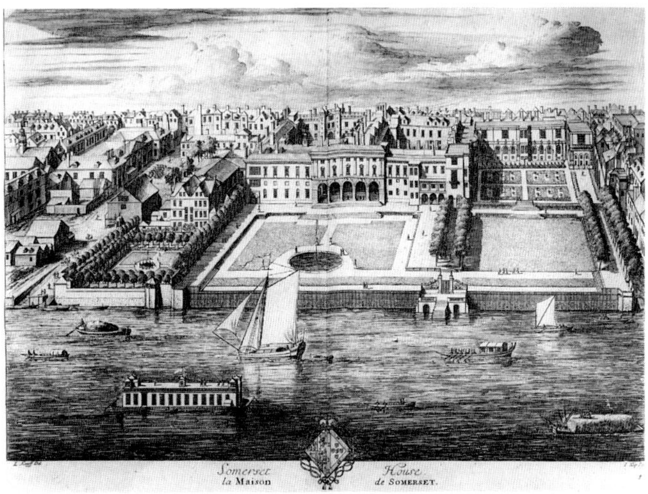

Fig. 56
Somerset House from the river, *c.* 1700, drawn by Leonard Knyff and engraved by Johannes Kip for *Britannia Illustrata* (1707)

Bibliography:
King's Works, iv, pp. 262–3

57 Design for a painted frieze with a female head in a roundel, a swag and cupids

Early 1630s

Pen and brown ink with grey-brown wash and graphite under-drawing

90 × 325 mm

Inscribed by Jones in faintly visible graphite within central wreath: *HMR*; and on *verso* with collector's mark in another hand: *308* λμξ

Ashmolean Museum, Oxford E/DBB 143

See colour illustration on p. 161

58 Design for a painted vertical panel with grotesque ornament and the cypher of Queen Henrietta Maria

Early 1630s

Pen and brown ink with grey wash and some pen shading; graphite under-drawing

306 × 120 mm

Inscribed on *verso* with collector's mark: *308* λμξ

Ashmolean Museum, Oxford E/DBB 144

These two exquisite presentation drawings for carved or painted panels can be associated with Jones's decorative work at Somerset House in the early 1630s. They were discovered by W. Grant Keith early this century in a volume of decorative designs by Jean Cotelle the Elder and others which had passed from Jones's office via the Talman collection to James Gibbs, who bequeathed his drawings to the Radcliffe Library, Oxford, in 1754. A third drawing by Jones from the same source and also now at the Ashmolean Museum, Oxford, is for a painted wall at Oatlands in 1637 (cat. no. 71). Keith and others have assumed that these two are for Oatlands, but stylistically they are earlier. Their fluently outlined and smoothly washed style is closer to drawings of the first two or three years of the decade, such as the proscenium and scene designs for the masque *Albion's Triumph* (performed January 1631) (cat. no. 95), than to drawings of 1637. They might be panel designs for the Cabinet Room, 1628–30, or for the Queen's Bedchamber at Somerset House, 1632–3, which we know had a bas-relief frieze by Thomas de Critz over the chimney-piece. Another possibility is the Queen's Bedchamber at St James's Palace, painted in 1629–30 by Matthew Goodrich with a frieze 18 in. deep having 'foliages like Marble and the ground of the work fair bleue'.

The prominent female heads in roundels, the 'HMR' insignia, and the rich classical ornament of swags, wreaths, grotesques and putti, announce Henrietta Maria's imposition of a lavish new style of interior decoration in the royal apartments of England in the French manner.

See colour illustration on p. 162

Bibliography:

W. G. Keith, 'Some hitherto unknown drawings by Inigo Jones', *Burlington Magazine*, xxii (1913), pp. 218–26

King's Works, iv, pp. 216, 249, 262–3, 266

D. Blayney Brown, *Ashmolean Museum Oxford: catalogue of the collection of drawings*, iv (Oxford, 1982), pp. 87–9

J. Harris, *The Design of the English country house* (London, 1985), pp. 84–5

59 Plan and elevation for the Chapel window at Somerset House, London, with detail of entablature

1632

Pen and dark brown ink over scorelines, black chalk and graphite

280 × 454 mm. Central vertical fold. Rectangular piece, 106 × 191 mm, cut away in upper left-hand corner

Watermark: disc showing peacock with spread tail, similar to cat. no. 97

Inscribed by Jones in pen and brown ink near bottom right-hand corner: *window for the/Queens Chappel/So: House/1632*

Scale: 5 ft = 3 in.

RIBA Jones & Webb 35

The new Catholic Chapel at Somerset House had been proposed with the St James's one in 1623, but then postponed. Jones had already produced a design, but it is not known if this was discarded for a new one seven years later. By the time the chapel was completed in 1635 it was a deeply considered building, perhaps one of the most refined of any by Jones. Unfortunately it is inadequately documented in matters of existing drawings. This window design is almost certainly one of the eight 'Great windows of Portland Stone', but there is no proof of this. Early in the 1720s Henry Flitcroft was ordered to measure and draw the ceiling (fig. 58), and in about 1731 Isaac Ware engraved the screen to the Royal Closet and the altar (fig. 59). The ceiling was of the flat ornamented beam type used at the Banqueting House and had a Roman coffered extension over the closet.

The enframement of the window by panelled pilasters topped by triglyphs and fluting, and by a frieze with a winged cupid's head and swags comes from a design by Domenico Fontana published in 1590 (fig. 57). Jones corrected the proportioning of Fontana's Mannerist entablature and set the frame around an arch instead of a square-headed opening. He returned to the same source for his St Paul's nave doorways in 1637 (cat. no. 80).

Fig. 57
Domenico Fontana.
Design for a Doric doorway. Engraving in his *Della Trasportatione dell'obelisco vaticano et delle fabriche di nostro signore Papa Sisto V . . . libro primo* (Rome, 1590), fol.18

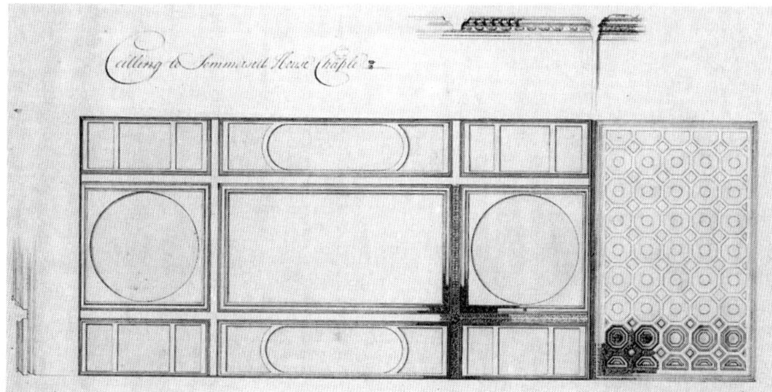

Fig. 58
Henry Flitcroft.
Measured drawing made for Lord Burlington in the 1720s of the Somerset House chapel ceiling

Fig. 59
Engraving of the Somerset House chapel screen made for Isaac Ware's *Designs of Inigo Jones and others*, c. 1731

Bibliography:
J. Summerson, *Inigo Jones* (Harmondsworth, 1966), pp. 75–9
King's Works, iv, pp. 263–6

Fig. 60
Engraving of the Somerset House chapel reredos made for Isaac Ware's *Designs of Inigo Jones and others*, c. 1731

Fig. 61
Fragment of a Roman entablature from Asia Minor (2nd century AD) from Lord Arundel's collection, now in the Museum of London

60 Sketch elevation for the Chapel niche, Somerset House, London

c. 1632

Pen and brown ink over graphite

272 × 204 mm. Trimmed sheet of smooth creamy paper, with 13 × 35 mm projection at bottom right-hand corner

Inscribed by Jones in pen and brown ink at bottom right-hand corner: *Scitzo for the/Neece with out the/chappell So: Ho:*; and on *verso* by an 18th-c. hand in pen and brown ink: *Niche.3.*

Mounted with cat. nos 61 and 62

RIBA Jones & Webb 36

Although this niche is inscribed for the Somerset House Chapel, none is mentioned in the accounts. Clearly it was, as inscribed, 'without' or outside the chapel proper, and it has been suggested that it might have adorned the exterior of the west transept, but this is unconvincing, unless there were to be three aedicules of this design. This sketch seems to represent an earlier idea than the more finished niche with the figure of Christ as Salvator Mundi (cat. no. 61). However, it should be noted that the niche in this design sits upon a cornice as if intended to have been elevated from the ground, whereas cat. no. 61 has no such cornice, and was perhaps intended to sit upon the ground. In fact, 'without' the chapel might mean in the Vestry House or vestibule behind the altar at the south end (cf. also cat. no. 123).

Bibliography:
King's Works, iv, p. 264

61 Elevation of a tabernacle frame with standing figure holding an orb, for exterior of Somerset House Chapel, London

c. 1632

Pen and brown ink over graphite and scorelines

265 × 182 mm

Inscribed on *verso* by an 18th-c. hand in pen and brown ink: *Niche.4.*

Mounted with cat. nos 60 and 61

RIBA Jones & Webb 37

Like the preceding niche, this design, on the right of the same mount, has joined composite pilasters flanking a fully-draped standing figure on a panelled plinth. The figure, which holds a globe in the left hand and makes a sign of benediction with the right, is presumably an image of Christ as Salvator Mundi and as such could only have been intended for Henrietta Maria's Catholic Chapel at Somerset House. The winged cherub's head in the frieze is a recurrent image in Jones's designs for religious buildings in the 1630s. It was used on several parts of Somerset House Chapel (cat. nos 59, 60, fig. 59) and crops up again over the nave aisle windows of St Paul's Cathedral (fig. 76) and on the rejected west front elevation (cat. no. 78). The image was popularized by the Jesuits as a symbol of the divine presence on their church façades and thus had strong Catholic associations (fig. 79).

Bibliography:
King's Works, iv, p. 264

62 Sketch elevation for a niche with a voussoired architrave surround containing a statue

Mid-to-late 1630s

Pen and brown ink over graphite and scorelines. Later red ink ruled border lines on left and right edges

265 × 182 mm. Central horizontal fold

Watermark: water-pot surmounted by coronet, quatrefoil and crescent moon

Mounted with cat. nos 60 and 61

RIBA Jones & Webb 38

The firm and vigorous style of pen shading place this design later than the Somerset House Chapel niche of 1632 on the left of the same mount (cat. no. 60). The figure is secular, and the rustic style suggests a wall feature in a garden setting. This may be a project for the relocation of some of Charles I's antique statues from the Duke of Mantua's collection, which at first were placed in the Sculpture Gallery at St James's Palace, 1629–30. In 1635–6 some were moved to the garden at Somerset House, and in 1637–8 three complete statues – an Apollo, a Bacchus and a Cupid – were restored and re-erected in the garden at St James's Palace. The shading on the right-hand side of the design suggests a return wall, with the niche and statue terminating the vista of a walk.

Bibliography:

A. H. Scott Elliott, 'The statues from Mantua in the collection of King Charles I', *Burlington Magazine*, ci (1959), pp. 218–27

King's Works, iv, pp. 249–51, 268–9

63 Design for a wainscot chimney-piece in Somerset House, London

1636

Pen and brown ink with brown wash over scorelines and slight graphite under-drawing

302 × 188 mm

Watermark: crest surrounded by scroll motif and surmounted by crown; beneath is a scroll plaque inscribed. *VENVRIS*

Inscribed by Jones in pen and brown ink at bottom of sheet: *for a chimny peese of wainscott So: House 1636*; and with *HMR* monogram in cartouche at top of overmantel; and on *verso* by an 18th-c. hand in pen and brown ink: *Chimney.20.*

Scale: 1 ft = $\frac{13}{16}$ in.

RIBA Jones & Webb 41

The location within the palace of this chimney-piece is unknown. It is the same date as the Cross Gallery design (cat. no. 65) and might initially have been intended for this location before Jones decided to adapt the existing one. The design stands out as uncharacteristic of Jones, for the reason that he was compelled (perhaps) to work from an existing French design submitted by an anonymous French architect or designer (cat. no. 64). His main alteration to the source was to remove the superimposed panel in the overmantel to create an oblong frame of more convenient shape to take a painting.

Bibliography:
King's Works, iv, p. 267

for a chimny peese of wainscott So: House 1636

64 Unknown French designer. Elevation for a chimney-piece

Early 1630s

Pen and brown ink with grey wash

344 × 203 mm. Thick paper

Inscribed on *verso* by an 18th-c. hand in pen and brown ink: *Chimney.19.*

Scale (in pieds): 1 ft = just under $\frac{13}{16}$ in.

RIBA Jones & Webb 42

This design was the model for Jones's wainscot chimney-piece at Somerset House in 1636 (cat. no. 63). The same unknown French designer supplied models for Jones's chimney-piece in the Cabinet Room of the Queen's House, Greenwich, in 1637 (cat. no. 75); for an unknown location (design in the Metropolitan Museum of Art, New York, from the Talman collection); and perhaps for the French ambassador's residence at Brooke House, Holborn, also in 1636 (RIBA Jones & Webb 9). This last design, however, is inscribed *from ye French ambasator* and may have been transmitted to Jones from France, via the ambassador, rather than being for the ambassador's residence. This intervention by a Frenchman who must have been favoured by the French Queen Henrietta Maria underlines the dominance of French sources in Jones's interior decoration in the 1630s.

The Frenchman's designs are characterized by framed panels bordering the hearth and overmantel, enriched with grotesques, mask-heads, swags and term figures, and by a stepped-forward panel on the overmantel. They are less heavily sculptured than those of Jean Barbet or Pierre Collot, both dating 1633 (figs 66, 73), but share a tendency to contain the upper pediment within a straight panel.

Bibliography:

J. Harris, 'Inigo Jones and his French sources', *Metropolitan Museum of Art Bulletin*, xix (May 1961), pp. 253–64

65 Design for the installation of a Jacobean chimney-piece with a new overmantel in the Cross Gallery, Somerset House, London

1636

Pen and brown ink over black chalk (rubbed away) and graphite, with under-scoring

403 × 326 mm. Central horizontal fold; tear near top left-hand corner

Inscribed by Jones in pen and brown ink at top right: *chimney peese for the cross gallery So: House/1636*; and with feet-and-inches dimensions in and around the overmantel frame; and on *verso* by an 18th-c. hand in pen-and-brown ink: *Chimney.8.*

RIBA Jones & Webb 40

The Cross Gallery was to the east of the main courtyard at Somerset House, on the north side of an open court overlooking the Privy Garden (figs 55, 56). It had been panelled in 1611–12, when Maximilian Colt, the King's Sculptor, had supplied a white marble chimney-piece. In 1635–6 the interior of the Cross Gallery was remodelled. The Jacobean panelling was reused and new panelling added in a design which included a rich cornice, dado rail and more than thirty pilasters, probably in a Corinthian order. Jones's design is for a new overmantel to stand above the cornice and Ionic terms of Colt's existing chimney-piece, and flanked by the original Jacobean pilasters. When installed in 1637–8, it was painted a 'timber cullor and gold'. The panelling was painted a 'sad colour' and many of the carved enrichments were gilded. It is possible that Jones made alternative designs for this overmantel, for three anonymous and rather amateurish drawings are to be found among the group for Somerset House at the RIBA (Jones & Webb 43–5), one copying the wainscot chimney-piece (cat. no. 63), the other two variations on the Cross Gallery overmantel.

The overmantel is of similar inspiration to the two Oatlands chimney-piece designs of the same year (cat. nos 67, 68). All three designs show broken and scrolled pediments and a classical style of detail and contrast with the panelled frames carved with grotesque ornament on Jones's chimney-pieces copied from French models in the same period (cat. nos 63, 68, 75). Jones may have been working from an Italian Mannerist rather than French source, although none has been identified. Copied by Lord Burlington for the gallery closet chimney-piece at Chiswick Villa in the 1720s, the upper part of the cornice of overmantel embodies the Vitruvian scroll, a motif dear to the eighteenth-century Palladians.

Bibliography:
King's Works, iv, p. 267
J. Harris, *The Palladians* (London, 1981), p. 123

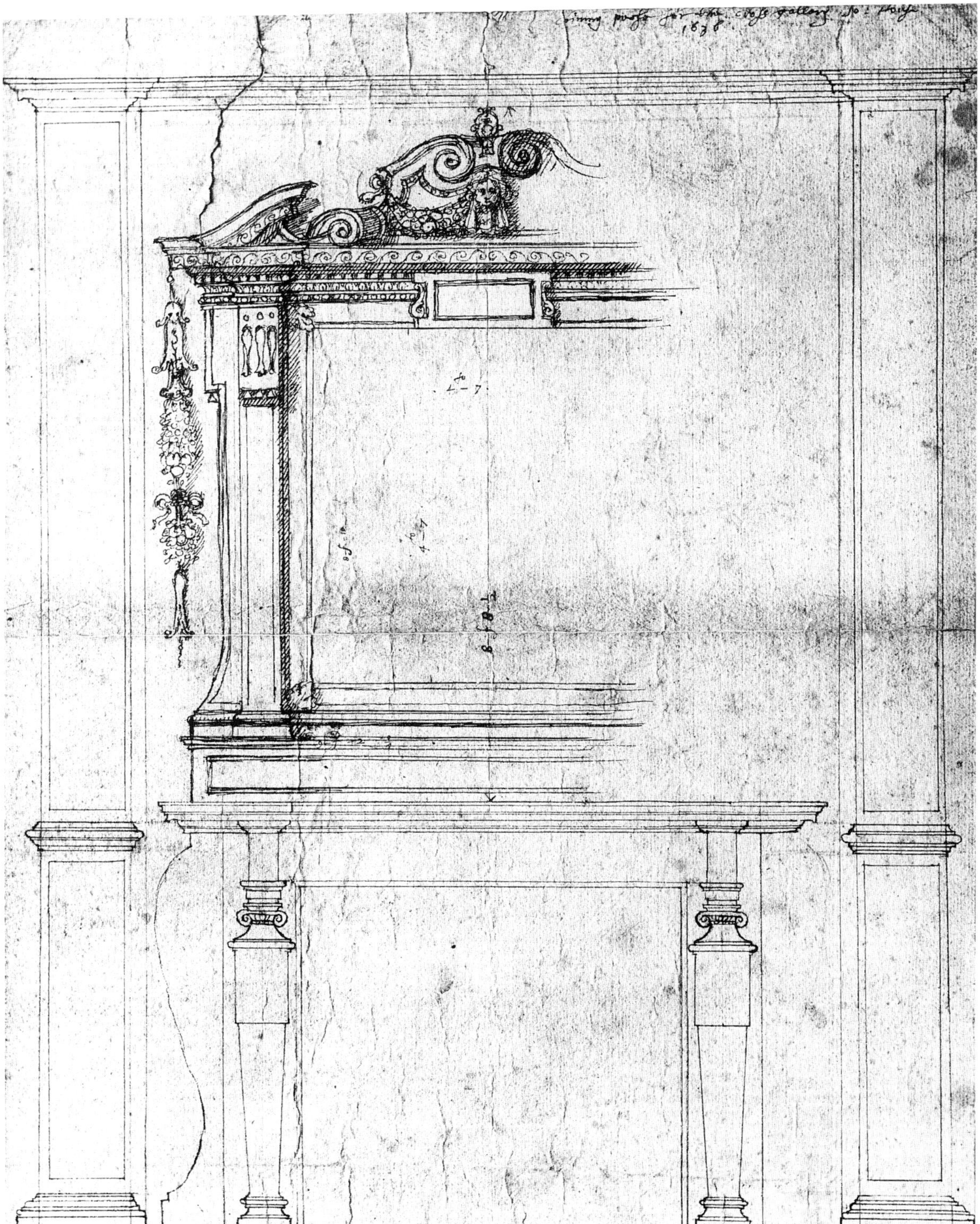

66 Design for a cistern house at Somerset House, London, and (below) a design for a water-gate, probably for Somerset House

1628–32

Pen and brown ink over thick graphite under-drawing

330 × 225 mm. Creamy paper with brown-yellow discolorations

Inscribed by Jones in pen and brown ink to right of upper design: *for the c∅r* [sic] *sesterne for / So House 1632 / to bee made in the outterc∅* [sic] *or base courte for / the youse of the garden*; and on *verso* by an 18th-c. hand in pen and brown ink: *Door.39.*

RIBA Jones & Webb 33

The fact that both are on the same sheet poses a problem, for if the lower drawing is indeed a rejected design for the water-gate at Somerset House (and there is no reason to think it is not), it must have been made when the 'new stairs' were projected in 1628, and certainly before 1630 when the masonry of the landing-place was erected. As built the stairs were modest, with a landing-stage and a pair of gate-piers with some ornamental sculpture (fig. 56). The young John Webb, then only aged seventeen, was apparently consigned this task by his master Jones.

Jones's design is for a powerful rusticated gate of the Hatton House type (cat. no. 44), with blocked Ionic columns and a pediment raised above a panel, upon which lean figures. The gate is set in a channelled ashlar wall topped by a heavy cornice supported on console brackets. The balustraded platform is probably seen in end-elevation and would have projected into the river.

This may have been a scribbled idea immediately rejected for the obvious reason that since Tudor times the palace had been visually open to the river over the grand terraced gardens. Jones's proposed wall could hardly have been less than 15 ft high, to judge by the double entrance door.

The problem concerns the rough black chalk sketch on the upper half of the sheet, for this relates to the new 'cisterne house' built in 1632 to supply water to the gardens. This discrepancy in dates may simply be due to Jones picking up the sheet with the rejected water-gate design and using it for roughing out a first idea for the cistern, which was built to a different design, 44 ft long and 12 ft wide, rather than in the tower-like form of Jones's sketch.

Bibliography:

King's Works, iv, p. 270

67 Perspective and two sketch plans for a fountain in the garden at Somerset House, London

c. 1633

Pen and brown ink with grey wash over black chalk

346 × 216 mm. Trimmed sheet. Laid down

Chatsworth (unnumbered)

It is known that Inigo Jones collaborated with Hubert Le Sueur in setting up a fountain in the garden of Somerset House in the 1630s, and that a 'large fountain of blacke marble' with attendant brass figures was moved from Somerset House to Hampton Court in 1656, later to be remodelled as the 'Diana Fountain' in the Privy Garden, but moved again in 1713 to Bushy Park, next to Hampton Court (fig. 62). As Geoffrey Fisher and John Newman have shown, this drawing is evidence that Jones was responsible for the initial design of the Somerset House fountain, and that some features of his design, notably the mermaids seated on dolphins, still survive at Bushy Park.

Fig. 62
The Diana Fountain in Bushy Park, Hampton Court

A site for the fountain had been prepared in 1633–4, and in 1637 Hubert Le Sueur received payment for 'brasse and Marble worke done by him for a Fountayne in her M^ats^ Garden at Somerset House according with severall Bargaines made with him by Inigoe Jones Esq. Surveyor of her M^ats^ workes'. Jones took the elements of his design from two prints: an engraving by Domenico Tibaldi dated 1570 of Giambologna's Neptune fountain in Bologna showing similar fish-bearing putti and a frontal mermaid, and another by Jan Muller (1602) of Adriaen de Vries's Hercules fountain in Augsburg, which has the large shells at the angles and a similar hexagonal basin. The crowning nude figure expressing water from her breasts may have been suggested by a statue of Ceres on Ammanati's Juno fountain, which stood in the Boboli Gardens, Florence, between 1588 and 1635, but there was no engraving of this fountain. In any event, Le Sueur's figure, which may originally have been intended to represent Diana, was more decorous. On the fountain at Bushy she wears a dress of antique style gathered at the waist and leaving one breast bare.

The drawing was probably made in 1633, and is revealing of Jones's mature figurative style. He is still indebted to mid-sixteenth-century Florentine Mannerists such as Parmigianino and Rosso Fiorentino for the gesture and turn of his figures but has evolved a more natural pose and anatomy. The vigorous pen outlines give the Diana a solidity that is entirely lacking in his drawings before 1613 (cat. nos 7, 9), although her slightly off-balance posture is a reminder that Jones was more confident when drawing children or the heads of figures. The ungainly perspective is not unexpected. Jones never completely mastered single-point perspective drawing in his masque sets, and this design, which has a stepped square podium seen at an angle within a hexagonal basin, would have tested the skills of the most competent of perspective artists.

Bibliography:

J. Harris, 'The Diana fountain at Hampton Court', *Burlington Magazine*, cxi (1969), pp. 444–7

G. Fisher and J. Newman, 'A fountain design by Inigo Jones', *Burlington Magazine*, cxxvii (1985), pp. 531–2

L. Stainton and C. White, *Drawing in England from Hilliard to Hogarth* (London, 1987), pp. 126–8

Basing House, Hampshire, c. *1633*

The great house of Basing was undoubtedly one of the most magnificent Tudor mansions in England. William Camden described it as 'overpowered by its own weight', and even after the siege, as shown in the anonymous etching (fig. 63), it was planned on a vast scale. Jones's connection with Basing House concerns John Paulet, 5th Marquis. It is unclear when Jones was employed at Basing for interior works as demonstrated by the design for the chimney overmantel (cat. no. 68), and naturally care must be taken in this matter as the design could have been for a London mansion. The etching shows a large three-bay pedimented frontispiece set between two octagonal Tudor towers, and to one side of this, and lower, a smaller pedimented front. At the site were once to be found several fine Corinthian pilaster capitals, probably of Jonesian date (fig. 64).

In the Civil War Basing became a centre for the Court and for those who had been attached to that of Queen Henrietta Maria, now exiled. According to a Parliamentary news sheet Jones was 'gotten thither for help to the House' in preparing it for the siege. When the house finally fell in October 1645, Jones was in celebrated company. William Faithorne the engraver was there, and so was the historian Thomas Fuller.

J.H.

Bibliography:

W. T. Warren (ed.), *The Story of the great siege of Basing House*, Hampshire Observer Office, Winchester (n.d.)

King's Works, iii, p. 156

Fig. 63
Basing House, Hampshire, after the siege of 1645. Anonymous etching showing classical additions (marked A)

Fig. 64
Fragment of one of several Corinthian capitals from a pilastered order, photographed at Basing House in 1959

68 Two half elevations for a chimney overmantel and (on *verso*), another half elevation, ascribed to Basing House

c. 1633

Pen and dark brown ink over thick black chalk

207 × 307 mm. Thick, dark paper

Watermark: small bunch of grapes beneath simple coronet

Inscribed on *verso* by Jones in pen and brown ink, in centre of design: *IF*; and on lower left, upside down by an 18th-c. hand in pen and brown ink: *chimney.2.*

RIBA Jones & Webb 69

These overmantel designs (fig. 65) have been ascribed to interiors at Wilton House from 1636 onwards, but the drafting is not mature enough for the later 1630s. The pen shading is not as clean and vigorous as on chimney-piece designs of 1636 and 1637 (cat. nos 69, 70, 76), although the technique as a whole certainly belongs to the same decade.

The coronets on each side of the sheet show strawberry-leaves separated by balls on points and are for a marquis. During

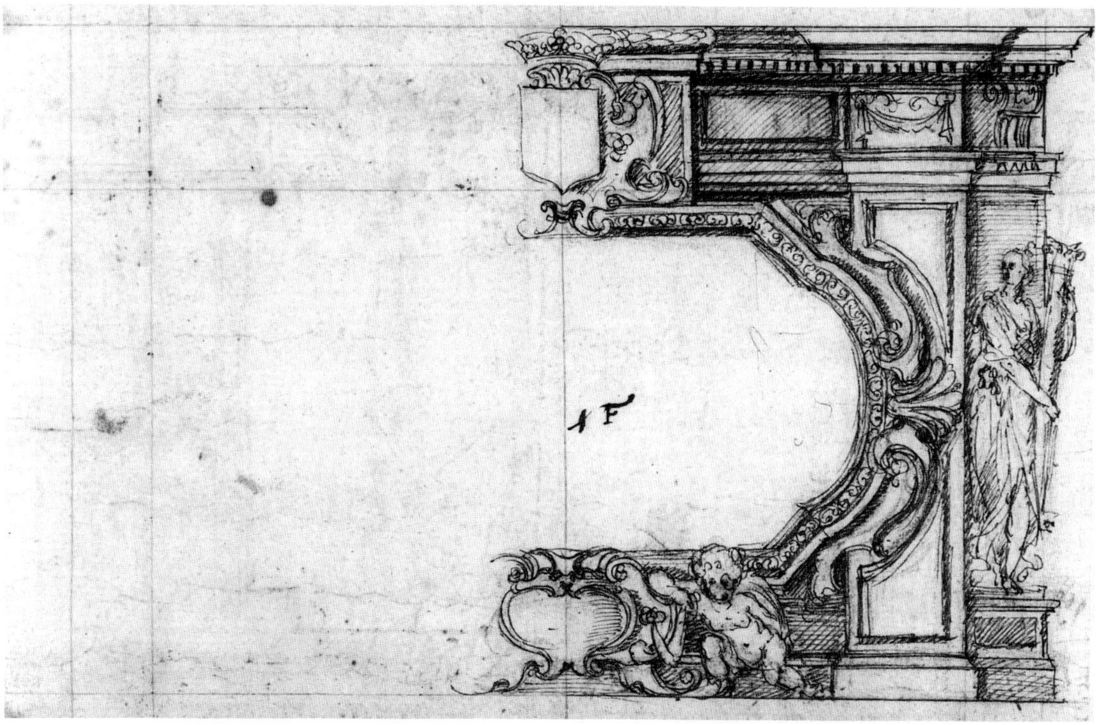

Fig. 65
Overmantel design on *verso* of cat. no. 68, *c.* 1633

Fig. 66
Pierre Collot. Engraved design for a chimney-piece and overmantel from *Pieces d'architecture où sont comprises plusiers sortes de cheminées* (Paris 1633)

the 1630s, John Paulet, who succeeded as 5th Marquis of Winchester in 1629, was the only member of the English peerage with that title, and we know that classical refurbishments to his ancestral Tudor home, Basing House in Hampshire, took place a decade or so before the buildings were ransacked and partly demolished by Cromwell's troops at the end of the siege on 14 October 1645 (when Jones was carried off in a blanket). The breadth of these overmantels, and the absence of any classical feature below them, suggest that they were intended to surmount a traditional hearth of Tudor dimensions. There is, however, no documented connection between Jones and Basing House in the 1630s.

The luscious carved ornament on the overmantels can be traced in part to a suite of engravings by Pierre Collot, *Pieces d'architecture où sont comprises plusiers sortes de cheminées* (1633) (fig. 66). Collot was an exact contemporary of Jean Barbet, whose designs inspired some of Jones's chimney-pieces at Greenwich in 1637 (cat. nos 72, 76). Jones emulated the deep modelling and distinctive horizontal shading of Collot's engraving, and copied features such as the dentilled cornice and pair of putti supporting a shield. He may also have seen drawings by the draftsman of the so-called 'Derain' volume of decorative designs in the Louvre (Cabinet des Dessins, 2027). One or two of the chimney-pieces in this volume have the lozenge panels and consoles enriched with fish-scale and drapery motifs which distinguish these overmantels from others by Jones at this period.

See colour illustration on p. 163

Bibliography:

J. Harris, 'Inigo Jones and his French sources', *Metropolitan Museum of Art Bulletin*, xix (May 1961), pp. 263–4

L. Stone, *The Crisis of the aristocracy* (Oxford, 1965), p. 758

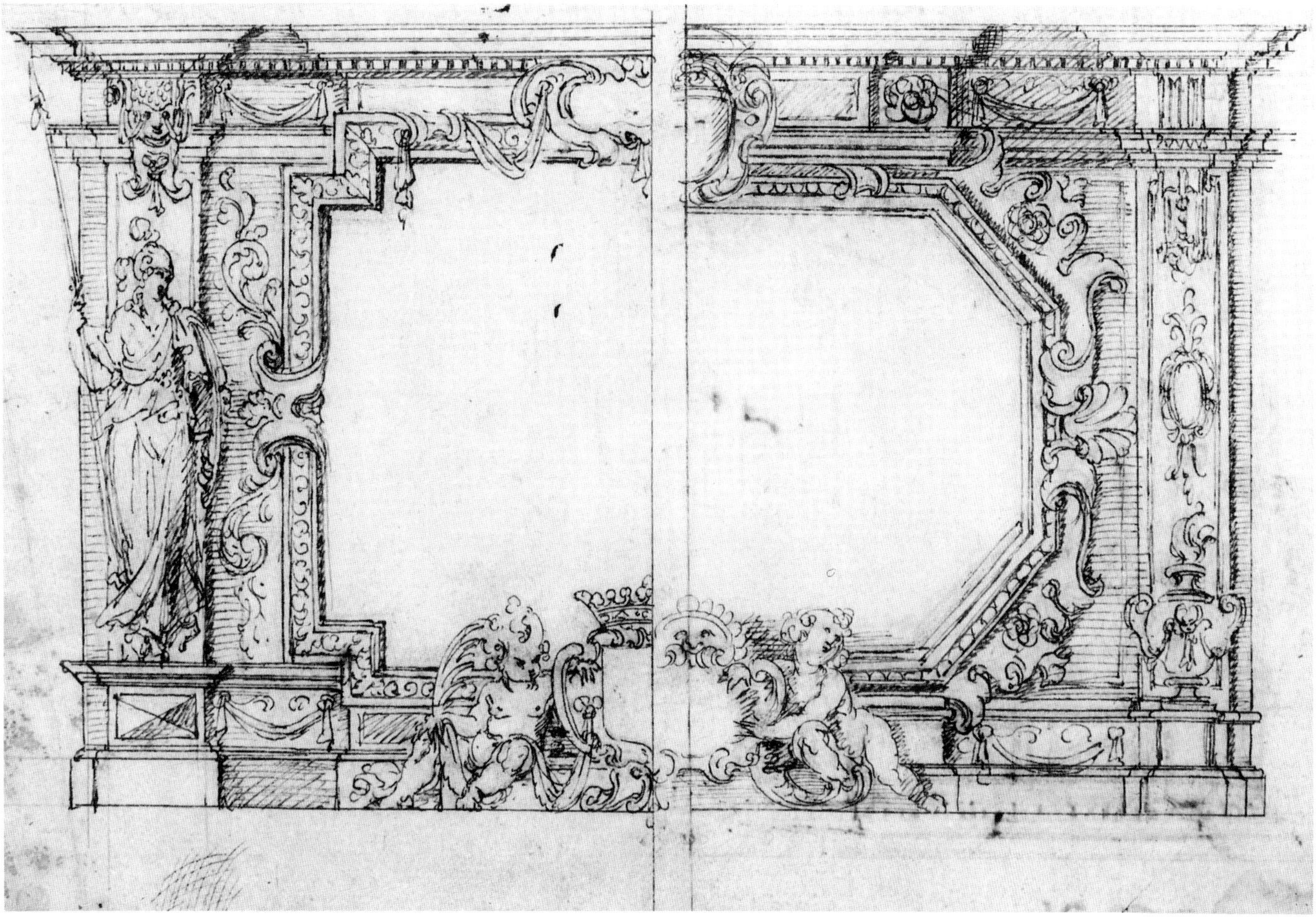

Oatlands Palace, Surrey, 1636–8

69 Sketch elevation for a chimney-piece with alternative overmantel designs for Oatlands Palace, Surrey

1636

Pen and brown ink over black chalk, graphite and scorelines

292 × 186 mm

Watermark: carafe motif, with large handles each side, surmounted by a bunch of grapes

Inscribed by Jones in pen and brown ink at bottom left: *first scitzo chimny peese for oatlandes/1636*; and on *verso* by an 18th-c. hand in pen and brown ink: *Chimney 22*

Scale: 1 ft = $\frac{5}{8}$ in.

RIBA Jones & Webb 67

For both Queen Anne of Denmark and Queen Henrietta Maria, Oatlands was a great set-piece Tudor palace, and neither ordered more than minor works and internal decorations. This chimney-piece coincides with decorative improvements begun for Henrietta Maria in 1635, including a new 'Queen's cabinet' and 'Queen's bedchamber'. For the 'King's attiring room' Nicholas Stone carved a chimney-piece. The Queen's Cabinet had a chimney-piece painted a white marble colour and gilded.

With this 'first scitzo' we can sense the immediacy of Jones's mind and hand, quickly and fluently experimenting with alternative treatments for the overmantel. In this period Jones worked out all the essentials in black chalk and graphite before applying the pen. He then redrew the outlines in ink, shading over unwanted portions rather than erasing the pen lines. The thickly modelled outlines are characteristic of sketch designs in the 1630s (cf. cat. no. 76).

The differing shapes of the overmantels were probably dictated by the paintings from the royal collections which they were to contain. The left overmantel is like the one for Somerset House Cross Gallery in the same year (cat. no. 65), and was eventually carried out for Lord Burlington in a taller form, over a chimney-piece in the Blue Velvet Room at Chiswick Villa in the 1720s.

See colour illustration on p. 164

Bibliography:

King's Works, iv, p. 216

J. Harris, *The Palladians* (London, 1981), p. 123

1636

70 Finished design for a chimney-piece and overmantel for Oatlands Palace, Surrey

1636

Pen and brown ink over graphite and scorelines

287 × 228 mm

Inscribed by Jones in pen and brown ink at bottom right: *for oatlandes 1636*; and in graphite in the chimney opening: *5 fo*, *4–6, 4–8, 4–2*; and on *verso* by an 18th-c. hand in pen and brown ink: *Chimney. 25.*

Scale: 1 ft = $\frac{5}{8}$ in.

RIBA Jones & Webb 68

Here Jones perfected his 'first scitzo', converting the preliminary study (cat. no. 69) into a tighter, more controlled, design in a form that could be transposed by his sculptors and carvers of wood and marble. The right-hand overmantel design of cat. no. 69 has been redrawn with slight alterations to the decoration of the frame and shape of the pediment scrolls, and the fireplace is lower with a more compact entablature devoid of modillions in the cornice. Jones has proportioned his chimney architrave with divider points to exactly a tenth (6 in.) the width of the opening and structured the entablature in a logical sequence of 6:7:8 for the architrave, frieze and cornice.

for Oatlands 1636

71 Design for painted frames in the lower gallery at Oatlands Palace, Surrey

1637

Pen and brown ink with brown wash over graphite underdrawing

165 × 255 mm

Inscribed on *verso* by Jones in pen and brown ink: *for the painting in oyle of/the open wale w*[th] *landscipes/in the garden at Oatlandes/1637/to be a landscip only and no compartements*; and with collector's mark in another hand: *308* λμξ

Ashmolean Museum, Oxford E/DBB 142

The *History of the King's Works* relates that in 1638–9 the walls and ceiling of the 'lower gallery' (below the Stone Gallery) fronting the Privy Garden at Oatlands Palace were painted by George Portman. This gallery was 80 ft long, 12 ft wide and 10 ft high, the ceiling painted with 'Cloudes and sky color'. Unique for England at this time was the series of large prospects of eight of the Queen's houses that included Pontefract Castle, Havering, Eltham, Nonsuch, Oatlands, Somerset House and Greenwich, painted by Portman 'in Landskipp in oyle'. There is a description of a 'leaning place, about three feet high and marbled', which was evidently a fence upon which to lean to view the pictures. No doubt Jones saw a visual connection between these landscapes and the Privy Garden seen through the arches or colonnades.

His design incorporates a female bust in a cartouche, like those in roundels in Jones's decorative panel designs in the same collection (cat. nos 57, 58). The ornamental style, however, is more free-flowing than on the earlier drawings and employs strap-work and mask-heads similar to details on the chimney-pieces by the unidentified Frenchman (cat. no. 64).

See colour illustration on p. 165

Bibliography:

W. G. Keith, 'Some hitherto unknown drawings by Inigo Jones', *Burlington Magazine*, xxii (1913), pp. 218–26

King's Works, iv, p. 216

D. Blayney Brown, *Ashmolean Museum Oxford: catalogue of the collection of drawings*, iv (Oxford, 1982), pp. 87–8

The Queen's House, Greenwich, 1630–40

The completion of the building for Queen Henrietta Maria was effected from about 1630 to 1640, although it is possible that it was never fully decorated internally before Civil War broke out. Both Queen Anne of Denmark and Queen Henrietta Maria may have seen the building more for the ceremonial reception of distinguished visitors and ambassadors than for royal residence, and it is surely significant that both by road and river Greenwich was the arrival point from Dover. The only surviving elevation of the Queen's House before the Restoration is a lost drawing of *c.* 1640 by an unidentified hand (fig. 67). It provides valuable evidence that the north front may have faced a reception area for the approach from the river. The front was intended to be painted with murals, and the use of iron pergolas to clasp the pairs of first-floor windows adds to the idea of assembly and observation. The curious stage set in front of the entrance to the galleried cube hall would also

Fig. 67
The Queen's House, Greenwich. Anonymous drawing of the north front with indications of mural paintings of trophies, sacrifices, triumphs etc., perhaps by an Italian artist, *c.* 1640

Fig. 68
View of the north front of the Queen's House, completed 1635

Fig. 69
Detail of the Queen's House from an anonymous painting, *c.* 1680, showing early glazing and Webb's infilling of the H-plan

Fig. 70
The south front of the Queen's House, from Colen Campbell's *Vitruvius Britannicus, i,* 1715

Fig. 71
Interior of the galleried hall of the Queen's House

seem to have been for ceremonial welcome. Visitors might land at Greenwich, progress to the Queen's House, be received by theatre or poetry, move into the galleried hall, and then to the loggia to view a contrived hunt.

After 1660 the architectural integrity of the building was abused, first by Webb filling in the spaces of the H to make it into a small palace, then in 1663 by the clumsy attempt to add pavilions to the angles. When Greenwich Palace was rebuilt for Charles II from 1663, the Queen's House became an embarrassment, and more so at the end of the century, when the incomplete palace was used as a hospital for seamen. It was always in the way.

Once the Queen's House passed into the pantheon of Palladian buildings in Campbell's *Vitruvius Britannicus* in 1715, it was revered but misunderstood. Lord Burlington and his draftsmen made a study of it, and parts were influential as fodder for the many pattern-book compilers throughout the eighteenth century. It was particularly crucial when Burlington was assembling precedents for his Tottenham Park and for Chiswick Villa in the 1720s. The 40 ft galleried cube hall was taken up by Campbell at Houghton in 1723, and had a resounding effect on the design of galleried halls for the following two centuries. Despite successive restorations by the Office of Works, the Ministry of Works, the Department of the Environment, now aided by the dreaded Property Services Agency, who are, at the time of writing, proposing to meddle with its interior, it remains a noble piece of architecture, a reminder of the deep intellect that Jones brought to bear upon his design in the 1630s.

J.H.

Bibliography:
G. H. Chettle, *The Queen's House, Greenwich*, London Survey Committee monograph, xiv (London, 1937)
J. Charlton, *The Queen's House* (London, 1976)
King's Works, iv, pp. 119–22; v, pp. 141–6, vi, pp. 326–8

72 Elevation for a chimney-piece in the room next to the back stairs (present North-West Cabinet Room), the Queen's House, Greenwich

1637

Pen and dark brown ink with grey wash over black chalk and graphite

206 × 202 mm

Watermark: water-pot surmounted by quatrefoil

Inscribed by Jones beneath elevation in graphite and erased: *for ye room next to ye backstairs grenwich / 1637*, and rewritten in pen and brown ink: *Grenwich 1637 / for the room next the bakstaiers / ~~below~~* [*sic*] *above*; and in bottom right-hand corner in graphite and erased . . . *under* . . . (rest indecipherable); and in another hand in pen and brown ink within mantel frame: *A*; and on *verso* by an 18th-c. hand in pen and brown ink: *Chimney 16*

RIBA Jones & Webb 22

The inscription tells us that the design was intended for the room next to the back stairs 'above'. This refers to the small Cabinet Room, served by a private staircase leading up to the roof platform, which adjoined the Queen's Bedchamber on the first floor in the north-west corner of the house. The indecision in the inscription, *below* or *above*, underlines the vagueness of the evidence for the decoration and functions of rooms in the original Queen's House: it would seem from this note that a similar chimney-piece was intended for a cabinet room below on the ground floor but the exact purpose of this apartment is not known.

Jones borrowed the herm figures and pronounced ovolo-moulded frame from Plate 9 in Jean Barbet's *Livre d'architecture*, but used the straight-topped panelled mantelpiece favoured in drawings by the unidentified French designer (cat. no. 64, fig. 72). This attractive model was copied by Lord Burlington for the west closet in the gallery at Chiswick Villa (late 1720s).

No accounts survive for the execution of Jones's chimney-pieces at the Queen's House; but that there may have been Barbet-style chimney-pieces has been demonstrated by the recent discovery in nearby Charlton House, Greenwich, of a chimney surround based on a plate in Barbet that may have been one of the chimney-pieces removed during alterations to the Queen's House in 1662–3.

Bibliography:

J. Harris, 'Inigo Jones and his French sources', *Metropolitan Museum of Art Bulletin*, xix (May 1961), pp. 254–5

J. Newman, 'Strayed from the Queen's House?', *Architectural History*, xxvi (1984), pp. 33–5

73 Sketch elevation for the Bedchamber chimney-piece, the Queen's House, Greenwich

c. 1637

Pen and dark brown ink with some brown wash over black chalk and graphite. Traces of later red ink ruled border lines on left and right edges of sheet

260 × 227 mm. Trimmed sheet

Watermark (or countermark): bunch of grapes surmounted by shield motif

Inscribed by Jones in pen and brown ink at top of sheet: *Grenwich/ for the bedchaˉber*

Mounted beneath cat. no. 74

RIBA Jones & Webb 23

74 Completed elevation for the Bedchamber chimney-piece, the Queen's House, Greenwich

c. 1637

Pen and dark brown ink with some brown wash over black chalk and scorelines

185 × 221 mm. Trimmed sheet

Inscribed by Jones in faint graphite across opening: *6½*, and vertically: *5 2.*

Mounted above cat. no. 73

RIBA Jones & Webb 24

As on the two drawings for the chimney-piece at Oatlands in 1636 (cat. nos 69, 70), Jones roughed out a half-elevation in freehand and then worked up a more careful and slightly adjusted finished design. Although the draped herm motif facing forwards and sideways comes from a plate in Barbet's *Livre d'architecture*, other details are apparently of Italian inspiration. In this respect the two drawings can be grouped with the Oatlands pair and the sketch for an overmantel in the Somerset House Cross Gallery (cat. no. 65); all have richly moulded cornices, console brackets and acanthus ornament. When borrowing more directly from the French sources, Jones placed greater emphasis on the panelling and the sculptural handling of herm figures and cartouches.

We have to imagine this chimney-piece beneath the lavishly painted Bedchamber ceiling, its coves covered with grotesque ornament and the central canvas framed by a broad soffit of acanthus scrollwork. The chimney-piece would almost certainly have had an overmantel reaching to the cornice of the room, and the whole feature would have been set off by tapestry hangings.

75 Sketch elevation for the Cabinet Room chimney-piece and overmantel, the Queen's House, Greenwich

1637

Pen and dark brown ink with grey wash over black chalk, and some graphite under-drawing

305 × 186 mm. Central horizontal fold

Inscribed by Jones in pen and brown ink at bottom right: *Grenwich 1637/Cabinet room aboue/behind y[e] round stair*; and beneath the pediment of the overmantel: *HENRIETTA MARIA REGNA*; and in graphite against projections on right-hand side, top to bottom: *1, 2, 3, 4, 5*; and with dimensions in graphite within chimney opening; and in pen and brown ink in lower right-hand corner of overmantel: *15*; and on *verso* by an 18th-c. hand in pen and brown ink: *Chimney. 21*.

RIBA Jones & Webb 25

The Cabinet Room is opposite the Bedchamber on the north side of the Queen's House and overlooks the River Thames. It was the first state room to be reached by the visitor after progressing up the great round staircase from the semi-public rooms of the ground floor. This was the principal reception room at the Queen's House, and would have been the most splendid of all – rivalling the Cabinet Room at Somerset House – had a plan succeeded in 1638–40 to commission Rubens or his pupil Franz Jordaens to paint twenty-one canvases of scenes from the story of Cupid and Psyche to cover the walls and ceilings. Eventually Jordaens started work but only completed eight paintings (since lost).

Jones's chimney-piece, like the one for Somerset House in 1636 (cat. no. 63) is taken directly from a drawing by the unknown French designer (fig. 72). The copying is very literal, but shows a similar modification to the frame of the overmantel, so that the overlapping planes of the originals are reduced to a single square border. Although there is no proof of execution, the mask-heads, cartouches and drops of fruit on the pilasters of the overmantel are repeated on the surviving wall pilasters in the Cabinet Room. Jones's version of the overmantel was used by Lord Burlington, together with chimney surround cat. no. 72, in the west closet at Chiswick. The drawing was engraved for Isaac Ware's *Designs of Inigo Jones and others* (c. 1731), Plate 4.

See colour illustration on p. 166

Fig. 72
Anonymous French designer. Model for Inigo Jones's Cabinet Room chimney-piece in the Queen's House (cat. no. 75)

Bibliography:
J. Charlton, *The Queen's House* (London, 1976), pp. 26–7

76 Sketch design for a chimney-piece for the Queen's House, Greenwich, and studies of putti

c. 1637

Pen and brown ink over graphite; large grey ink brush marks on right side of sheet

193 × 295 mm. Reinforced on back, Paper eaten away in places by acidic action of the ink

Inscribed by Jones in pen and brown ink above putti: *for Greenwich*, and vertically along right edge of sheet: *the pillor in hight 4 diameters and* $\frac{1}{2}$; and within overmantel: *HMR*

RIBA Jones & Webb 21

Aesthetically this is one of the most attractive sheets of drawings in Jones's *œuvre*, not least for its spontaneity, and the vigorous drafting of the putti. It presumably dates from 1637 and like cat. no. 72 is based on a design by Jean Barbet (fig. 73). Jones has rationalized his French source by separating the sections of pediment in the mantelpiece and raising up the picture above the sculptural ornament. In this way he created a more sympathetic surround for the painting and gave greater definition to the powerful chimney frame, which now culminates in putti holding up a crown above the insignia of Henrietta Maria. A variant sketch design for the same chimney-piece is at Chatsworth (cat. no. 124).

Fig. 73
Jean Barbet. Engraved design for a chimney-piece and overmantel from *Livre d'architecture, d'autels, et de cheminées* (Paris, 1633)

Bibliography:
J. Harris, 'Inigo Jones and his French sources', *Metropolitan Museum of Art Bulletin*, xix (May 1961), pp. 255–7

Wimbledon Palace, Surrey, c. *1639*

77 Sketches for friezes of entablatures at Wimbledon Palace

c. 1639

Graphite, drawn over on upper design in pen and brown ink

152 × 268 mm

Watermark: scrolled cartouche containing crozier and horn motif; beneath is a panel inscribed *DVRAN*

Inscribed by Jones in pen and brown ink in centre of sheet: *for freeses at wimbelton/part of Reliue parte painted*

RIBA Jones & Webb 70

The history of Wimbledon as a royal work has been insufficiently examined. It was the last gift of King Charles to his 'dear consort the Queen', purchased late in 1638, for by 1642 Queen Henrietta Maria had fled to Holland. To ascertain what might have been effected to the Elizabethan mansion built by Sir Thomas Cecil in 1588 it is necessary to compare Robert Smythson's survey of 1609 at the RIBA with the two invaluable views etched by Henry Winstanley in 1678 when it was in the possession of the Earl of Danby (fig. 74).

Despite the unpropitious times, much must have been done. In December 1638 the King leased a brickfield and early in 1639 John Betz, brickmaker, was paid for burning 124,000 bricks for 'the Queen's majesty's work at Wimbledon'. What these were for can only be guessed, but Jones's involvement is not only demonstrated by this sketch for a frieze, perhaps for some quite complex break in the entablature of a room or for a chimney projection, but by a payment made 29 March 1649 by warrant from the Queen in The Hague, of £558.10s.11d. 'for building and repairing at our house at Wimbledon'.

Winstanley's etchings suggest the rebuilding of Cecil's kitchen range on the west side in a brick style sympathetic to the earlier house, providing a new entrance with a classical door with a broken segmental pediment. Although there is a record of payments to Nicholas Stone and his men for minor work to chimney-pieces in July 1641, it is not possible to be more specific as to what new interiors there might have been. Outside, it is another matter. Early in April 1642 André Mollet was paid £50 for half a year's work. This is uncommonly interesting, for this great gardener's whereabouts between leaving Holland *c.* 1640, returning to France and arriving in Stockholm in 1648 is imprecisely recorded. Now we know that he was employed by Queen Henrietta Maria and thus introduced the Mollet style to English royal gardens long before he published his *Le Jardin de plaisir* in 1651. His work at Wimbledon can be detected in the *parterres de broderie* laid out on the south front divided by a broad central walk. Beyond, to the east side of the house, is Cecil's sunken Privy Garden with a new 'Orange House', and on the north front between the outer and inner courts, one below the other, Cecil's oval stairs have been replaced by an open classical ascent, perhaps by Jones, for the centre part comprises a voussoired arch flanked by Tuscan columns, and topped with a balustraded parapet.

Bibliography:
C. S. Higham, *Wimbledon Manor under the Cecils* (London, 1962), p. 30ff.
R. Strong, *The Renaissance Garden in England* (London, 1979), pp. 191–7

Fig. 74
Wimbledon Palace. Etching by Henry Winstanley, 1678, showing the main garden front and sunken orange garden

Restoration of St Paul's Cathedral, London, 1633–42

The greatest of all Jones's undertakings while Surveyor of the King's Works was the restoration of old St Paul's Cathedral. The cathedral had been badly neglected in Tudor times and severely damaged when lightning struck the spire in 1561 and set fire to the roof. When James I came to the throne the decay of the building, and its abuse by loiterers, horse-traders, gamblers and money-lenders, who gathered in the nave and at the west door, had become a public scandal. In 1608 James initiated a survey of the building, which resulted in an estimate of £22,537.2s.3d. for the cost of repairing the fabric and rebuilding the steeple. To this year belongs Inigo Jones's design for a new termination to the Gothic tower of St Paul's (cat. no. 4). No further action seems to have been taken until 1620, when a Royal Commission was appointed with Jones as one of the members. A national subscription was launched and large quantities of Portland stone were brought to the site, but again there was a lapse of interest. It required the energetic William Laud, Bishop of London from 1628 to 1633, to spearhead the effective restoration campaign which began in earnest with the setting-up of a new commission for gathering funds on 5 January 1631. Jones was appointed honorary architect for the restoration on 4 February 1633, by which time some £5,000 had been collected, including a promise of £500 annually for ten years from King Charles.

By 15 May 1633 it was decided that enough money had been collected to start repairs on the Gothic choir. This work lasted about two years during which time further funds were collected for the recasing of the Romanesque nave and transepts. Laud's elevation to the See of Canterbury in September 1633 added impetus to the subscription, but the great benefaction came on 23 April 1634, when King Charles wrote to Laud promising to pay for the entire west front himself, over and above his existing bounty. The Archbishop was required

Fig. 75
St Paul's Cathedral, London. Engraved by Wenceslaus Hollar, from William Dugdale, *The History of St Paul's Cathedral* (London, 1658)

Fig. 76
St Paul's Cathedral. Detail from Wenceslaus Hollar's engraved view of north elevations of transept and nave, from William Dugdale, *The History of St Paul's Cathedral* (London, 1658)

'to call upon our Surveyor to use all care and industry for the setting forward of this work'. Jones's lost design for the executed west front, copied by Henry Flitcroft and published by William Kent in 1727 (fig. 78), must have been made soon after April 1634. To the same period belongs a preliminary design for the north transept front (cat. no. 79). The surviving west front design (cat. no. 78), hitherto dated to both the 1608 and 1620 campaigns, belongs stylistically to this period but may predate the King's letter, as it carries no reference, in the form of inscription or statuary, to the royal benefactor. The other St Paul's design dates from 1637 and is for the north and south nave doors (cat. no. 80). By this time work on the recasing of the Romanesque walls must have been well advanced, for in January and March 1635 workmen were setting up experimental plaster-cast models of the upper and lower cornices at the south-east and north-east ends (presumably the transepts). Work on the west portico was slower and more painstaking. The foundations had been dug in November 1635, but in 1638 and 1639 Jones was still refining the details. He ordered the erection *in situ* of wooden 'modells' and 'paterns' after his designs of the doorways, portico entablature and main cornice of the west front, evidently with the purpose of seeing the effect of these features himself before allowing them to be carved in stone. John Webb, who as clerk engrosser was on the task from beginning to end, later reported that Jones had reached an interpretation of Vitruvius' obscure passage about *scamilli impares* at St Paul's and had had the portico set out with what he concluded to be the Roman method of optical correction. Judging by Jones's notes on the subject in his copy of *I Quattro libri* and Daniele Barbaro's *I Dieci libri dell'architettura di M. Vitruvio Pollio* (Venice, 1567) this would have concerned the visual relationship between the balustrade of the portico and the column shafts below, rather than a sophisticated curving upwards of the portico in the centre (as the *scamilli impares* passage is understood today). It may be in this connection that a payment was made in the west front account in June 1638 'To Peter Penson joyner for the making of a Modell for part of the Church of St Paules being of Wainscott & Peartree with the Seuerall Ornaments therto belonging . . .' (Guildhall MS.: W.A.9, p. 53). Jones's design methods must have changed radically during the St Paul's restoration as the sheer scale of the work forced him to abandon the drawing-board and seek verification on the building site or through scale models.

In 1640 and 1641 models were still being set up at the west end, the last being of the scrolls which screened the ends of the aisle roofs between the towers and the central gable. Work continued until at least September 1642, when everything except the repair of the central tower had been completed and over £80,000 had been spent on the entire work. During the Civil War the cathedral was used for the quartering of horses and Jones's splendid portico was filled with makeshift shops and lofts. It was to stand intact for no more than a quarter of a century before the Great Fire of London of 1666 left the whole edifice a gaping ruin. The portico was finally demolished in 1687 to make way for Wren's west front.

Fig. 77
Hieronymous Cock. Detail from an engraving of the Baths of Diocletian, Rome, from Sebastiaan van Noyen, *Terme Diocletiana Imp.* . . . (Antwerp, 1558)

Fig. 78
St Paul's Cathedral. Engraved drawing of the west front from William Kent's *Designs of Inigo Jones* (London, 1727)

In nearly ten years' continuous building Jones had recased the nave and transepts, transforming the Romanesque windows into classical openings, changing the buttresses to pilasters and crowning the eaves with heavy block cornices (figs 75, 76). His main inspiration was the architecture of ancient Rome. The rusticated walling follows Palladio's woodcuts of the Pantheon and engravings by Hieronymous Cock of the Baths of Diocletian, which show a similar eaves cornice of lion's heads alternating with triplets of drop motives (fig. 77). The giant west portico is based on Palladio's reconstruction of the Temple of Venus and Rome with details from that of Antoninus and Faustina (fig. 78). As at the Pantheon, the majestic portico is seen against a huge expanse of plain wall, a dramatic and unique solution for a church façade in Europe at this date.

G.H.

Bibliography:
Guildhall Library, London, MS. 25, 473 (W.A. 1–11, 13–15)
Lambeth Palace Library, London, Fulham Papers, 321 (W.A. 12)
King's Works, iii, pp. 147–52

78 Elevation for the west front of St Paul's Cathedral, London

1633–4

Pen and brown ink with grey wash, over scorelines and graphite

456 × 505 mm. Sheet trimmed on all sides and around pediment gable. Laid down

Watermark: Crozier of Basle

RIBA Jones & Webb 31

This famous project for the west front of St Paul's Cathedral has been associated with each of the three campaigns to restore the cathedral, in 1608, 1620 and 1633–42. J. A. Gotch and Rudolf Wittkower assumed that the drawing was made for Laud's restoration, begun in 1633, but in 1964 Sir John Summerson assigned it to the earliest proposals of 1608. He compared the central attic with those on the New Exchange design of that year (cat. no. 3) and the rustication with Jones's scene design, 'Oberon's Palace', for the masque *Oberon, The Fairy Prince* in 1610 (cat. no. 8). This early dating was rejected in 1973 by John Harris who suggested that the closest similarities were with Jones's Banqueting House designs of 1619.

The technical and stylistic evidence make it certain that the drawing belongs to William Laud's restoration campaign of 1633–42. Characteristics of Jones's drawing technique in the mid-1630s are the smooth and accurate outline style, particularly in the drafting of the column shafts, the cleanly handled and evenly slanted pen shading lines, the sparsely applied wash in narrow bands and neatly ruled graphite under-drawing. Specific similarities may be noted with Jones's drafting of columns and draped standing figures on the Winchester Cathedral Choir Screen design of 1637–8 (cat. no. 81), and the Somerset House Chapel niche design of 1632 (cat. no. 61). The presence of statuary and cherubs' heads on the elevation reinforces the connection with Laud's restoration, for the use of imagery accorded with his reforming measures in the Church of England which stressed ritual, ceremony and outward beauty. In the so-called Laudian Revival of the 1630s communion tables were removed to the east end of the chancel, surplices and vestments were reintroduced for officiating ministers, music was encouraged and images of the saints and the Virgin were set up on choir screens and reredoses. Jones's elevation would have been unthinkable in the predominantly puritan atmosphere before the accession of Charles I in 1625.

The terms of reference of the Laudian Revival were often those of the Roman Catholic Church, although the intention behind the movement was not to lead England back to Rome. Jones's elevation is redolent of Roman Catholic Italy, as it is modelled on Jesuit church façades. One was Il Gesù in Rome (1571), a monumental two-tiered west front, advanced in the centre through the use of half columns rather than pilasters, and the other was the façade of San Ambrogio in Genoa (1589–1606), as engraved in Peter Paul Rubens's *Palazzi di Genova* in 1622 (fig. 79). Both the Italian façades have paired orders, statuary in niches, and a crowning 'IHS' monogram in a sunburst, a favourite Jesuit symbol. The Genoese façade is the source for the winged cherub heads in the upper frieze, which are also found over the aisle windows of the finished St Paul's elevations (fig. 76), and on the Somerset House Chapel designs (cat. nos 59–61). Jones's drawing probably dates before King Charles's offer to pay for the west front on 23 April 1634. As a mere skin on the existing fabric it would have been much less costly than the executed portico and it bears no reference to the royal benefactor.

Fig. 79
Façade of the Jesuit Church of San Ambrogio, Genoa, from Ruben's *Palazzi di Genova* (Antwerp, 1622) Pl.xxiii

As Jones's most ambitious exercise in the use of orders on

a two-tiered façade, the design has attracted critical attention. In 1928, Gotch thought that the elevation fell 'below the standard that we are accustomed to associate with [Jones's] name', and in 1964 Summerson dismissed it as derivative and immature. Wittkower, in an influential paper on Jones's architectural theory in 1953, acknowledged that the elevation was less than satisfactory but went on to consider Jones's proportioning method. He deduced that the façade was set out over a net of incised lines determined by the module of the main order column diameter. In particular, he noted that the main order pilaster shafts were divided into three parts, $2\frac{1}{2}$ modules each, and that the lower third was marked with a horizontal scoreline which determined the central line of the outside bay and the height of the doors of the aisles. Moreover, he observed that 'the basis of the columned aedicule in the outside bay was fixed $\frac{1}{2}$ module below this line'. He assumed that a total modular system was at work on the façade, in view of the fact that the 'diameter of the upper order is $\frac{3}{4}$ module, that of the columns of the central order $\frac{2}{3}$, that of the dwarfed pilasters of the towers $\frac{1}{2}$, and that of the column of the aedicules underneath $\frac{1}{3}$ module'. Wittkower's interpretation of the drawing stemmed from his view that Jones subscribed to a 'rational mathematical interpretation of beauty' which was 'founded on the metaphysical belief in the universal efficacy of number'. A closer inspection of the proportioning of this elevation reveals, however, that abstract modular patterning was not Jones's chief concern. His main preoccupation was visual harmony through coordination of levels and through adjustment of proportions to allow for the optical factor on tall façades.

The scoreline which crosses the elevation at a third of the height of the main order column shafts is actually $2\frac{3}{4}$ modules above the bottom of the shaft. This line marks where the shafts begin to taper inwards to form the 'entasis' of the columns. Although it serves to define the outer bays as twice a third-column-shaft proportion across, it also corresponds with a point at exactly two-thirds the height of the column shafts of the central door. In this way the larger and smaller orders on the lower stage are coordinated through three-part divisions of their respective shafts; that is to say, they are *visually* coordinated through the entasis motif. The scoreline below this, running through the basis of the niche, is at a distance of just under $\frac{5}{8}$ module, not $\frac{1}{2}$ module. It seems to have been positioned without reference to the column diameter, and was a means of aligning the niche with the ears of the door architrave and the middle rail of the central door. The upper order of the façade is indeed $\frac{3}{4}$ the diameter of the lower order. It would not be correct to assume, however, that the rest of the upper order is in a 3:4 relationship with the lower order, for Jones has 'stretched' the proportions of these upper columns in order to counter the effect of diminution which would result when they were viewed from the ground. Palladio's recommended proportions for the Composite order are the same as for the Corinthian: 10 diameters for the columns, including $1\frac{1}{6}$ modules for the capital, and 2 modules for the entablatures. Jones followed these proportions for his lower, Corinthian order, but for his upper order he used proportions of $10\frac{1}{2}$ modules for the columns, $1\frac{1}{3}$ modules for the capitals, and about $2\frac{1}{6}$ modules for the entablature. Moreover, he enhanced the entablature with bold and simple detailing, giving deeply projecting square modillions to the cornice and a pronounced cymatium to the architrave. These adjustments to standard Renaissance formulae reflect Jones's understanding of the Vitruvian concept of optical correction, which demanded that set ratios be modified according to the distance a feature was from the eye. The same principle lay behind Jones's use of full-size experimental models during the restoration of St Paul's between 1635 and 1641. It also prompted him to make a number of comments against illustrations in his copy of Palladio's *I Quattro libri.* He wrote complainingly of Scamozzi above Palladio's example of the Composite order on page 50 of Book I:

> noat the ancientes when a cornish stood farr from the eye maad the members great and som times Put modiglions in the freese w[ch] mad Arrchitraue freese and Cornish sheau affar of all on cornish. this Secrat Scamozio being purblind under stoode nott. Se y[e] Colloseo y[e] upper order. Ser:. fo.65 Li.3.

Jones's conviction that visual factors should take precedence over academic rules of design accounts for some of the awkwardness of this elevation. By stretching the proportions of the Composite order, Jones contributed to the top-heavy feeling at the nave section of the design, a feeling enhanced by the tall attic above the upper entablature. This attic, modelled on the Arch of Constantine in Rome, was Jones's method of classicizing the proportions of the steep Gothic roof gable, which is still visible in the graphite under-drawing. No doubt Jones felt that these tall features would recede from the eye, but on paper the solution is unconvincing, and it is not hard to see why he abandoned an articulated façade for a plainly rusticated front with projecting portico (fig. 78). The executed front allowed the masses of the Romanesque building to speak for themselves. Jones retained the roundels over the aisle doors and in the main gable, but changed the outer niches to windows and removed all statuary to the balustrade of the portico.

See colour illustration on p. 167

Bibliography:

J. A. Gotch, 'The Burlington Devonshire Collection of drawings with special reference to the relations between Inigo Jones and John Webb', *RIBA Journal*, xviii (1911), pp. 319, 321

J. A. Gotch, *Inigo Jones* (London, 1928), p. 175

R. Wittkower, 'Inigo Jones, architect and man of letters', *RIBA Journal*, lx (1953), pp. 84–5 (repr. 1974)

J. Summerson, 'Inigo Jones: lecture on a master mind (1964)', *Proceedings of the British Academy*, l (1965), pp. 183–4, and *Inigo Jones* (Harmondsworth, 1966), pp. 28, 99

J. Harris in *King's Arcadia*, pp. 141–3

C. V. Wedgwood, *The King's Peace, 1637–41* (London, 1955; repr. Harmondsworth, 1983), pp. 91–123

79 Elevation for the north transept front of St Paul's Cathedral, London, incorporating, on left, a sectional outline of the east aisle and a side elevation of a buttress

c. 1634

Graphite outlines over scorelines; pen and brown ink for the central door, left-hand gable scroll and sectional outline. Graphite studies of gable scrolls and cornice profile at bottom of sheet; brown ink blots on lower right of elevation

600 × 452 mm. Trimmed sheet of thick paper

Watermark: large bunch of grapes above an inverted fleur-de-lys, between which is a scroll marked 'FOLEVE' (?)

Inscribed with modern pencil catalogue number in top right-hand corner: *46c* in circle

Scale: 7 ft = 1 in.

Worcester College H & T 14

This preparatory elevation corresponds with Hollar's engraved view of 1658 of the north side of the old cathedral (fig. 76), except for the treatment of the aisle bays. Jones shows arched and square-headed windows on straight walls where Hollar shows niches and roundels on walls with large end-buttresses. The buttresses would have helped to disguise the unequal widths of the aisle walls, since the east aisle on the left was about 3 ft wider than on the west. That Jones may have felt uncomfortable with this inequality is shown by his having redrawn the left-hand wall and its cornice profile 3 ft in from the edge. The experimental nature of the design is further demonstrated by his reworking of the gable scroll and door embellishments, and by the study of a wall section at the left edge of the sheet. No projecting wall was built at this point, but Jones may have reused this side of the drawing for a side view of the deep buttresses which were built out from the central section of the south-transept front. The loose sketching of the gable is another sign that Jones's ideas at St Paul's evolved in a gradual, piecemeal fashion, to the extent that many larger features were refined during the building work itself.

80 Elevation for north and south nave doors at St Paul's Cathedral, London

1637

Pen and dark brown ink over graphite and scorelines

380 × 268 mm. Trimmed sheet

Inscribed by Jones in graphite at top of sheet: *Doures of the south and north/sides St Pauls 1637*; and below this in pen and dark brown ink: *the first draught Taken*; and half-way up the left side of the sheet, in graphite: *as much to y^e spaces as/to y^e fluttes*; and below: *the dropes to com/eune with y^e pila-/starell*; and on *verso* by an 18th-c. hand in pen and brown ink: *Door. 23.*

Scale: 1 ft = approx. $\frac{23}{32}$ in. (11 ft = 8 in.)

RIBA Jones & Webb 32

Jones's mature technique is superbly illustrated in this powerful design for the doorways in the centres of the north and south sides of the nave of St Paul's Cathedral. After setting out the design with dividers and scorer, he drew the cornice and triglyph profiles in graphite before applying his pen. In the ink drawing he modified the drops (guttae) beneath the triglyphs two or three times. Jones then noted his preferred solution for the triglyphs in two pencilled instructions on the left side of the sheet: the flutes and spaces between them were to be equal in width and the drops were to project flush (or 'even') with the pilasters alongside the architrave moulding. This 'first draught' was then passed on as the 'Taken' (accepted) scheme.

The doorway combines two ideas from Jones's earlier designs for entrances: the continuous arch, without imposts, enclosed by a pediment (as in cat. nos 46 and 48), and pilasters topped by triglyphs. The pilasters derive from a doorway design by Domenico Fontana (fig. 57), but have been stripped of their mouldings in tune with the severe, astylar mood of the St Paul's elevations. The channels and roundels of the triglyphs are the most prominent details of Jones's door, and seem to echo the giant arched windows surmounted by roundels in the aisles of the nave (fig. 76).

Bibliography:

R. Wittkower, 'Inigo Jones, architect and man of letters', *RIBA Journal*, lx (1953), pp. 84–5 (repr. 1974)

Winchester Cathedral, Hampshire, 1637–8

81 Preliminary elevation and half plan for the Choir Screen at Winchester Cathedral

1637–8

Black chalk and some brown wash over scorelines

304 × 393 mm. Central vertical fold

Watermark: small, elaborate coat of arms surmounted by cross

Inscribed by William Kent in pen and brown ink below elevation: *of Inigo for y^{e} Skreen of Winchester Ch*; and on *verso* by John Talman in pen and brown ink: *54:* [illegible]:

Scale: 10 ft = $2\frac{7}{8}$ in.

RIBA Jones & Webb 71

The story of the building in this suggestive sketch design begins with the poor state of the Norman pulpitum, or choir screen, in 1636. Bishop Wren of Ely reported to Archbishop William Laud

Fig. 80
Winchester Cathedral, Hampshire. The Choir Screen drawn by Charles Woodfield, 1714

Fig. 81
The centre bay of the Winchester Choir Screen, now in the University Museum of Archaeology and Anthropology, Cambridge

on 20 October that year that when Charles I visited Winchester on progress in 1635 he expressly disapproved of the pulpitum. By April 1637 a decision had been taken to replace the pulpitum, apparently with the advice of Laud, and Jones's drawing was probably made about this time. There are cathedral accounts in 1638 for £234. 4s. 0d. that include 'erecting ye new building before ye Quire', and on 17 June the sculptor Hubert Le Sueur was engaged by the King 'to cast in brasse two statues' of James I and Charles I to be 'delivered to the surveyor of his Maties workes in March ensuing', in other words to Jones in 1639 (figs 82, 83). In 1640 payments were made for setting up the statues, a terminal date for the work.

It was a tragedy that the screen was dismantled in 1820 by the architect William Garbett, presumably acting on instructions from the Chapter who regarded it as a 'misplaced design by its justly celebrated Architect'. The remains were removed to the triforium of the north transept, plundered by cathedral masons for stone, and after being rejected in 1909 as a gift by the Victoria

of Inigo for y Skreen of Winchester Ch

Fig. 82
Hubert Le Sueur's statue of King Charles I, Winchester Cathedral, 1638

and Albert Museum, the centre bay, including the two innermost pilasters, was given to the University Museum of Archaeology and Anthropology at Cambridge, where it incongruously remains (fig. 81). To anyone visiting Cambridge, the fragment is majestic. Indeed, it is higher than Jones's surviving Beaufort House gateway and a better demonstration of the power that he could instil into the entrances that he so enjoyed designing. Some masonry is still in the Winchester triforium, and the statues are at the west end of the cathedral.

In John Webb's annotated copy of Serlio at the RIBA there is an associated study for the screen by Webb which locates the initial source for the drawing in Book VII of the treatises (fols. 85*r.* and 87*r.*). The common inspiration of the Laudian Revival for this design and Jones's rejected elevation for the west front of St Paul's Cathedral, *c.* 1633–4 (cat. no. 78), is illustrated by their many shared features: the central door aedicule surmounted by reclining statues, the pedimented niches with standing saints and the panelled attic crowned with flaming candelabra.

Fig. 83
Hubert Le Sueur's statue of King James I, Winchester Cathedral, 1638

Bibliography:

J. A. Gotch, 'The Choir Screen in Winchester Cathedral', *RIBA Journal*, xxxvi (1929), p. 46

King's Works, iii, p. 153

J. M. G. Blakiston, 'The Inigo Jones Screen', *Winchester Cathedral Record*, nos 45–7 (1976–8)

Triumphal arch at Temple Bar, Fleet Street, London, 1636–8

82 Sketch elevation for a triumphal arch at Temple Bar

1636

Pen and brown ink with brown wash over graphite and scorelines

331 × 311 mm. Two small oblong sheets, each 48 × 77 mm, are pasted over cut-out oblongs above the side arches, and two circular sheets, 45 mm in diameter, are pasted over cut-out circles in the attics

Watermark: same as cat. no. 21

Inscribed by Jones (?) on the roundels in pen and brown ink: *LAETITIA PVBLICA* and *HYLARITAS PVBLICA*; and by Jones on *verso* of left roundel in graphite: *medal(?) fro[m] y Ki[ngs](?)/Printes(?)*

Sketch detail of Corinthian capital on right-hand side of sheet

Scale: 10 ft = $1\frac{9}{16}$ in.

RIBA Jones & Webb 52

83 Longitudinal section for a second scheme for a triumphal arch at Temple Bar

1638

Pen and dark brown ink shaded with ochre and red wash, over graphite under-drawing, scorelines and compass marks. Later red ink ruled border lines on left and right edges of sheet

392 × 319 mm. Including pasted strip at bottom, 57 × 316 mm, which is in two pieces, 144 mm and 177 mm long, with 6 mm overlap

Inscribed and signed by Jones in pen and dark brown ink on right of bottom strip: *Purfill of the Arch tempell barr/how the brik-work is to bee within/1638/Inigo Jones*

Scale: 10 ft = $2\frac{5}{32}$ in.

RIBA Jones & Webb 54

The Temple Bar marked the border between Westminster and the City of London. Here the monarch would pause and be welcomed. Jones would have remembered the triumphal arches erected by Stephen Harrison when James I royally progressed from the Tower to Westminster in 1604. Although Jones was not officially in charge of buildings in the City, he exerted an influence through his powerful presence on various building commissions and as the Royal Surveyor with a voice on the Privy Council. In 1636 the Council directed certain Aldermen, the Recorder of the City and Jones to confer about a gate at the Temple Bar. The present drawing probably belongs to that year, the date on a copy elevation by John Webb of an alternative design (fig. 85).

In 1636 his great Roman portico on the west front of St Paul's Cathedral was building, paid for by Charles I as an act of piety. There was no portico like it north of the Alps, and it too was thoroughly Roman. It is tempting to associate this portico with the Temple Bar, an arch leading via a triumphal way to the classical frontispiece of the cathedral. However, there is no evidence that this was Jones's intention, and as triumphal arches have always been entrances, such an arch at the Temple Bar would have come naturally to mind had the St Paul's portico never existed. Nevertheless, both arch and portico symbolize Stuart aspirations to Imperial grandeur.

a

Fig. 84(a)–(d)
Inigo Jones. Sketches for relief panels on *verso* of elevation by John Webb for Temple Bar Arch (fig. 85)

b

c

d

Fig. 85
John Webb. Elevation, after Inigo Jones, for Temple Bar Arch, 1636

e

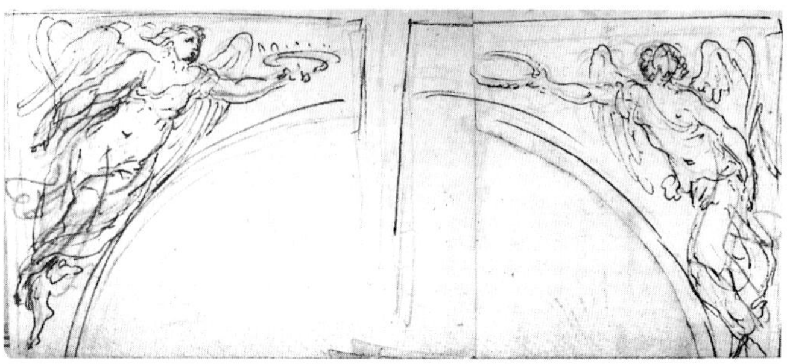

Fig. 84(e)
Sketch for spandrel figures on *verso* of sheet formerly attached to cat. no. 83 (as shown in photo)

The wonderfully fluid and spontaneous sketch in cat. no. 82 is one of the most attractive of all Jones's compositions. He proportioned the arch as a square of 60 ft, the central arch 15 ft wide and the proportions of the lower order to the upper attic, 3:2, or 36 ft to 24 ft, the latter being exactly the height of the Corinthian columns. Although he has taken the Roman arches of Septimus Severus and Constantine as his models, these are wider than they are high, and in heightening his arch Jones has exercised himself as the modern Vitruvius.

The oblong sketches pasted above the side arches are probably based on engravings of the victorious Marcus Aurelius on the Arch of Constantine in Rome, and the roundels in the attic are apparently copied from prints of Roman coins (as Jones indicates in a note on the back of the left roundel). They declare the joyfulness (Laetitia) and good humour (Hilaritas) of the body politic and are complemented by another pair of roundels depicting shipping and commerce in a group of four finished drawings for the panels which were originally pasted on the back of Webb's elevation (figs 84 a–d). Webb's drawing of the arch has a more pronounced military theme. Flanked by Neptune on the left and Ceres on the right, the laurel-crowned Charles rides in armour, the master of the sea and land.

Jones's longitudinal section (cat. no. 83) belongs with Webb's drawing and is proof that two years later the project was still under consideration. A sketch by Jones for the equestrian statue of Charles I was until recently attached to the bottom of this sheet, and has on the *verso* a study for Victory figures in the spandrels (fig. 84e). In this second design much of the proportional subtlety is lost. The proportions are now 2:1 between the lower order and the attic, rather than 3:2, although the whole elevation is still square. The attic and the equestrian statue look ungainly. Did Jones tire of the project and hand it over to his faithful but unimaginative assistant?

See colour illustrations on pp. 168–9

Bibliography:

J. Summerson, *Inigo Jones* (Harmondsworth, 1966), pp. 122, 124

LÆTITIA PVBLICA
HYLARITAS PVBLICA

Late Presentation Designs, *c*. 1638

By 1638 the pace of royal building work had begun to slacken. Interior decoration for the Queen at Somerset House, Oatlands Palace and Greenwich was either complete or well advanced, and no new works were put in hand for Henrietta Maria until the purchase of Wimbledon late in that year (cat. no. 77). Charles's funds were exhausted by preparations for the Scottish War in 1639, a futile campaign to impose the new Anglican *Book of Common Prayer* on the Presbyterian Kirk which led to the King's humiliation in the Long Parliament convened in November 1640. Not surprisingly, no royal masques were staged in January and February 1639. This gave Inigo Jones at least eighteen months respite from the onerous task of designing sets and costumes, between the performance of William Davenant's *Luminalia* in February 1638 and work for the same author's *Salmacida Spolia* (performed 21 January 1640). Although grandiose schemes were afoot for a new Palace of Whitehall modelled on the Escorial in Madrid and for a huge classical front to Somerset House in the Strand, all the surviving drawings for these projects are in the hand of John Webb, who was assuming increasing responsibility for major tasks in the Office of Works in the late 1630s. For the first time since the accession of Charles I and Henrietta Maria, Jones had time for small private commissions, and returned to a highly finished style of presentation drawing.

The following eight drawings all belong to the period around 1638 and share a common style of draftsmanship and architectural detail. They are in a meticulous outline technique and have their classical ornaments pared down to a few minimal features. The rich palazzo style of Jones's early domestic designs has given way to a restrained manner that anticipates the Restoration country-houses of Pratt and May or the Georgian terraced houses of the following century. Jones has reduced his window cornices to single, large mouldings, stripped away running mouldings from wall surfaces, contracted his main entablatures to block cornices of the Roman type, and abandoned sculptural ornament. The severe style has affinities with brick domestic architecture surviving in Hertfordshire from the mid-seventeenth century, notably in the use of ovolo mouldings on the chimney-stacks (cat. nos 84, 86), and large cyma mouldings for the floor bands and eaves cornices (cat. no. 87). If these house designs were indeed for an all-brick rather than brick-and-stone construction they represent a shift in idiom from designs of 1616–19, such as Fulke Greville's house in London and the Prince's Lodging at Newmarket Palace (cat. nos 22, 30, 31). They would also reflect a trend towards brick ornament on London houses which is exemplified by the work of Artisan-Mannerist builders at the 'Dutch House', Kew, *c*. 1631 (fig. 90), or Cromwell House, Highgate, 1637–8. But on these Artisan houses brick is used merely to emulate the Italianate stone details which Jones had introduced two decades earlier. In his own designs of the 1630s Jones pioneered a classical idiom suited to the soft and richly textured character of the brick material, which demands large, easily carved mouldings and responds to broad areas of plain wall. It was a style, however, which found no immediate imitators. None of Jones's late domestic designs was apparently built, and his restrained treatment of brick was out of step with the mood of the Artisan builders, who were anxious to prove that they could surpass the stone-mason in richness of carving.

Underlying the severe detailing of the three late house façades is a feeling for the plainness and simplicity of the Tuscan order. The brew-house design (cat. no. 90), previously ascribed to Newmarket in 1616 but consistent with the late period in drafting techniques and architectural style, has a portico with a simplified version of Scamozzi's Tuscan order and a door with a single-moulding cornice. The rest is bare wall, without quoins or string-courses. The design should be compared with the elevation for a house with a hexastyle portico where the order seems to combine Corinthian and Tuscan features (cat. no. 86). From the brew-house design it is only a short step to the much-debated drawings for a playhouse, currently ascribed to the Cockpit Theatre, Drury Lane, London, in 1616–17, but here redated to the late 1630s and tentatively assigned to a theatre project by William Davenant in 1639 (cat. nos 91, 92). The minimal lower order of the gallery and the slender door-frames are very close to details on the brew-house drawing, as is the technique of the plan and the rudimentary style of the elevation. Around the eaves of the building is a cove cornice like the one on Sir Peter Killigrew's house, *c.* 1630 (fig. 108). The remaining two drawings in this late group, a pair of enigmatic cupola designs, display that rigorous compulsion to reduce the classical vocabulary to its most vital elements which is the hallmark of Jones's mature architectural style (cat. nos 88, 89).

G.H.

84 Elevation for a five-window house for Lord Maltravers' development at Lothbury, London

1638

Pen and grey ink with grey wash over faint scorelines and slight graphite under-drawing

404 × 308 mm. Single sheet of thin, grainy paper with central horizontal fold, the bottom half blank (identical paper to cat. no. 85)

Watermark: water-pot, the lid made of a quatrefoil surmounted by a crescent moon

Inscribed by Jones in pen and grey ink in top right-hand corner: *uprightes for my lo Maltravers/his house at loathbury 1638*; and to left in pen and black ink by a modern hand: *55* in circle

Scale: 1 ft $=\frac{11}{128}$ in. (10 ft = 21.5 mm)

Worcester College H & T 6

85 Elevation for a row of warehouses, 152 ft long, for Lord Maltravers' development at Lothbury, London

1638

Pen and dark brown ink over faint scorelines

307 × 405 mm. Thin, grainy paper

Watermark: same as cat. no. 84

Inscribed in the top right-hand corner in pen and black ink by a modern hand: *58D* in pencilled circle

Scale: 1 ft $=\frac{11}{128}$ in. (10 ft = 21.5 mm)

Worcester College H & T 8

Lord Maltravers was the courtesy title of Henry Frederick Howard, son of Thomas Howard, 2nd Earl of Arundel. In the 1630s he was granted a lucrative patent to mint royal farthing tokens and established an office on the family property at Lothbury for the issue and change of these tokens.

Although the terrace design is uninscribed (cat. no. 85) it clearly belongs with the house elevation (cat. no. 84) because it repeats the treatment of the two main floors and roof, and is drawn to the same scale on identical paper. With only two entrances on a thirteen-bay front, it would seem to be for commercial rather than domestic use. Neither design was apparently executed, but there seems to be a link between these elevations and the Restoration country-house type established by Sir Roger Pratt at Coleshill in the 1650s, where Jones is said to have given advice. Coleshill (burnt, 1952) was particularly close to the Maltravers façade in its use of two equal floors over a cellar, pedimented dormer windows, a Roman-style block eaves cornice and balconied windows set against a bare wall.

Bibliography:
J. Summerson, *Inigo Jones* (Harmondsworth, 1966), p. 114
O. Hill and J. Cornforth, *English country houses: Caroline 1625–1685* (London, 1966), pp. 15–18, 90–6

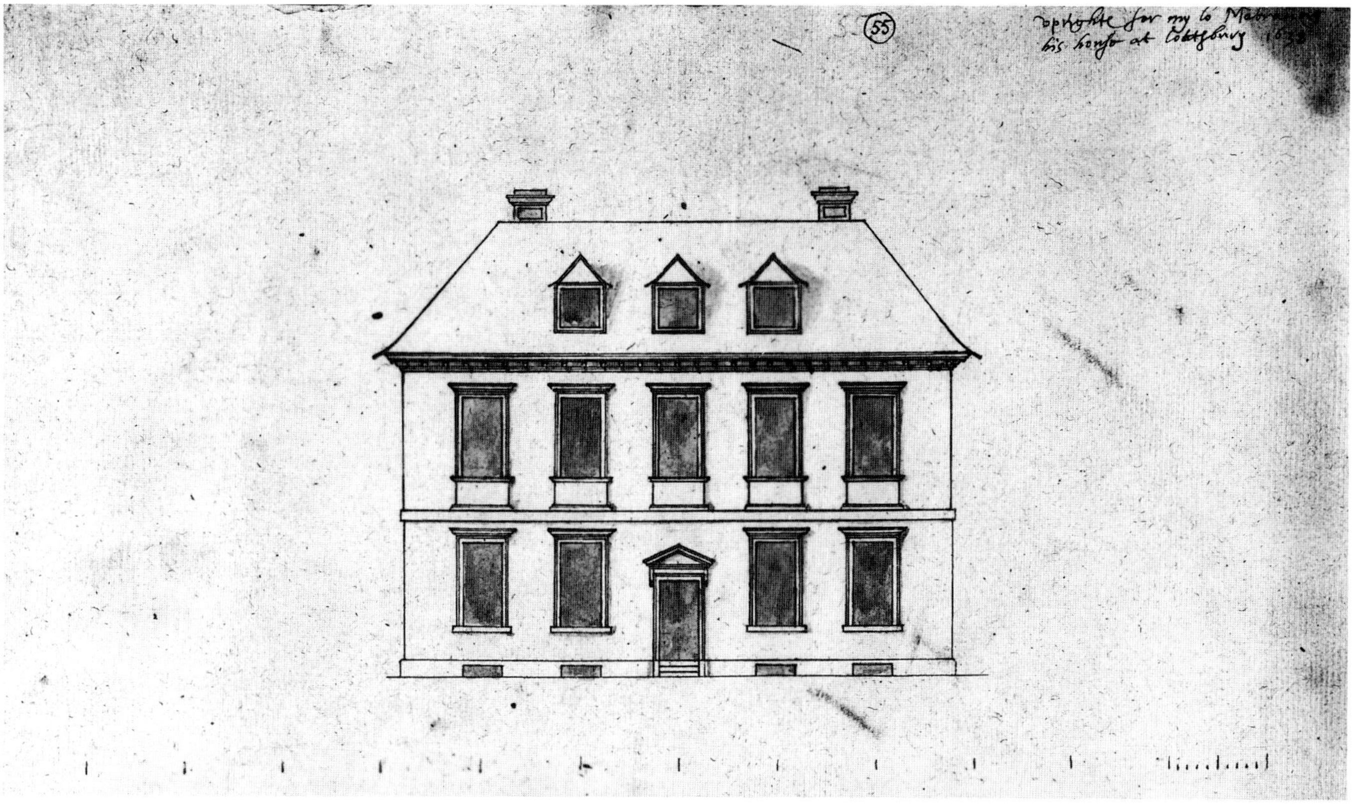
55

86 Elevation for a house with a hexastyle portico and balconied roof platform

c. 1638

Pen and brown ink over graphite and scorelines, with additions in graphite

225 × 280 mm. Thin, grainy paper. Two sheets showing windows pasted on left and right sides of basement (25 × 18 mm and 22 × 18 mm), and a sheet with graphite drawing of balcony pasted on top of roof (28 × 55 mm)

Inscribed by Jones in pen and brown ink *5* to *60*, right to left above scale of feet at top of sheet, and *5.10*, 16 and *10* up right-hand side of elevation for dimensions of basement, main floor and attic (including main entablature) respectively

Scale: 10 ft = fractionally less than 1 in.

Worcester College H & T 7

Although very close to cat. nos 84 and 85 in drafting style and detail, there is nothing to link this elevation positively with the two Maltravers drawings. The design is probably for a suburban or rural house, rather than a town house, its portico and roof balcony commanding a view over some open land. This type of roof balcony became a popular feature of the Restoration country-house, for example at Roger Pratt's Coleshill, *c.* 1657, and John Webb's Amesbury Abbey, *c.* 1658 (fig. 104), where it rises above a similar pedimented portico.

The elements of Jones's façade are Palladian – the hexastyle portico with paired end-columns and the attic above the main entablature – but all the details have been radically simplified. In the cornice of the portico, for instance, Jones has omitted the square-ended corona moulding leaving the two cyma mouldings one above the other, separated only by a fillet.

Bibliography:

J. Summerson, *Inigo Jones* (Harmondsworth, 1966) p. 114

J. Bold, *Wilton House and English Palladianism* (London, 1988), pp. 95–124

87 Elevation for a seven-window house with an iron pergola

c. 1638

Pen and brown ink with grey wash over fine graphite under-drawing and light scorelines

177 × 196 mm

Watermark: fleur-de-lys within shield above which is a crown and below a 4M insignia

Inscribed in pen and black ink by modern hand in top right-hand corner: *55A* in circle

Scale: 1 ft = $\frac{3}{32}$ in.

Worcester College H & T 68

Omitted by J. A. Gotch from his 1913 catalogue of the Worcester College and Chatsworth drawings, this meticulous elevation was not published until 1973, when it was dated to the 'Arundellian' phase of Jones's career, *c.* 1615–*c.* 1618.

The drawing is in the thick, uniform and fully ruled outline style of the Maltravers designs of 1638 (cat. nos 84, 85). The outlines on the drawing meet with great precision and are exact to the smallest detail: Jones has cleanly drawn the thin iron posts of the pergola, the profile of its rail and the slender fillet mouldings of the first-floor window cornices. No dated drawings before about 1634 have this degree of accuracy and uniformity (cf. cat. no. 79). As on the Maltravers elevations, Jones's handling of the outlines is very firm, with minimal thickening at the ends of the lines or in the profiles of the cornices. The under-scoring is tidy and neatly applied, and has been supplemented by a fully ruled graphite technique.

The wide iron balcony which links the three central openings implies a prospect over a park or garden and therefore a rural or at least a surburban location for the house. That the design was for a self-contained residence rather than for a hunting-lodge is indicated by the service basement, and by the implied main living floor through the enrichment of the upper floor windows with cornices. We know of no royal residence built to this pattern in the later 1630s, so the design was almost certainly made for a courtier or gentry patron.

The house has two main floors of equal height, and the walls are plain, without the quoins, voussoirs and continuous balcony rails found on the design for Sir Peter Killigrew's house of about 1630 (fig. 108), or on the richly articulated palazzo type of façade which formed the basis of Jones's domestic style in the period from 1616 to 1619 (e.g. cat. nos 22, 30, 31). Instead of a full entablature over the principal windows Jones has applied a single large cyma moulding. The cyma motif is repeated on the string-course which runs between the floors, and on the main eaves cornice, which is modelled on the Roman block cornice and takes the place of the standard Palladian cornice used on the earlier domestic designs.

See colour illustration on p. 170

Bibliography:
King's Arcadia, p. 111

55A

88 Plan and elevation for a cupola, surmounted by baluster and flag

c. 1638

Pen and dark brown ink with grey wash over scoring with a rounded point

421 × 321 mm. Horizontal fold in centre of sheet

Watermark: same as cat. no. 21

Inscribed in modern pen and black ink in top right-hand corner: *92* in circle

Scale: 1 ft = $\frac{3}{8}$ in.

Worcester College H & T 66

89 Alternative plan and elevation for a cupola with hexagonal centre-piece and low roof

c. 1638

Pen and dark brown ink over faint graphite and scoring with a rounded point

421 × 327 mm. Identical paper to cat. no. 88

Inscribed in modern pen and black ink in top right-hand corner: *93* in circle

Watermark: same as cat. no. 21

Scale: 1 ft = $\frac{3}{8}$ in.

Worcester College H&T 67

These two curious designs are variants for the same structure: a small feature, rising from a podium, and consisting of a rectangular peristyle surmounted by a circular or hexagonal one, with pilasters on each level 3 ft high. The base of the structure is treated in stepped fashion, but there is no provision for access from the podium to the peristyle, or from the lower to the upper stages of the feature. The designs may show a roof cupola, possibly surmounting a stair-tower, although unlike most examples of this type on seventeenth-century country-houses (e.g. John Webb's Amesbury Abbey, Wiltshire, *c.* 1658, fig. 104) there is no access from the cupola to a roof platform.

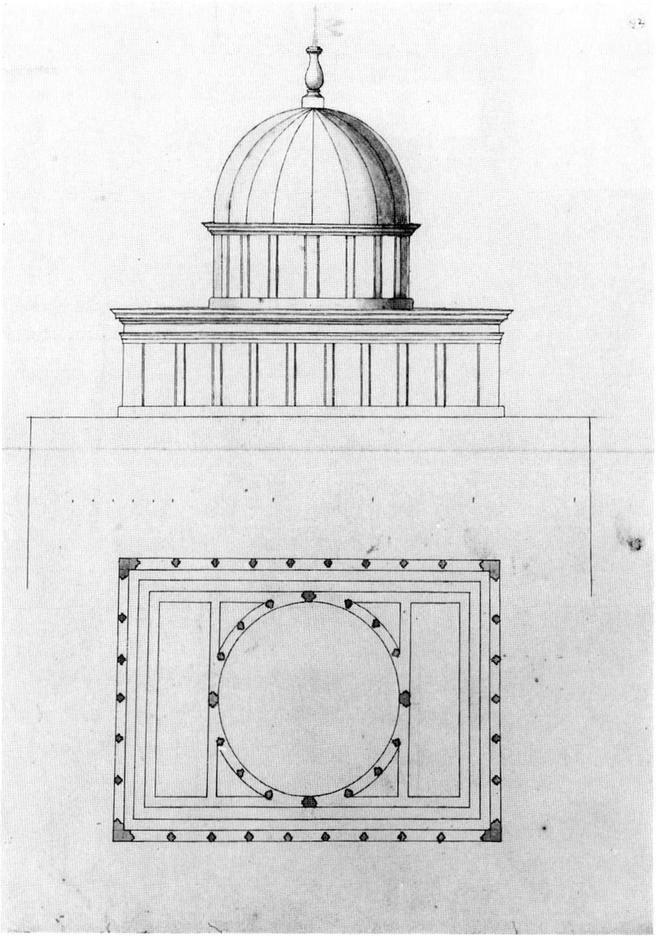

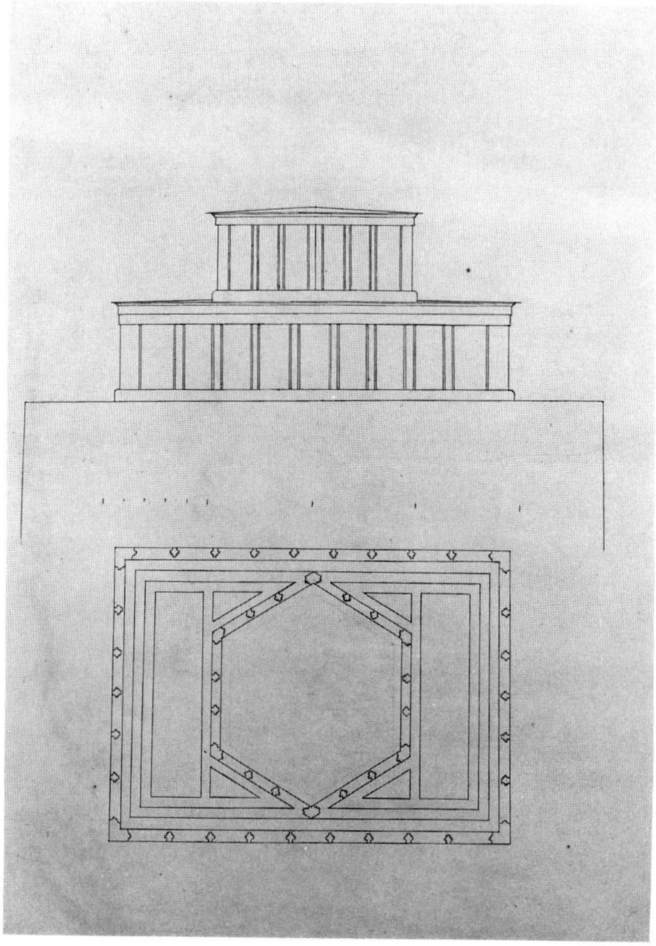

90 Plan and elevation for a brew-house, ascribed to Hassenbrook Hall, Essex

c. 1638

Pen and brown ink with grey wash over graphite under-drawing and scoring with a rounded point; dimensions in graphite. 18th-c. red ink ruled border line around edge of sheet

348 × 218 mm. In three pasted sheets, the top sheet for the elevation, 152 × 217 mm, with 5 mm overlap beneath the middle sheet (bearing the plan) which is 185 × 217 mm, with 4 mm overlap beneath the bottom sheet, which is 55 × 218 mm

Watermark (on central sheet): same as cat. no. 21

Signed: *Inigo Jones* in pen and brown ink on bottom sheet. Inscribed by John Webb with feet-and-inches dimensions in graphite on plan, and to right of elevation. Inscribed by an 18th-c. hand in pen and brown ink in top right-hand corner: *27*.

Scale (prick marked on bottom sheet): 10 ft = $1\frac{5}{32}$ in.

RIBA Jones & Webb 58

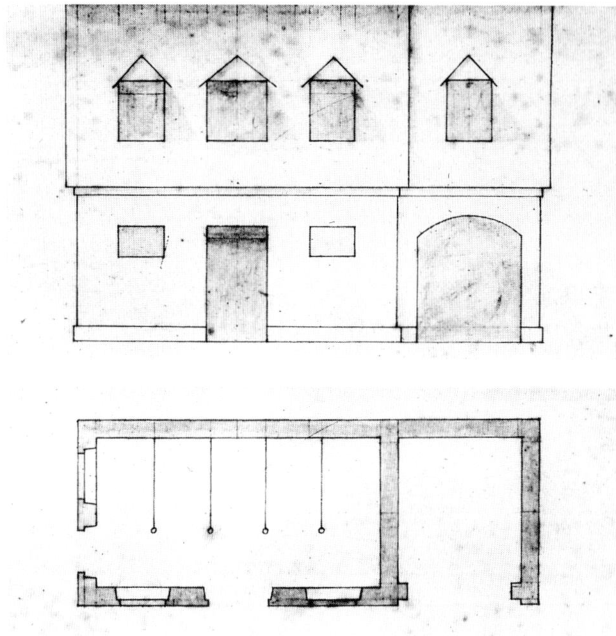

Fig. 86
John Webb. Plan and elevation for stables at Hassenbrook Hall, Essex, 1638

Like the stable elevation at the RIBA (cat. no. 9), this design has been associated with works at Newmarket between 1615 and 1617. At Newmarket, however, the brew-house was nearly twice the size of the building in this drawing, and had a twin-pitched roof and no portico.

The pen outlines of the design are in the thick, uniform style of Jones's *c.* 1638 drawings, and the sheet, which is in three pieces of good-quality paper, bears Jones's signature in a style similar to that on the 1638 sectional drawing for the Temple Bar arch (cat. no. 83). This style of signature, with the 'J' of 'Jones' much smaller than the 'I' of 'Inigo', and with relatively simple flourishes at the beginning and end of the name, is much less elaborate than on the three signed drawings of 1616–17 (cat. nos 17, 18, 21). Moreover, the graphite dimensions on the drawings are in the hand of John Webb who joined Jones's office in 1628. They have been inscribed over the ink drawing and have Webb's characteristic use of 'fo' as an abbreviation for 'feet' written alongside (rather than above) the numbers, his usual chevron markings, and his secretary-style lower-case 'd' with a backward sloping looped stem (in 'dia' on the plan of the portico). Other late drafting characteristics include the under-scoring with a rounded point and the very precise joining of ruled lines at the angles and profiles.

All these factors suggest a date around 1638 and Webb's involvement with the drawing may provide a location for the design. John Webb's earliest known private commissions in 1638 include a stable design for Henry Fetherstone's Hassenbrook Hall in Essex at the RIBA (fig. 86). The Hassenbrook stable design has undressed doors and windows, dormers of two sizes like those on the brew-house elevation, and walls 1 ft 2 in. thick – the dimensions which Webb inscribed on the walls of Jones's brew-house plan. We have no evidence, however, of any buildings by Webb or Jones at Hassenbrook, and Jones's brew-house design might equally have been prepared for Wimbledon Palace in 1639–41 (cat. no. 77), where a large brick service range was added to the west side of the west wing at about this time.

The order of the brew-house portico is Tuscan. This was an appropriate order for an ancillary building, but also underlines Jones's fondness for the most rudimentary of the five Roman orders in his late designs. He derived the Tuscan portico from a plate in Scamozzi's *L'Idea della architettura universale* (Part II, p. 58), but as on the two Tuscan designs of *c* .1630 from the same source (cat. no. 48), he simplified the details, eliminating the abacus of the capital and the triglyphs of the frieze and reducing the cornice from five to three members.

See colour illustration on p. 171

Bibliography:

J. Harris, 'Inigo Jones and the Prince's Lodging at Newmarket', *Architectural History*, ii (1959), pp. 26–40
C. S. Higham, *Wimbledon Manor under the Cecils* (London, 1962,) p. 30ff.
King's Works, iv, pp. 146–7
J. Lever and M. Richardson, *The Art of the architect* (London, 1984), p. 44

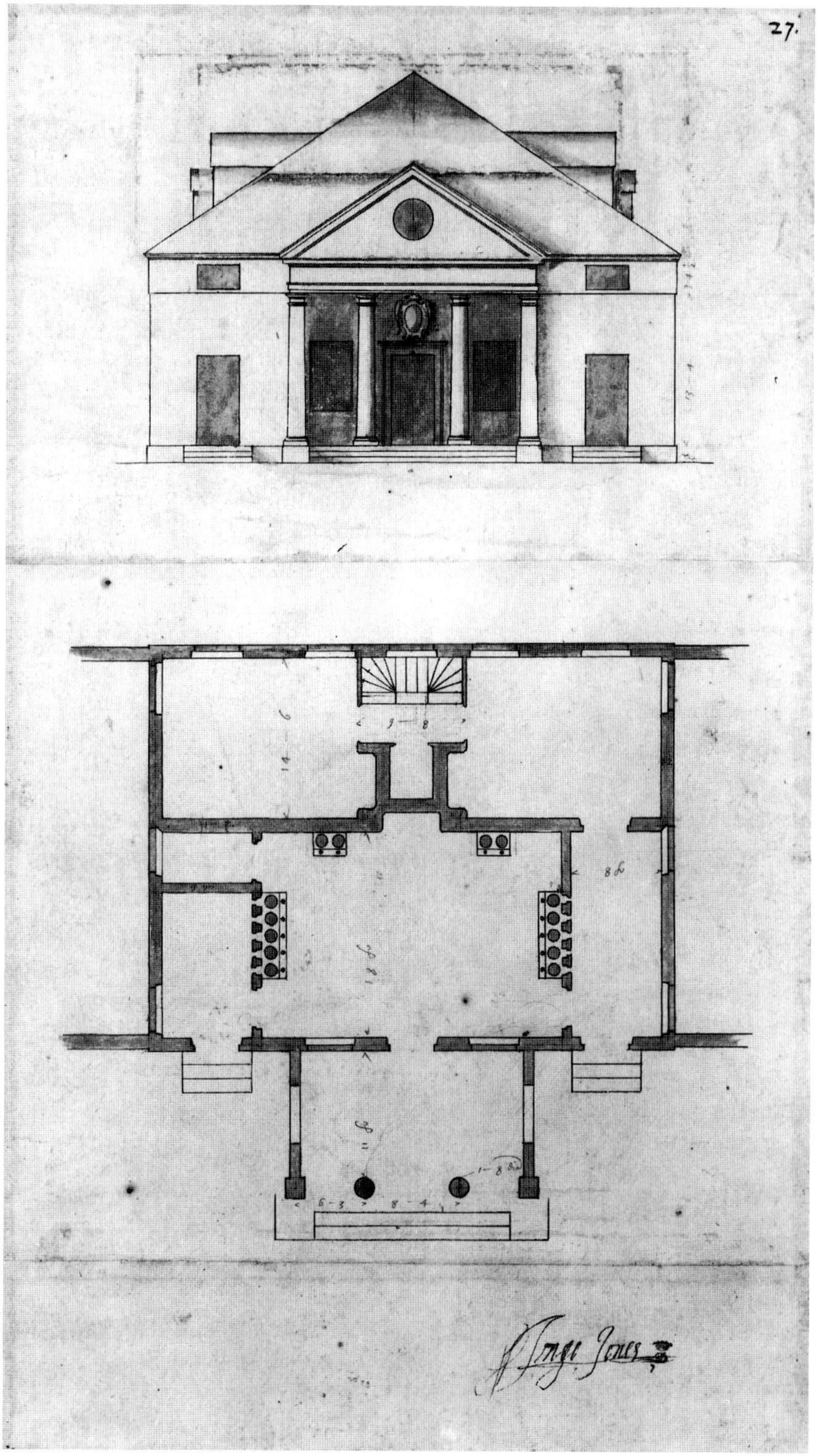

91 Elevation and plan for a playhouse, possibly for Sir William Davenant's unexecuted theatre project in Fleet Street, London (1639)

c. 1638

Pen and brown ink with brown wash over graphite under-drawing and scorelines

324 × 422 mm. Laid down. Vertical fold in centre of sheet

Watermark: same as cat. no. 21

Scale: 10 ft = $1\frac{3}{8}$ in.

Worcester College H & T 10

92 Two transverse sections of the above design, the left one showing the auditorium and the right one the stage end

Pen and brown ink with brown wash over graphite under-drawing and scorelines

325 × 420 mm. Laid down. Vertical fold in centre of sheet

Watermark: same as cat. no. 21

Scale: 10 ft = $1\frac{3}{8}$ in.

Worcester College H & T 11

Since first published by Don Rowan in 1969 these two immaculate presentation sheets have attracted a wider range of scholarly discussion than any other architectural drawings by Inigo Jones. They show an indoor playhouse, a type of theatre which existed alongside the outdoor playhouses of Shakespeare's and Ben Jonson's time, but which did not become the dominant form until the Restoration, when the introduction of a full scenic stage demanded a closed-in setting. Dating before the Civil War, these drawings represent the earliest known design for a purpose-built indoor playhouse and are therefore of enormous interest for our understanding of the development of English theatre buildings.

Glynne Wickham suggested that the drawings were made for the Salisbury Court Theatre, 1629–30, but in 1973 John Harris put forward the view that the drawings belonged stylistically to Jones's 'Arundellian' period, *c.* 1616 to *c.* 1618. In the same year Iain Mackintosh made some striking observations which seemed to link the drawings with the Drury Lane Cockpit, a building which was converted from a cockpit to a playhouse between 1616 and 1617 and became one of the most popular commercial theatres in seventeenth-century London. He pointed out that the pit of the playhouse, shown in the left-hand sectional view, had the characteristics of a cock-fighting pit, and that the dimensions of the stage were exactly those of a stage plan by John Webb in the British Library for William Davenant's opera *The Siege of Rhodes*, which was performed at the Drury Lane Cockpit in 1658–9. He also noted that the front of the stage had a set-back on each side for the fitting of a proscenium arch, the height and width of which were similar to those of a proscenium and scene design by Inigo Jones at Chatsworth inscribed 'for y[e] cokpitt for my lo Chambralin 1639' (which had previously been associated with the Cockpit-in-Court Theatre at Whitehall). Mackintosh's conclusions were reinforced by John Orrell in a detailed study of these two drawings published in 1977. Orrell noted that the overall width of the playhouse did not seem to fit the proportional scheme of the whole interior and was therefore likely to have been a predetermined dimension, a factor which complied with indications that the owner of the Drury Lane Cockpit, Christopher Beeston, had not built his playhouse *de novo* in 1616–17 but as an extension to a pre-existing cockpit. According to Orrell, Jones's involvement can be inferred from Beeston's apparent success in by-passing a court action enforcing a royal building proclamation, and from the fact that the playhouse was regularly used by Queen Anne's Men, an acting company patronized by Anne of Denmark. In a chapter devoted to the Drury Lane Cockpit in *The Theatres of Inigo Jones and John Webb* in 1985, Orrell enlarged on the later history of the playhouse, showing that not only John Webb's stage plan for Davenant's *The Siege of Rhodes* (at the British Library) but his frontispiece at Chatsworth for the same opera could be made to fit Jones's design almost precisely.

Although the exact correspondence between Webb's stage designs and the stage in the Worcester College drawings seems to suggest that the design was made for a building which housed Davenant's opera, the case for assigning the drawings to Christopher Beeston's Cockpit of 1616–17 hinges on the stylistic dating. All the other evidence is circumstantial or conjectural. Close inspection of their style, technique and architectural detail now shows that the drawings cannot have been made in 1616 but belong more than two decades later, near the end of the 1630s.

The drawings are in Jones's thick outline style of about 1638. Ruled and compass lines on the plan and elevation are flawlessly joined; constructional and decorative details on the sections are cleanly and firmly handled. The two sheets should be compared with the brew-house design of *c.* 1638, which has an identical handling of stairs, door reveals and other features on the plan, and the same firm drawing of a cartouche on the elevation (cat. no. 90). Other indicators of a late date include the tidy underscoring which is neatly followed in the ink lines, the ruled graphite under-drawing (visible in the right-hand section), and Jones's use of a folded sheet to display one drawing on each side of the open folio. The washed shading has been hastily applied, giving a patchy effect like that in the windows of the 1638 Maltravers design (cat. no. 84).

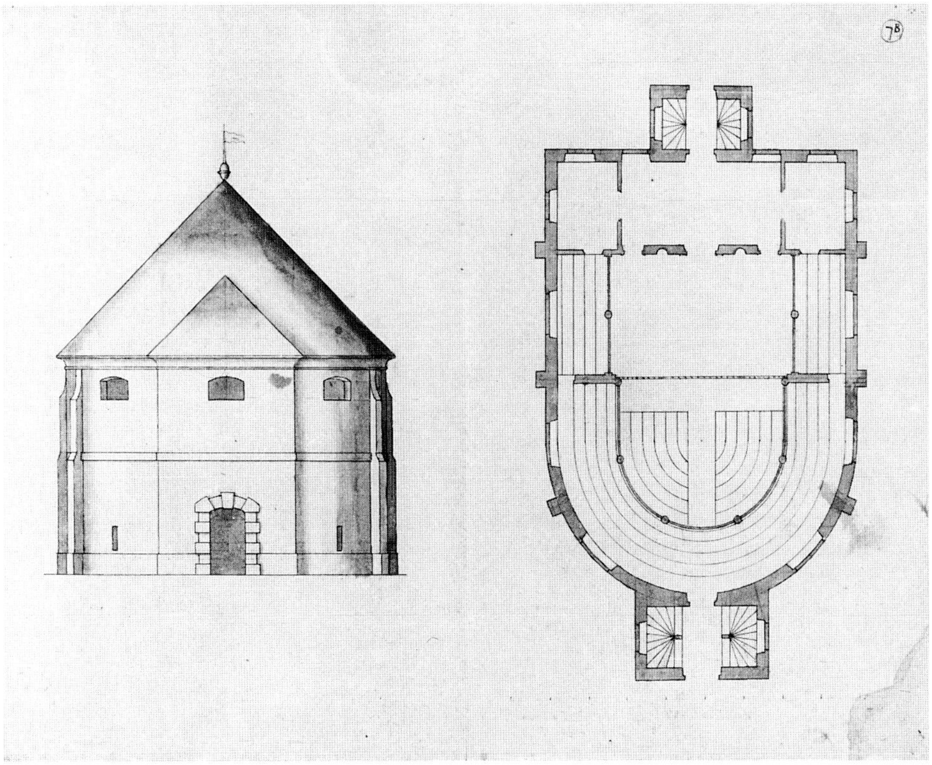

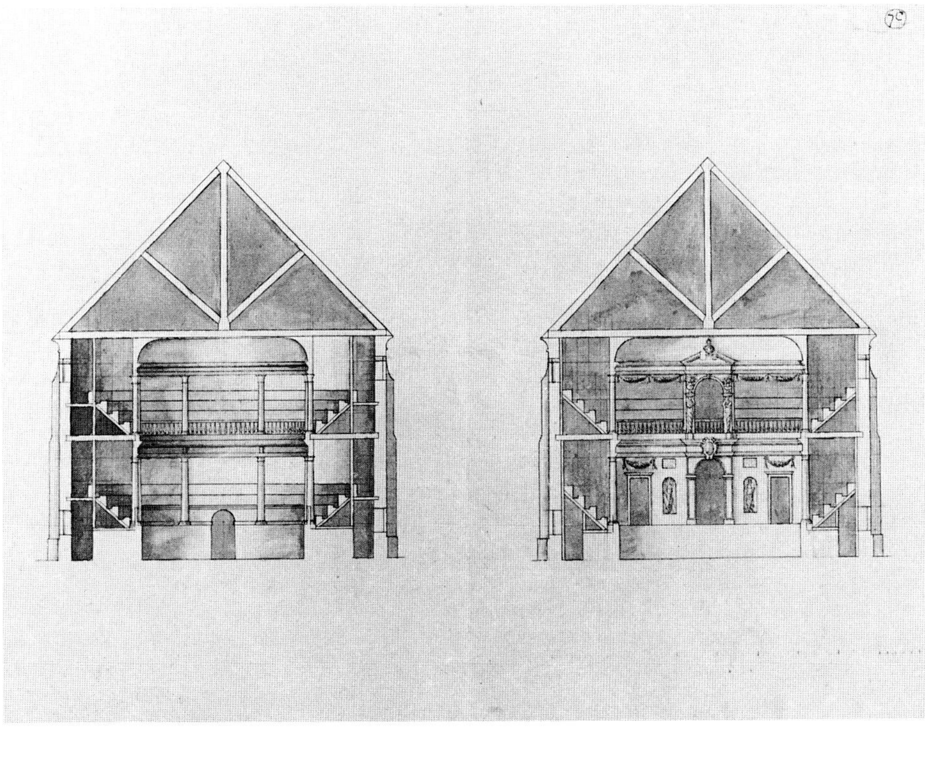

The *c.* 1638 date rules out any possibility that the drawings were made for a rebuilding of the Drury Lane Cockpit. There is no evidence for any reconstruction work at the Drury Lane Cockpit in the late 1630s, notwithstanding much other detailed information which we have of the turbulent fortunes of its owners in that period. Nor could the drawings be fair copies of earlier designs. The designs are consistent with Jones's late elevational style in their simplified classical detailing, and there are redrawings and cancellations in the scoring and under-drawing which indicate a design rather than a copy. We must look elsewhere for an attribution, and it happens that there was one scheme afoot for a new purpose-built indoor playhouse at that time, the requirements of which are well satisfied by the present drawings. This was the theatre projected by William Davenant in 1639 for a site in Fleet Street. Davenant's scheme is described in a licence, dated 26 March 1639, which granted him permission to build '. . . a Theatre or Playhouse, with necessary tireing and retiring Rooms and other places convenient, containing in the whole forty yards square at the most, wherein Plays, musical entertainments, Scenes or other like Presentments, may be presented' (Calendar of State Papers Domestic, 1638–9, p. 604 [doquet]; see Bentley). The area specified is apparently that of the plot of ground, not necessarily that of the building, and it was to be 'at the most' forty yards square. The building itself was to serve several functions, including plays and 'scenes'. This distinction between plays and scenic performances is repeated further on in the licence, where it states that Davenant and his 'Players and Persons' have permission 'to act Plays in such House, so to be by him or them erected, and exercise Musick, musical Presentments, Scenes, Dancing or other the like . . .'. Outwardly the 'Theatre or Playhouse' was to be 'made or built of Bricke or Stone, according to the tenor of our Proclamations in that behalf'.

The dual purpose of Davenant's theatre as a house for plays and scenic productions implies a building that could be converted from the usual open-stage format of Elizabethan and Jacobean playhouses such as the second Blackfriars Theatre (1596), the Swan (1599) and the second Globe (1614), to a proscenium-fronted stage of the kind designed by Inigo Jones at the Paved Court Theatre in Somerset House (1632–3), or for *Florimène* in the Great Hall at Whitehall in 1635. The present drawings are for just such a convertible theatre. The clear division across the central transverse axis between the auditorium and stage ends of the plan (a disjunction which encouraged Mackintosh and Orrell to view the stage end as an addition to the 'round' of a cockpit) implies a theatre with a scenic stage capable of being viewed exclusively from the auditorium, while the seating at the sides of the stage and in the first-floor gallery of the *frons scenae* indicate that when non-scenic plays were performed the audience could view the stage from all sides, as in the traditional Jacobean playhouse. That Webb's designs for *The Siege of Rhodes* can be made to fit precisely into the stage of the drawing confirms that the stage was designed for a proscenium arch and perspective scenery while at the same time establishing a connection between Jones's designs and Davenant's proposal. Jones designed the sets and costumes for Davenant's masques *The Temple of Love* (1635), *Britannia Triumphans* (1637), *Luminalia* (1638) and *Salmacida Spolia* (1640). He would therefore have been the natural collaborator in a venture to bring the sophisticated settings of Court scenic drama into the world of the commercial theatre where the non-scenic, open-stage theatre was still the dominant form.

Soon after Davenant's licence had been issued in 1639 he began recruiting actors, much to the annoyance of Richard Heton, manager of the nearby Salisbury Court Theatre. Davenant had obtained the necessary passage for his patent through the Great Seal and was in a position to start building, but on 2 October 1639, an indenture was made between King and Davenant forbidding the latter to build 'upon the said parcell of ground in Fleet Street' or 'upon any other parcell of ground lying in or neere the Citties or Suburbs of the Citties or London or Westminster' without renewed approval for the site under a royal warrant. Evidently Davenant's rivals in the neighbouring Salisbury Court and Blackfriars Theatres had brought influence to bear from among the courtly patrons to quash Davenant's plan. But though the indenture laid strict conditions on the siting of the building, it revoked none of Davenant's essential privileges, and his proposed theatre was still referred to as a valid establishment in a state paper of 1660–1 (C.S.P.D., 1660–1, p. 114). The survival of Davenant's scheme into the 1650s might explain why John Webb's stage designs for *The Siege of Rhodes* can be fitted into Jones's plan and elevation. Jones's small stage, 23 ft 10 in. across and 15 ft deep, would have provided Webb, the inheritor of these drawings, with a ready-made format for the first stage of *The Siege of Rhodes* at Rutland House, where the space available was, in Davenant's words, 'confin'd to eleven foot in height and about fifteen in depth'. His theatre project having come to nothing, Davenant may have asked Webb to make what use he could of Jones's designs for the setting at Rutland House.

The *frons scenae* of Jones's design should be compared with that of the Cockpit-in-Court Theatre at Whitehall, 1629–31, as recorded in a drawing by John Webb after repairs to the building in 1660–2 (fig. 87). Webb shows a similar two-storey setting with a central *porta regia* surmounted by a pedimented opening for the upper stage. Just as Jones's playhouse makes a clear distinction between scenic stage and auditorium so in the plan of the Cockpit-in-Court he disposes the audience in front or nearly in front of the stage. Both sets of drawings anticipate the axial stage and auditorium of the Restoration theatre, when the scenic spectacles of the Court masque entered the mainstream of English public drama.

See colour illustrations on pp. 172–3

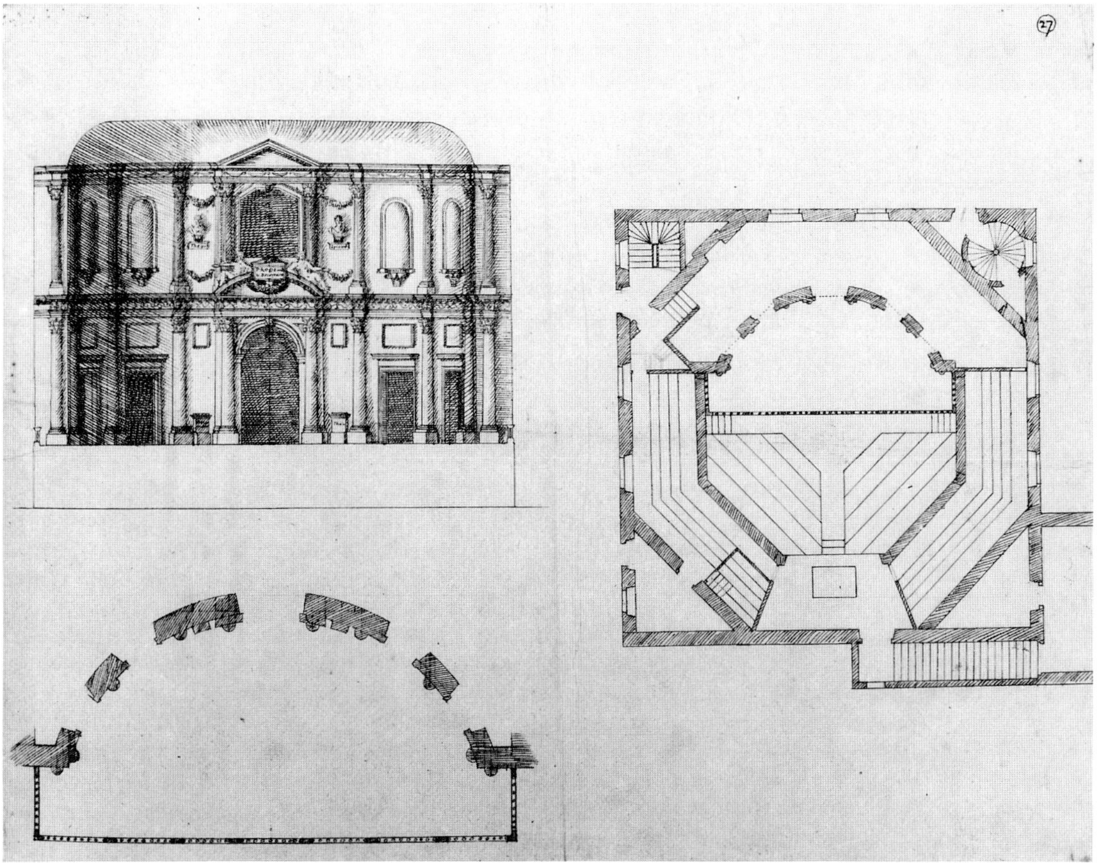

Fig. 87
John Webb. Plans and stage elevation of the Cockpit-in-Court Theatre, Whitehall, London (1629–31), as restored by Webb, 1660–2

Bibliography:

G. E. Bentley, *The Jacobean and Caroline stage* (7 vols, Oxford, 1941–68), vi (1968), pp. 304–9

D. F. Rowan, 'A neglected Jones/Webb theatre project: "Barber-Surgeon's Hall writ large"', *New Theatre Magazine*, ix (1969), pp. 6–15

G. Wickham, *Early English stages, 1300–1660* (3 vols; ii, part 2, London, 1972), pp. 144–7

J. Harris in *King's Arcadia*, pp. 107–9

I. Mackintosh, 'Inigo Jones – theatre architect', *TABS*, xxxi (1973), pp. 99–105

J. Orrell, 'Inigo Jones at the Cockpit', *Shakespeare Survey*, xxx (1977), pp. 157–68

A. Gurr, *The Shakespearean stage, 1574–1642*, 2nd ed. (Cambridge, 1980), pp. 147–50

G. Higgott, 'Inigo Jones in Provence', *Architectural History*, xxvi (1983), p. 31

J. Orrell, *The Theatres of Inigo Jones and John Webb* (Cambridge, 1985), pp. 68–77

M. Edmond, *Rare Sir William Davenant* (Manchester, 1987) pp. 75–6, 130–2

J. Orrell, *The Human stage: English theatre design, 1567–1640* (Cambridge, 1988), pp. 168–84

Stage Designs

Jones's achievement in stage design was no less revolutionary than in architecture. He introduced and perfected a type of stage developed in sixteenth-century Italy, which attempted to create an illusion of reality by means of painted, changeable scenery in a unified perspective scheme. After the Restoration in 1660, the scenic stage replaced the simple apron stage of the Elizabethan and Jacobean playhouses, and became the basis of English dramatic spectacle until the re-emergence of the theatre-in-the-round in the present century.

His earliest stage settings for the masques of Queen Anne of Denmark between 1605 and 1609 consisted of a series of 'pictures' in which the courtly actors played out symbolic roles. Moving sets, derived from medieval pageant cars, carried the actors across the stage, or from an upper, 'celestial' stage, to the 'earthly' stage below. Scenes were changed by withdrawing painted curtains, or by use of a revolving set (*machina versatilis*) (fig. 8). The costumes of the masquers were as important to the spectacle as the scenery, and in the early period were exceptionally lavish (cat. no. 2).

With Prince Henry's patronage of the Court masque from 1609 to 1612 scene changes became more numerous and sophisticated. Instead of curtains, the scenes were painted on flats or shutters divided in the middle and running in grooves on the stage floor (*scena ductilis*). These could be slid apart rapidly, and gave a firmer base for the painted scenery, which for the first time assumed a definite architectural character (cat. nos 7, 8). Sliding shutters were the basis of Jones's mature scenic technology and by the early 1620s he was using a full picture stage framed by a proscenium arch. The scene consisted of three side wings with two or more sliding shutters at the back for changing the scene. Behind these were 'scenes of relieve' (cut-out scenery) and above was an upper stage with seating for masquers, who would appear in a tableau. A variant of the flat side shutter was the angled 'book' wing, which had the inner face canted towards the backshutter to give a deeper, more realistic perspective effect (fig. 88). Derived from Serlio's *Il Secondo libro di perspettiva* (Venice, 1560) it was first used for the setting of the play *Artenice* in 1626, and ten years later for another pastoral, *Florimène* (cat. nos 96, 97). The illusion of recession was enhanced in *Florimène* by the raking of the stage.

By the early 1630s Jones was changing shutters at the sides as well as the back of the stage. The first scene of *Albion's Triumph* (cat. no. 95) gave way to a forum, then to an amphitheatre, and next to 'a pleasant grove of straight trees' with a temple in the background. The most complex of all Jones's changeable perspective scenes was his last, for the masque *Salmacida Spolia* in 1640. John Webb's annotated stage plan in the British Library shows four sets of side wings, each with four movable shutters, four backshutters, a scene of 'relieve' where the King and masquers sat in tableau, and above this a cloud machine in which the Queen descended to the stage.

Movable side shutters led to the complete detachment of the proscenium arch from the standing scene. In the design for a hunt scene of *c.* 1621 the proscenium seems to be incorporated within the front shutter (cat. no. 93), but in *Albion's Triumph* of 1631–2 it is drawn on a separate sheet, the first of several proscenium designs by Jones for masques of this decade, each of which bears allegorical motifs summing up the essential theme of the entertainment.

The enormous technical advance in Jones's stage designs between 1605 and 1640 corresponds with a development in his drafting skills no less remarkable than in the architectural drawings. To the early period, from 1605 to 1613, belong all Jones's watercolour costume designs (cat. nos 2, 10). Thereafter, Jones relied exclusively on pen and brown wash, or pen shading, the latter technique becoming the dominant one in the 1630s. By the very end of this decade, Jones's pen handling is extraordinarily bold and suggestive (cat. no. 98).

Almost all Jones's stage designs were copied from printed sources, but the copying was rarely literal: as with architectural designs Jones often amalgamated two or three sources in a single drawing, tightening the original compositions and classicizing the architectural settings by reproportioning façades and stripping away fussy, Mannerist details. In the early period his borrowings were extremely diverse. He knew of Bernardo Buontalenti's sets and costumes for intermezzi at the Florentine Court in 1589 (cat. no. 10), but drew equally from French Renaissance designs by Rosso Fiorentino or engravings by Jacques Androuet Du Cerceau (cat. no. 8). The main inspiration for his mature stage sets were later Florentine intermezzi by Giulio or Alfonso Parigi, notably *Il Giudizio di Paridi* (1608) (cat. no. 95). French sources, however, remained influential. The most important were the picaresque scenic views of Jacques Callot, which yielded numerous ideas for incidental buildings and backshutters. Another quarry was *Le Livre de la conqueste de la toisin d'or* (1563) by René Boyvin after Léonard Thiry, a suite of ornamental engravings from the School of Fontainebleau which inspired several of Jones's proscenium borders (cat. no. 96). Although the dominant spirit of Jones's late masque designs remained Italian, French engravings enlarged Jones's vocabulary of ornament and range of architectural types and reflect the influence of Henrietta Maria's taste.

G.H.

93 Proscenium and hunt scene, possibly for an unknown masque of 1621

c. 1621

Pen and brown ink with brown wash over graphite and black chalk, the proscenium in pen and dark brown ink over rough black chalk. Squared with scorer and graphite for enlargement, and splashed with brown-red scene-painter's distemper

439 × 461 mm. Single sheet of thick, whitish paper, trimmed at top and bottom. Central vertical fold

Watermark: shield containing bear, surmounted by crown. Beneath is a D above 3 balls: the mark of the Düring family mill, Basle

Chatsworth O & S 110

This large and beautiful drawing is one of a group of forest scenes dated tentatively by Orgel and Strong to the early 1620s, and associated with the Arcadian settings for *Pan's Anniversary or the Shepherds' Holiday* performed 19 June 1620 or (in this case) with an unknown masque of the following January. If correctly dated, the design is Jones's earliest to show a complete set framed by a proscenium arch, and can be related to a plan on one of the accompanying drawings (O & S 111) depicting a shallow stage with three pairs of wings and two sets of moveable backshutters. In the sky of this design is a circle drawn in graphite, indicating the use of an upper stage for a celestial tableau.

The full structure of Jones's scene, however, is far from clear. The wings are very loosely defined, and the proscenium arch is apparently drawn as part of the setting rather than as a detached feature. Vivaciously and suggestively handled, the drawing stands at the beginning of the evolution of Jones's mature stage technology, when the various elements of his changeable perspective scenery were not yet interpreted as distinct facets in his compositions.

94 Scenery design for 'Cupid's Palace' in an unknown masque

After *c.* 1619

Pen and dark brown ink, with pen (or brush) and light brown ink for outer portions of design; graphite under-drawing and squared graphite lines (10 mm apart) over whole sheet for transference

533 × 417 mm. Composite sheet. The central portion showing Cupid's palace is 417 × 280 mm. Overlaid left and right are two strips cut from the same sheet, the left one 412 × 88 mm and the right 410 × 68 mm (including 6 mm overlaps). Overlaid above is a rectangular strip of two pasted sheets, the left one 128 × 254 mm and the right 129 × 169 mm (with 3–8 mm overlaps). Horizontal folds through centre and upper third of whole sheet

Watermark (divided between left- and right-hand strips): complicated shield surmounted by coronet and quatrefoil

Inscribed by John Webb in graphite at bottom centre: *Cupids Pallas*. The *verso* of the central sheet has a sketch in black chalk of a domed hall with three arched openings, framed by an arch. This is inscribed by John Webb in graphite *eaves purple*(?); on left of sheet is a graphite thumbnail stage plan by John Webb inscribed as 51ft 8in. across and 18 ft deep, and also inscribed: *betweene y^e^* [. . .] *of Joyst 38/betwene ye galleries (?) / 43*

Chatsworth O & S 113

The actual masque remains unidentified, but Orgel and Strong comment that it may relate to the lost productions of 1619 and 1621, and that the 'Cupid's Palace' motif would have been apposite at a time when negotiations for a match between Prince Charles and the Spanish Infanta were under way. On grounds of drawing technique, however, the design might be a decade later. The broad pen shading of the flanking buildings and the fine pen outlines of the palace may be compared with designs for *Shepherd's Paradise* of 1632–3 (O & S, 245–74). Moreover, the sketch on the *verso* showing a domed room framed by an apse resembles the interior of a 'Temple with Tombs' from act v, scene 8 of this pastoral play (O & S, ii, p. 329 and O & S 249).

Although Summerson and others have alluded to the relationship of the tripartite arrangement of windows on the Cupid's Palace with designs for the Prince's Lodging at Newmarket Palace in 1619 (cat. nos 30, 31) and the Queen's Chapel at St James's Palace of 1623–5 (fig. 48), Peacock has rightly located the germ of the colonnaded portico idea with an architectural perspective by Vredeman de Vries in *Scenographiae sive perspectivae* (1560). He has also suggested that the urban palace fronts relate to a tragic scene by G. B. Aleotti, published in Ferrara in 1618. But the sources for the palace fronts matter less than the fact that Jones is here working out a design for a grand town house or public building with one and a half storeys spanned by a giant order, of the kind he had intended for the Star Chamber in 1617 (fig. 31). It is also worth observing that the small arched openings in the basements of these façades are similar to those shown on Van Stalbemt and Van Belcamp's painting of the incomplete Queen's House in *c.* 1632 (fig. 16).

Bibliography:

J. Summerson, *Inigo Jones* (Harmondsworth, 1966), pp. 73–4

O & S, ii, pp. 328–9

J. Peacock, 'Inigo Jones's stage architecture and its sources', *The Art Bulletin*, lxiv, no. 2 (June 1982), pp. 209–11

95 Scenery design for the masque *Albion's Triumph* (1632): scene 1: 'A Roman Atrium'

1631

Pen and brown ink with brown wash, over graphite underdrawing and scorelines marking perspective lines to two vanishing points; splashed with greyish-green scene-painter's distemper on left and right

368 × 403 mm. Laid down on thick paper. Central vertical fold, torn in lower half of sheet

Chatsworth O & S 191

The source of this setting of scene 1, 'A Roman Atrium', in this masque of *Albion's Triumph*, is Giulio Parigi's 'Tempio della Pace' in *Il Giudizio di Paridi*, Florence, 1608. Peacock has shown that in matters of the sculptural accompaniments, Jones turned to Lord Arundel's celebrated collection of antique sculpture as source material. The frieze of the colonnades is based upon the Roman fragment of a frieze with heads and consoles, the latter replacing the normal triglyphs, similarly used by Jones for the Chapel Screen at Somerset House at about that time (figs 59, 61). There are other identified sources: the statues between columns seem based upon similar arrangements in Scribonius' *Le Triomphe d'Anvers*, 1550, and some statues are to be found in G. B. Cavalieri's *Antiquarum statuarum urbis Romae* . . . 1585. There is clear allusion here to the superiority of Arundel's collection as well as to the fact that the King had recently acquired the statues from the Gonzaga collection at Mantua. As a Roman triumph in Albion (Great Britain), with Albanactus as the King and Alba the Queen, this allusion to the richness of British collections is understandable. Scene 3 was of a Roman amphitheatre, either borrowed from Panvinius' *De Ludis circensibus*, 1581, or from its original source in an engraving by Du Cerceau. In the printed text Aurelian Townshend wrote, 'Master Inigo Jones and I were employed in the Invention'.

See colour illustration on p. 174

Bibliography:

D. Howarth, *Lord Arundel and his circle* (New Haven and London, 1985), pp. 108–9

J. Peacock, 'Inigo Jones and the Arundel marbles', *The Journal of Medieval and Renaissance Studies*, xvi, no. 1 (1986), pp. 75–90

96 Proscenium and standing scene for the play *Florimène* (1635)

1635

Pen and brown ink over black chalk and graphite

296 × 354 mm. Laid down

Chatsworth O & S 326

Florimène was a French pastoral play performed in honour of the King's birthday by the Queen's Ladies in the Great Hall at Whitehall Palace on 21 December 1635. It was both a dramatic and a spectacular entertainment with five acts separated by intermezzi during which the backshutters of the standing scene parted to reveal cut-out scenes of the Seasons. Drawings of the *Florimène* theatre by John Webb in the British Library include a plan of the stage showing a proscenium arch, four angle wings, three movable backshutters, three scenes of 'relieve' and a backcloth (fig. 88). In Jones's drawing the stage is shown at the beginning of the play, with the first of the backshutters (cat. no. 97) in place. The proscenium arch, incorporating a shepherd and shepherdess playing instruments and a frieze of children enacting pastoral rites and sacrifices, is one of Jones's most fluent masque border designs, and like the standing scene is predominantly French in inspiration. Jones looked at decorative borders in René Boyvin's (after Léonard Thiry's) *Le Livre de la conqueste de la toison d'or* (1563) for the figurative groups and turned to various etchings by Jacques Callot for the rustic cottages among trees in the wings of the standing scene.

Bibliography:

J. Peacock, 'New sources for the masque designs of Inigo Jones', *Apollo*, cvii (February, 1978), pp. 103–4

—, 'The French element in Inigo Jones's masque designs' in D. Lindley (ed.), *The Court masque* (Manchester, 1984), pp. 155–65

J. Orrell, *The Theatres of Inigo Jones and John Webb* (Cambridge, 1985), pp. 128–48

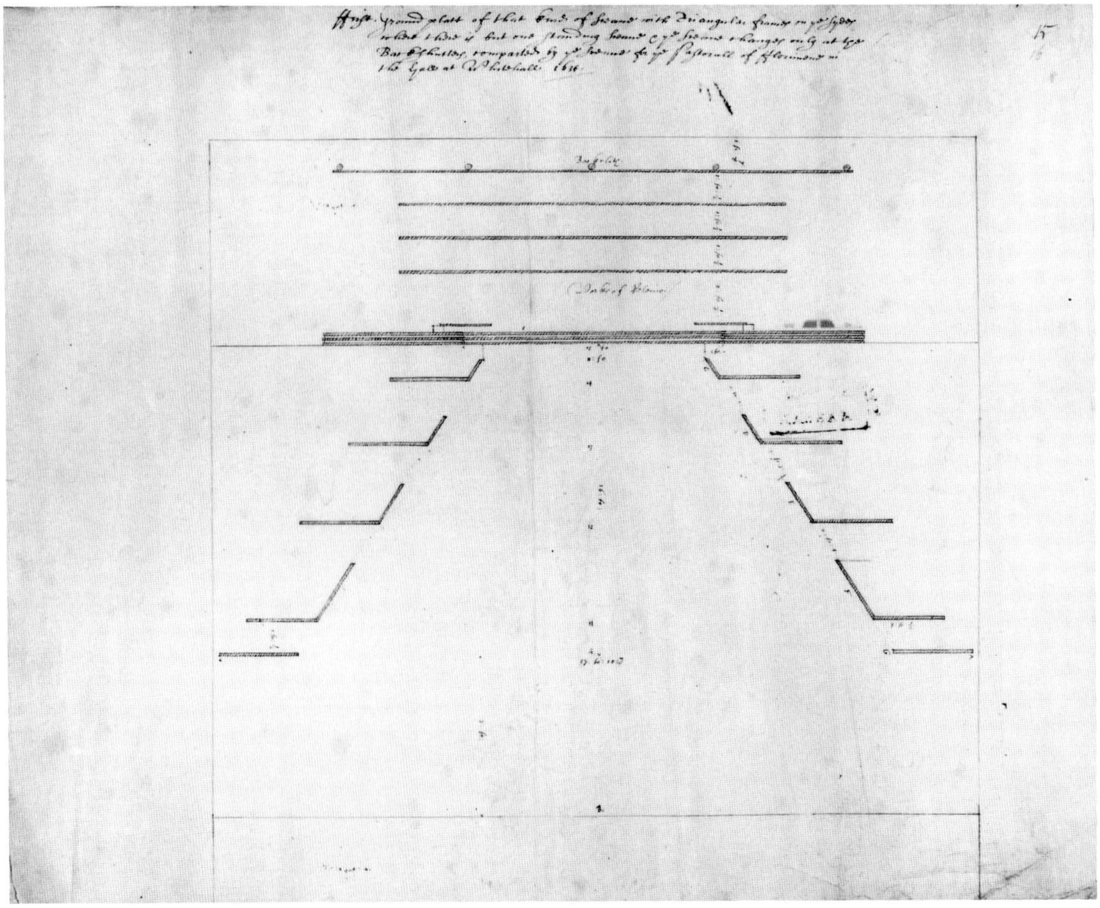

Fig. 88
John Webb. Interpretive plan of the stage for *Florimène* in the Great Hall, Whitehall Palace, 1635

97 Scenery for the play *Florimène* (1635): backshutter for the standing scene: 'The Isle of Delos'; and sketches for figures on the proscenium arch. On *verso* is a right-half sketch for the proscenium and standing scene

1635

Pen and brown ink over black chalk; studies in black chalk, graphite and red chalk; the sheet splashed with blue, green, red, black and white scene-painter's distemper. The sketch on *verso* is in pen and brown ink with black chalk

345 × 231 mm. Trimmed sheet, mounted on frame of paper

Watermark: peacock with spread tail in circle

Inscribed by John Webb in black chalk at top left-hand corner: *the shutter / [o]f the Isle of / [D]elos being for / [t]he standing sceane*; and below in pen and brown ink in an 18th-c. hand: *No. 31*, and below in graphite: △*24*

O & S 327 and (*verso*) 325

This backshutter design accompanies the proscenium and standing scene (cat. no. 96) and is one of the liveliest and most attractive of Jones's masque sketches, not least for conveying the immediacy of the artist at his drawing-table. Splashed with scene-painter's distemper, it demonstrates how Jones's fluid pen-sketching technique in the 1630s allowed him to pass a first draft straight to the craftsmen for full-sized rendering. The two right-hand sketches are studies for the shepherd and shepherdess on the pilasters of the proscenium arch. A study on the *verso* shows the proscenium and standing-scene design in gestation, with loosely grouped cottages and trees and a low horizon line.

See colour illustration on p. 175

98 Costume design for King Charles in the masque *Salmacida Spolia* (1640)

1640

Pen and dark brown ink over black chalk, corrected in places with white gouache

290 × 168 mm. Laid down

Inscribed by Jones in pen and brown ink in bottom left-hand corner: *for ye kinge 1640*

Chatsworth O & S 432

Salmacida Spolia was the final royal masque that the tragic king played in before the outbreak of the Civil War in 1642. Charles was portrayed as Philogenes, the lover of his people, a Divine King whose 'secret wisdom' quelled the forces of disorder. This poignant drawing is one of several preparatory studies for the costumes of the King and masquers, who towards the end of the masque appear in a tableau among 'craggy rocks and inaccessible mountains . . . sitting in the Throne of Honour, his majesty highest in a seat of gold and the rest of the lords about him'. The masque was performed on 21 January 1640 in Jones's temporary masqueing room next to the Banqueting House and was repeated thrice in February.

Figurative Drawings

John Peacock

Figurative design was part of Jones's working routine from 1605 onwards. It was required for the sets and proscenia, and especially the costumes, of the Court masques. Later, particularly during the 1630s, figure drawing was needed for statuary on buildings, for example the west front of the remodelled St Paul's and the Choir Screen at Winchester Cathedral (cat. nos 78, 81). It also contributed to schemes of interior decoration, and there are studies of children or putti where experiments in form merge into decorative programmes for the Queen's House (cat. nos 76, 124). What may be called pure figure drawing only makes a significant appearance in Jones's work in the 1630s; and the majority of the surviving sheets – about 1,800 in all – date from the later 1630s and the 1640s, the last phase of his career.

There are some full-length figures, standing or reclining, and half-lengths, but more instances of single bodily features: eyes, noses, mouths, ears, hands, legs and feet. The majority, however, are studies of heads. These occur singly, in pairs and in groups. Sometimes the pairings and groupings have a formal and psychological rationale, sometimes they are arbitrary, a matter of the artist's convenience – although on the more crowded sheets it can be difficult to make a hard and fast distinction, and, as often happens with drawings of this kind, arbitrary relationships may look intriguing or striking. So it is a pity that many of Jones's original sheets have been cut up, and neighbouring heads separated. John Webb may have begun this, in an attempt to classify the motifs into types, as in the mount of nine female heads, nearly all in three-quarter face looking upwards (cat. nos 100–8). In the same way he classified house-plans, or types of window and other architectural details stemming from Jones and Palladio.

Most of these drawings are now mounted in two volumes at Chatsworth, with a sizeable minority at Worcester College, from which four of our five examples come. But our first exhibit is the Roman Sketchbook, also preserved at Chatsworth, which contains a rich sample of Jones's figure drawing, illuminated by notes and comments (cat. no. 99).

Long before the period to which the drawings belong there is a theoretical space reserved for figuration in his œuvre, waiting to be filled out and populated. There are two overlapping contexts for Jones's figure drawing, and these help to explain its relationship to the rest of his work: Renaissance Vitruvianism, and Vasari's concept of *disegno*. Vitruvius had declared that well-proportioned architecture should follow the proportions of the well-shaped human body,[1] so making the architect a figurative artist in an abstract sense. He pointed out that the units of measurement which the architect used were derived from parts of the body, and claimed that the columns of the classical orders were modelled on different body types.[2] Renaissance architects and theorists, deeply impressed by the Vitruvian analogy, often pushed it further. Palladio wrote that the house, like the body, should have its nobler parts displayed and its meaner parts concealed;[3] Vasari said that a palace should 'represent' the human organism, almost in an allegorical sense;[4] Daniele Barbaro compared the architect drawing a cross-section to a physician, because he can show the anatomy of a building.[5] This idea, somewhere between a metaphor and a doctrine, of architecture as body, links up with the ruling concept of *disegno* developed in the later sixteenth century. Vasari called design the father of the arts,[6] and his *Lives* gave publicity and authority to the Florentine tradition that *disegno* was fundamental to the practice of any art. This doctrine tended to assimilate the arts to each other, and – since Vasari made clear that the elements of *disegno* consisted in learning to represent the human body – to base them all on the discipline of figure drawing.

Jones's response to these ideas can be read in the Roman Sketchbook, in a note on folio 76*v*. dated 19 January 1614 (Old Style, i.e. 1615 New Style):

> As in dessigne first on Sttudies the partes of the boddy of man as Eyees noses mouthes Eares and so of the rest to bee practicke in the partes sepperat ear on comm to put them toggethear to maak a hoole figgure and cloath yt and consequently a hoole Storry wth all ye ornamentes
>
> So in Architecture on must Studdy the Partes as loges Entranses Haales Chambers Staires doures windoues. and then adorrne them wth colloms. Cornishes. sfondati. Stattues. Paintings. Compartimentes. quadraturs. [. . .]

He expounds the primacy of figuration, and the Vitruvian analogy, in terms derived from Alberti, who had written the first Renaissance texts on painting and architecture.[7] Alberti particularly stressed the relation between parts and whole, both in building (which he too compared to a body or natural organism) and in an *historia* – that dramatic, complex figurative narration which he held out to be the painter's highest project. Jones calls it 'Storry', and spells out Alberti's key concept of *compositio*: the combination of surfaces into bodily parts or members, of members into bodies, and of bodies into the total *historia*.[8] This seminal note bears fruit in Jones's much later experiments 'to bee practicke in the partes sepperat' of the human figure.

Of course these experiments came too late in his career to have the results theoretically predicated for them. He never did gain full command of the drawing of the 'whole figure' – as the ungainly anatomy of his nudes shows (cat. no. 67) – let alone the complexities of 'historical' composition. But some of his limitations may have been self-imposed. The drawings hint at a voluntary restriction of scope, as if he wanted to dwell on the study and composition of heads. He often lines them up in close contrasts of profile and character, or sets them apart while at the same time suggesting a kinship (cat. no. 113). There is an elaborate network of cross-references, and certain heads recur or undergo subtle metamorphoses, in the handling or the pose

– quite often being reversed, as seen on the right-hand page which we show from the Sketchbook. These these moves and variations have a fascination of their own, but are also a form of marking time, as if he were foreever detained by an interest in the parts rather than the whole. Perhaps the analytical compulsion is inevitable in the make-up of a classical architect.

But to do Jones full justice, we should stress the wider relation of these drawings not only to his architecture but to his stage design. There is no doubt that he saw figure drawing connected, intrinsically and not just expediently, with costume design for the masques. On various sheets from the 1630s studies of heads, half-lengths or nudes occur alongside masquers' costumes, in what seems symbiotic proximity. Next to a design for Charles I as the emperor Albanactus in *Albion's Triumph* (1632) Jones has sketched (after a print) one of the *ignudi* from the Sistine ceiling;[9] and a sheet showing an exotic headdress for Henrietta Maria in *The Temple of Love* (1635) is shared by various other head studies,[10] including a Venus type recognizable from the Roman Sketchbook and elsewhere in the figurative corpus. These apparently casual associations are full of meaning. Costume designs always ended up as presentation drawings; Jones's experience in figure drawing helped to make his costume designs more than presentable. He could meet, in fact surpass, the demands of the art-loving Stuarts and the connoisseur grandees who dominated their Court, by representing them to themselves (as did Van Dyck) with an idealizing virtuosity studied from the great Italian figurative tradition.

With the same aesthetic power he represented them to the world, or at least to that privileged part of it admitted to watch the masques. Large-scale figurative allegories had to be designed for the proscenium arches – cat. nos 93 and 96 are excellent examples – which he described as 'picture qualified with moral philosophy'.[11] But he came to see the masque scenes altogether as monumental figuration, 'and indeed these shows are nothing else', he wrote, 'but pictures with light and motion'.[12] For Vasari, one of the goals towards which painting progressed was *vivacità*:[13] the *tableaux vivants* of Jones's theatre could realize this ideal literally. So in a sense his figure drawing did lead to grand 'historical' compositions.

But the best of these drawings cannot be logically fitted into Jones's œuvre, since they almost certainly belong to the time when he was *désœuvré*, no longer a Court artist. They are done for aesthetic motives, in pursuit of *la bella maniera*. They follow an instruction he had long ago marked with special approval in his copy of Vasari:

> La maniera venne poi la piu bella, dall' havere messo in uso il frequente ritrarre le cose piu belle; & da quel piu bello o mani, o teste, o corpi, o gambe aggiungerle insieme; & fare una figura di tutte quelle bellezze. . . .[14]
>
> One's style gains in beauty by the frequent practice of copying the most beautiful things, and by combining the finest hands, heads, torsoes and legs, to produce a figure from all those fine features. . . .

This alludes to the story of Zeuxis, the famous painter of antiquity, who composed a Helen from the most beautiful features of various women.[15] Jones wrote a paraphrase in the margin: 'gudd manner cums by Copiinge ye fayrest thinges'. For him, the 'fayrest thinges' in the figurative repertory were certain poses of the head deriving from Raphael and the creative derangement of his work by the first generation of Mannerist painters, especially Parmigianino (1503–40). Jones was fascinated by Parmigianino's etchings, and by the imitations, revisions and pastiches of them made by Schiavone (d. 1563); and in those compositions it is often the posing and relation of the heads which provide a formal dynamic. Jones's studied pose and composed heads in a similar but looser style, without the tension of a thematic programme.

The original themes were as often as not religious ones. Free of their Holy Families and Mystic Marriages, no longer implicated in an overruling divine scheme of things, the heads retain and acquire a singular suggestiveness. Some of them Jones redrew again and again, gradually refining his technique. He tried to soften the outline of the face by defining contours with shading, or redrawing the lines that would otherwise mark a too precise contour. In a few late drawings he painted over outlines with white gouache. Working within a narrow range of motifs, he approached mastery within that range. In figurative design he perfected the drawing of the head, just as in architecture he perfected the design of the gate.

Notes

1. Vitruvius, *The Ten books on architecture*, trans. Morris Hicky Morgan (Harvard, 1914); repr. Dover, New York, 1960), p. 72 (III, i, 1)
2. Ibid., p. 73 (III, i, 5) and pp. 103–4 (IV, i, 6–9)
3. *I Quattro libri*, Book II, p. 3
4. Giorgio Vasari, *Le Opere*, ed. Gaetano Milanesi, 9 vols (Florence, 1878–85), i, p. 146
5. *I Dieci libri*, p. 30
6. Vasari, op. cit., p. 168
7. Jones possessed both printed in the same volume: Leon Battista Alberti, *L'Architettura . . . tradotta in lingua Fiorentina da Cosimo Bartoli. . . . La Pittura tradotta per M. Lodovico Domenichi*, Monreale, 1565
8. Alberti, *On painting and on sculpture*, ed. and trans. Cecil Grayson (London, 1972), p. 71f.
9. O & S 204; engraving, by Adamo Scultori, repr. Stefania Massari, *Incisori mantovani del '500* (Rome, 1980), p. 53, no. 62 [but illustration erroneously numbered 63]
10. O & S 316
11. O & S, ii, p. 730, line 67; the phrase occurs in the text of Davenant's *Salmacida Spolia*, the descriptive part of which Davenant ascribes to Jones
12. O & S, ii, p. 480, lines 49–50, in Aurelian Townshend's *Tempe Restored*, the descriptive parts here too ascribed to Jones
13. Vasari, op. cit. iv, pp. 12–13
14. Vasari, *Delle Vite de' piu eccellenti pittori scultori et architettori. . . . primo volume della terza parte*, (Florence, 1568) [Jones's copy at Worcester College], sig. *****2 *verso*
15. The story is told in Pliny, *Historia Naturalis*, XXXV, 64

99 Roman Sketchbook

Opened at folios 9*v*. and 10*r*. showing studies of heads, in pen and brown ink over black chalk (later 1630s)

Quarto volume (203 × 133 mm) in limp vellum, rebound probably in 19th c. in original bindings, using newer paste-downs and 2 fly leaves at front and back. 89 unnumbered folios, excluding the 4 fly leaves. Three of four original leather tags survive

Folio size: 198 × 130 mm. Some folios missing. Folio 26 torn off near binding (32 mm wide), folio 29 trimmed at edge (104 mm wide)

Watermarks: bird standing on three mounds some with the initials S.M. at the sides of the mounds. Italian paper, perhaps made by the Mariotti family of the Fabriano paper mill

Inscribed by Jones in pen and brown ink on fol. 1 *recto*: *Roma: / Altro diletto che Imparar non trouo / Inigo Jones / 1614. /*; and below, in pen and brown ink, probably by John Talman, the code marks: *245:* , and below, in same hand: *This Book Containeth 29: Pages each full of / Drawings*. Folio 9*v*. inscribed by Jones in pen and brown ink at top: *thes heades looking dounwardes have binn hild hard to doo / but if the ~~purfile or~~* [*sic*] *designe & outerlines bee well understoode it is as / easi as thos in purfile this must bee lerned from the life and / heades in relieuo*; and below middle left-hand female head: *thes heades in purfile are / in remenbrance of y[e] venus / gidio* [*sic*] *and Joue iṇ tolomais / medaile*. Folio 10*r*. inscribed by Jones in pen and brown ink above central head: *dell polidor / in dessegnio*.

The sketchbook has 31 pages of pen and brown ink figurative sketches on both sides of folios scattered throughout the volume, a sketch in graphite of a section through a dome (fol. 9*v*.), a slight sketch in black chalk of a group of trees and a church with a Hertfordshire spike (fol. 69*v*.), and a pen and brown ink sketch of the poop of an antique ship, among notes on that subject (fol. 77*v*.), all by Jones. At the beginning of the book are 4 folios of pen and brown ink notes on drapery and types of antique clothing (fols 2–5), dated 21 January 1614. The longest sequence of notes is from fols 14 to 19 inclusive, dated 20 and 24 February (1614; New Style), which are copied from Palladio's *L'Antichità di Roma* (Venice, 1588). There are two groups of notes translated from Lomazzo's *Trattato dell'arte, della pittura, scoltura, et architettura* (Milan, 1585), on the proportions of children (fols 22*v*., 32*v*.) and colouring (fols 73*v*., 74*r*.). Folio 76*r*. and *v*. has notes dated 20 and 19 January 1614 (Old Style, i.e. 1615) respectively; another note (on antique ships) of the same period is on fols 77*v*. and 80*r*. The remaining folios are blank. Other blank folios include 35–44 and 53–62.

Chatsworth (unnumbered)

The key to the Roman Sketchbook is Jones's motto, inscribed at the beginning, 'Altro diletto che Imparar non trouo', 'I find no other pleasure than learning'. This is adopted from Barbaro's commentary on Vitruvius (p. 32), but it has a more fundamental context in antiquity: Aristotle's discussion of *mimesis* in the *Poetics*. To account for the pleasure which human beings take in imitation Aristotle explains it as a means of knowledge. Nearly everything in the Roman Sketchbook, whether written or drawn, is copied; and imitation is central to all Jones's work. In referring to the unique pleasure of learning, the motto implicitly characterizes the contents of the book, as exercises in acquiring knowledge through imitation. The two leaves which we show make sense in precisely these terms: using models from the work of other artists, Jones practises drawing the head in different and sometimes difficult poses.

Strictly speaking, 'Roman Sketchbook' is a misnomer. The book was begun in Rome, but also used later in Jones's career; and as well as sketches or drawings it also contains notes and longer prose passages. Gordon Higgott's study of Jones's handwriting and graphic style, together with some dates and other external evidence, make it possible to distinguish two periods of use. In Rome in 1614, Jones made notes on the representation of drapery, especially in antique costume, and the design of 'Chariotes and Poops of anticke shipes'; he seems to have had one eye on antiquity as such, and the other on pastiche *all' antica* for modern Court festivals. Elsewhere in the book he translated passages on the topography of ancient Rome from Palladio. Most interesting are two pages of personal reflection on architectural design, dated 19 and 20 January 1614 (Old Style, i.e. 1615 New Style), when he was back in London (see above, pp. 55–6, 284–5). In the 1630s he returned to the book, adding passages translated from Lomazzo (on the proportions of children, and the colours to use in representing the four traditional complexions or humours), and a wide range of drawings. Some of these are copied from original sheets by Raphael, Perino del Vaga and Polidoro da Caravaggio. Others are copied from the drawing manuals of the early seventeenth century, by Odoardo Fialetti, Palma Giovane and Guercino, which show how to draw parts of the body at different stages of realization, and how to draw the head in foreshortening with the aid of simple linear schematisations. Jones turned the analytical approach of the manuals back on to two ambitious compositions or *historie* of the sixteenth century: Bandinelli's *Martyrdom of St Laurence*, engraved by Marcantonio and lavishly praised by Vasari, and Michelangelo's *Last Judgment*, engraved by Martino Rota. He exerpted figures, heads, hands and feet, and studied them individually. The same analysis was made of smaller compositions

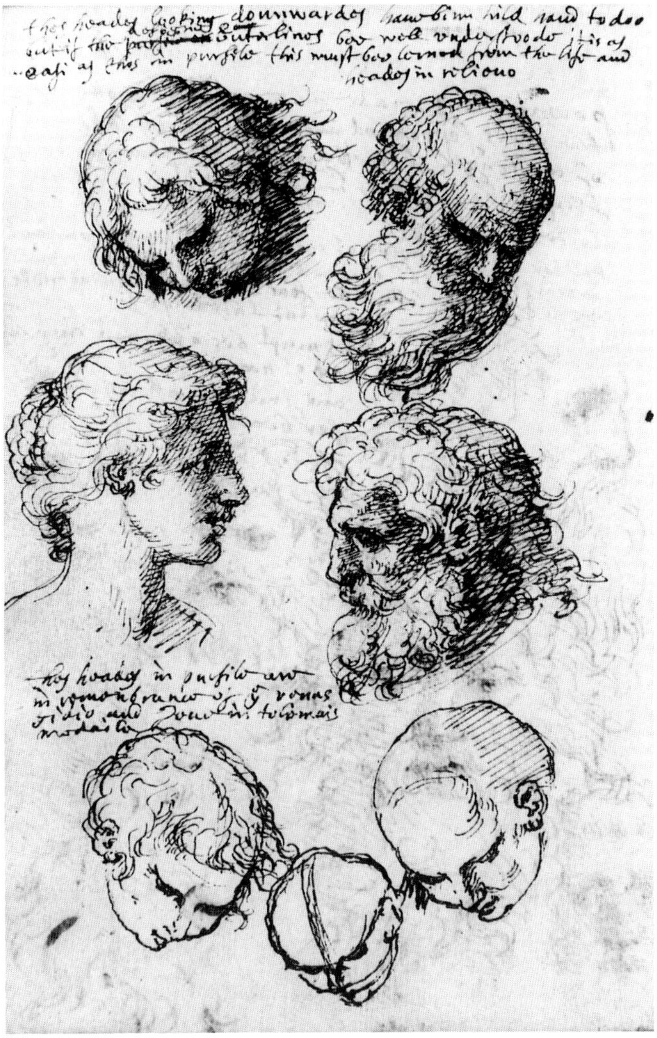

in the etchings of Parmigianino and Schiavone. In one respect, the book is a breviary of Jones's figurative design.

Our two sheets show studies of heads, important here as elsewhere in Jones's figurative work. Folio 9*v*., on the left, contains two antique profiles – Zeus, from a Hellenistic medal (possibly in Charles I's collection ?), and the Venus of Cnidos, 'the most beautiful statue in the world', according to Pliny. Around these classic norms it concentrates on one modern problem, 'heads looking downwards'. The head top left and the three at the foot of the page are all the same, one posed in reverse. The schematized outline (it recurs a few pages on) is adapted from Fialetti, and is gradually realized more fully in the other versions.

The opposite folio has two principal heads. The full face at lower right recurs on a later page as 'Venus Cnidio' – another pose of the Venus of Cnidos' head. The head looking down top right is taken from a Polidoro drawing of the Annunciation; the original, or a version, is now in the Louvre. Jones has varied it twice, reversing the pose and elongating the neck. He is using an analytical method inspired by the academic classicism of the seventeenth century on earlier Mannerist figure imagery, with intriguing results. The pleasure taken in learning is of a rather sophisticated kind.

John Peacock

Bibliography:

E. H. Gombrich, *Art and illusion* (3rd ed., London, 1968), ch. V, section V: 'On German, Italian, Netherlandish drawing books'

Vincenza Maugeri, 'I manuali propedeutici al disegno, a Bologna e Venezia, agli inizi del Seicento', *Musei Ferrarese 1982, Bollettino Annuale 12* (Florence, 1984), pp. 147–56

Joan Sumner Smith, 'The Italian sources of Inigo Jones's style', *Burlington Magazine*, xciv (1952), pp. 200–7

100 Female head in three-quarter view, looking up to right

1630s

Pen and brown ink

102 × 81 mm. Laid down

Worcester College H & T 72, Mount 7(a)

101 Female head with veil over her hair, looking up to right

1630s

Pen and brown ink

69 × 61 mm. Laid down

Worcester College H & T 72, Mount 7(b)

102 Female head in three-quarter view, looking up to left

1630s

Pen and brown ink

92 × 85 mm. Laid down

Worcester College H & T 72, Mount 7(c)

103 Female head in three-quarter view, looking up to right

1630s

Pen and brown ink over black chalk

71 × 49 mm. Laid down

Worcester College H & T 72, Mount 7(d)

104 Female head in three-quarter view, looking up to left

1630s

Pen and brown ink over black chalk

93 × 104 mm. Sheet cut away by 15 mm on upper half of left side. Laid down

Worcester College H & T 72, Mount 7(e)

105 Female head in three-quarter view, looking to right

1630s

Pen and brown ink

67 × 45 mm. Laid down

Worcester College H & T 72, Mount 7(f)

106 Female head in three-quarter view, looking up to right

1630s

Pen and brown ink

102 × 75 mm. Sheet cut away by 10–12 mm on lower half of left side. Laid down

Worcester College H & T 72, Mount 7(g)

107 Two female heads in three-quarter view, one seen from behind

1630s

Pen and brown ink

65 × 90 mm. Laid down

Worcester College H & T 72, Mount 7(h)

108 Female head in three-quarter view, looking to right

1630s

Pen and brown ink. Laid down

103 × 62 mm. Laid down

Worcester College H & T 72, Mount 7(i)

These nine studies of female heads may have been cut from larger sheets of multiple figure studies by John Webb in the 17th century. They are on 18th-century secondary supports and were mounted together in the present century. All are copied or derived form 16th-century Italian sources. The top left head is taken from an engraving by Cherubino Alberti, after one of Raphael's frescoes of the *Legend of Cupid and Psyche* in the Villa Farnesina in Rome (*c.* 1511) showing Venus with Juno and Ceres (Jones's head is the Venus; see Bartsch XVII.84.106), while the next head on the right (cat. no. 109) is a variant of the Virgin's head from Parmigianino's etching, *The Annunciation* (repr. J. Sumner Smith, figs 20, 21; Bartsch XVI.6.2). The central study (cat. no. 104) illustrates Jones's sensitive handling of light and shade through variations in the thickness and spacing of hatched lines. Broader-spaced lines beneath the cheek suggest the shadow being modified by reflected light.

Bibliography:

A. von Bartsch, *Le Peintre graveur*, 21 vols (Vienna, 1803–21)

J. Sumner Smith, 'The Italian sources of Inigo Jones's style', *Burlington Magazine*, xciv (1952), pp. 200–7

109 Study for the three ages of woman, in side, frontal and three-quarter views

1630s(?)

Pen and brown ink

97 × 199 mm. Sheet trimmed unevenly on left

Worcester College H & T 72, Mount 9(a)

110 Studies of five heads, including bust of woman with hand to chest

Late 1630s

Pen and brown ink

140 × 179 mm. Laid down on thick paper with pencil border

Worcester College H & T 72, Mount 9(b)

111 Group of six heads in black chalk and graphite

1630s

Graphite reinforced with black chalk or charcoal

72 × 198 mm. Laid down on thick paper with pencil border

Worcester College H & T 72, Mount 9(c)

Crowded head studies are typical of Jones's mature figurative technique. In the middle sheet he used vigorous horizontal pen shading to bind the composition together. The bottom drawing combines black chalk or charcoal with the harder and greyer graphite medium in the manner of some of his architectural drawings (e.g. cat. no. 15). The top study, showing the Three Ages of Woman (or possibly the three Fates), seems to depend on the same source as the bust in cat. no. 112.

112 Head of man looking down, bust of woman in three-quarter view, detail of hand and part of face (rest cut off)

1630s

Pen and brown ink over graphite

208 × 182 mm. Laid down

Worcester College H & T 72, Mount 1(a)

Studies of heads looking down and bearded heads with flowing hair are a preoccupation in notes and sketches in the Roman Sketchbook (cat. no. 99). The bearded man comes from an engraving by Ugo da Carpi, after Parmigianino's chiaroscuro woodcut, *Diogenes*. The right-hand figure, possibly of a boy rather than a woman, should be compared with the central bust of cat. no. 109.

Bibliography:

A. von Bartsch, *Le Peintre graveur*, 21 vols (Vienna, 1803–21), XII.100.10

113 Group of eight heads in various positions, and on *verso*, group of seven heads including half-length female nude figure

1630s

Pen and brown ink

191 × 307 mm. Backed by modern paper frame, 10–15 mm wide all round

Watermark: water-pot inscribed DV and surmounted by a crescent moon

Worcester College H & T 72, Mount 1(b)

This is one of the most beautiful of all Jones's figurative sheets and illustrates his methods of extemporizing on printed sources by redrawing the same head in a variety of poses. On the *recto* sheet, showing eight heads, the frontal head near the centre is turned in a downward three-quarter view immediately to the right, while the profile next on the right is modified in the two larger profiles at the edge of the sheet. On the *verso* (fig. 89) the head of the half-length figure is repeated in reverse on the left and is possibly from the same source as the head directly below.

See colour illustration on p. 176

Fig. 89
Sketches of seven heads on the *verso* of cat. no. 113, 1630s

The Courtier or Subordinate Style, 1615–50

John Harris

Despite Jones's example and the sophistication of royal buildings from 1615 to 1640 due to his grip upon standards of design, few courtiers (out of very many) sought his services, and no-one from the trading or banking classes. In fact the term 'courtier style', as far as Jones is concerned, is a misnomer. As a great house such as Blickling Hall, Norfolk, demonstrates, here was an old-fashioned design for Lord Chief Justice Hobart as late as 1623. The gap between Hobart and Arundel was a yawning one.

The 'Dutch House' at Kew (fig. 90) may be a virtuoso performance in cut brick, but for 1631 it can only be described as 'Artisan', and is an accurate measure of the type of country-house favoured by the merchant classes and the gentry. Swakeleys in Middlesex, built in 1638 for a Lord Mayor of London, is another. Engraved Italianate elements may be recognizable, but the translation is crude and one marvels that such a house was built in the very year of Jones's minimal design for Lord Maltravers (cat. no. 84). The term 'Artisan Mannerist' has been invented for Swakeleys and many houses like it, and this implies that the rules of design are broken in ignorance of what was proper.

Through the 1630s to the 1650s, there is a multitude of these 'Artisan Mannerist' or (as I prefer) 'Subordinate', houses that borrow the scrolled and pedimented gable, and the pergolas or balconies, from those early courtier houses in London which Jones designed between 1615 and 1619. These were the houses, like Lady Cooke's in Holborn, that John Smythson examined with care when he came to London from Nottingham in 1619. Nearly all the exit streets (fig. 91) from Covent Garden after 1630 were sequences of gabled and balconied fronts, not unlike a street in Augsburg. Isaac de Caus may well have been responsible, if not Edward Carter.

But what of the 1620s, that richly productive decade demarcated by the Prince's Lodging at Newmarket Palace and the works at Somerset House? Surprisingly, we can almost seek in vain for buildings that might come up to the standards of Jones's revolution in the Office of Works. Even a high courtier such as the Marquis of Buckingham who had employed Jones at New Hall in Essex in 1622–3, was ambivalent in matters of good and bad in design, for in 1627–8 Sir Balthazar Gerbier gave him a thoroughly subordinate front to York House (fig. 92). It could only be described as 'Artisan Italianate', with its ill-proportioned attached giant order, secondary wall spaces punctuated by oval windows, and crude pilastered attic. Gerbier would have us believe it compared favourably with the Banqueting House; in fact it was a mockery of it.

Only one house after 1620 can be truly described as Jonesian: Raynham Hall, Norfolk, building slowly and empirically from 1621 (fig. 93). It is magisterial, and alludes so strongly to designs by Jones,

Fig. 90
The 'Dutch House', Kew Gardens, London, *c.* 1631

Fig. 91
View of James Street exiting north from Covent Garden, by an unknown French painter, *c.* 1640

Fig. 92
York House, Westminster. Detail of drawing by Jacob Esselens of Sir Balthazar Gerbier's front of 1627–8

Fig. 93
Raynham Hall, Norfolk *c.* 1621–35

Fig. 94
Sir John Danvers's house at Chelsea, *c.* 1622–3, drawn by John Aubrey, 1691

Fig. 95
Kirby Hall, Northamptonshire, north range by Nicholas Stone, 1638

Fig. 96
An unknown house in the Stone style, a family residence of Mary Fairfax, Duchess of Buckingham. Detail from portrait of Mary Fairfax by John Michael Wright, after 1657

that Jones would not have disavowed it as his own. However, its owner Sir Roger Townshend had visited Newmarket Palace, and one suspects connived with Jones, if only with his designs in the drawing office.

Apart from Raynham, and the circumstances of its birth are exceptional, only one other house can command respect: Sir John Danvers's at Chelsea, building about 1622–3 (fig. 94). John Aubrey recollected that its garden was the third in England of the great pre-Civil War layouts in the Italianate taste. Wilton House was the other, and the third was Danvers's at Lavington in Wiltshire. The façade of Chelsea was the first example in England to be described as Serlian, based upon elements found in Serlio's treatise. This is the style of Elias Holl in Augsburg, and was the trademark in the 1630s of Nicholas Stone. The front is composed of an arrangment of circular and oval voids with a crypto-Palladian window, all concentrated upon the central frontispiece which projects both upwards and forwards. It is tempting to attribute this to Jones, but it rather breathes the invention of an amateur genius, perhaps Danvers himself.

If houses such as Fulke Greville's or Sir Edward Cecil's motivate the later true courtier style, Danvers's is the model for a type of house that was not a parody of Jones by virtue of ignorant imitation, but one that had an authority in its own right. There is a danger in responding to a house by Nicholas Stone by demoting it by comparison with Jones's pure Italianism. Out of Danvers's Chelsea emerges a robust and indiosyncratic country-house style characterized by Stone's north range of Kirby Hall, Northamptonshire, 1638 (fig. 95), the unidentified house in the background of a portrait of Mary Fairfax, Duchess of Buckingham, painted after 1657 (fig. 96), and Tart Hall, Westminster, built by Stone for the Countess of Arundel in 1638, if that is the house shown in a composition representing *Spring* engraved by Hollar in 1643 (fig. 97). Both Kirby and the Buckingham (or Fairfax) house have frontispieces that are grander versions of Danvers's. Tart Hall is a good example of the fashion for the uneven grouping of windows of various shapes, combined with pergolas and 'Dutch' gables.

This Serlian fashion for juggling with uneven layers of windows can be also be observed on the front that remains from the early 1630s

Fig. 97
Tart Hall, Westminster(?) by Nicholas Stone, 1638. Detail from engraving by Wenceslaus Hollar, appearing in *Spring*, 1643

Fig. 98
Woburn Abbey, Bedfordshire. North front, probably by Isaac de Caus, early 1630s

Fig. 99
Isaac de Caus. Design for a reduced version of the south front of Wilton House, Wiltshire, *c.* 1636

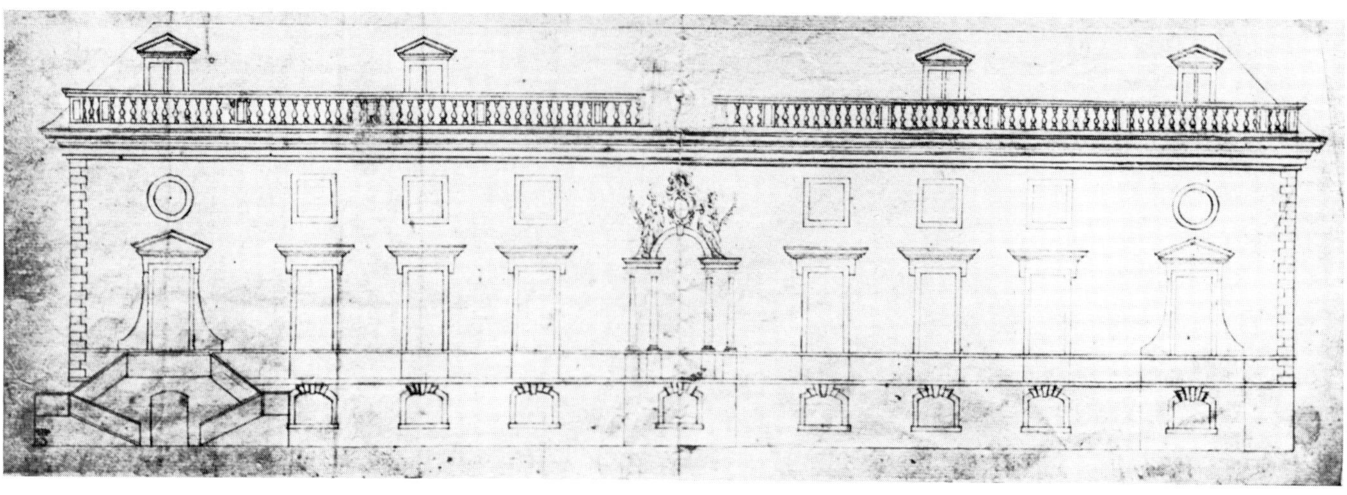

Fig. 100
Chevening, Kent, before 1630(?), from an estate map, 1679

Fig. 101
Castle Ashby, Northamptonshire, the screen front, *c.* 1636

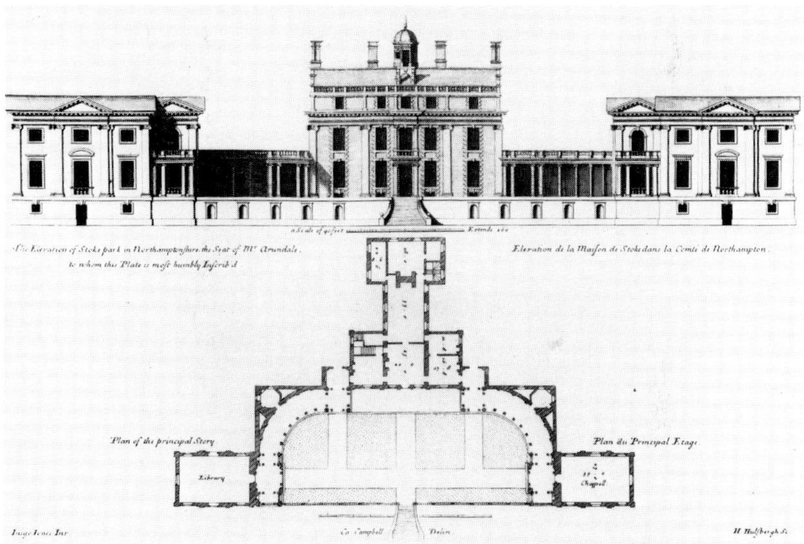

Fig. 102
Stoke Bruerne, Northamptonshire, *c.* 1630. Engraving from Colen Campbell's *Vitruvius Britannicus, ii*, 1717

rebuilding of Woburn Abbey, Bedfordshire (fig. 98), attributed to Isaac de Caus by virtue of his grotto behind it. De Caus was then acting for the Earl of Bedford at Covent Garden, and so was Edward Carter, building Jones's church there, and soon to be his deputy in rebuilding old St Paul's Cathedral. Both de Caus and Carter explode the myth of Jones as the sole renovator of the country-house.

There is now no doubt that de Caus designed the famous south front at Wilton House long venerated as a masterwork by Jones. It was begun in 1636, gutted by fire in 1647, and renovated by Webb from 1649 when he made it into a Palladian tower house. In any case we can now recognize that de Caus's front (fig. 99) speaks a quite different language to that of Jones. What is precious about Wilton is not the front, but Webb's surviving state rooms, for they are all that we possess to remind us of the ambience of the kind of rooms lived in by King Charles and Queen Henrietta Maria (fig. 103).

Carter's claim to reassessment is even greater than de Caus's. His unexecuted design for William Trumbull at East Hampstead Lodge, Berkshire, was made after 1626. It stands alone, outside of Jones's office, for its classical purity and is singular in being derived from Rubens's *Palazzi di Genova*, published in 1622. It is tempting to attribute to Carter Chevening in Kent (fig. 100), said to have been built for the 13th Lord Dacre, who died in 1630. Chevening is also Genoese in feeling with its tall silhouette, balustraded platform, and massive architectonic chimney-shafts. Now that Carter has been identified as the London 'surveyor' for building the famous screen front at Castle Ashby, Northamptonshire, in 1636 (fig. 101), another myth has been exploded. Thus Carter emerges as an architect who demands respect.

When Campbell perpetuated this myth of the universal Jones in his trilogy of *Vitruvius Britannicus* he threw in the cross-wing of Cobham Hall, Kent, built by Peter Mills in 1661; Stoke Bruerne, Northamptonshire (fig. 102), for which one must now believe family tradition that Sir Francis Crane 'brought the design from Italy, and in the execution of it received the assistance of Inigo Jones' about 1630; and four major buildings by John Webb: Amesbury Abbey, Wiltshire, *c.* 1658 (fig. 104), Gunnersbury House, Middlesex, *c.* 1659 (fig. 105), the New Gallery of Somerset House, 1662 (fig. 106), and the King Charles II Block at Greenwich, 1664.

Webb is the one exception in the whole of Jones's career of an architect who was not incomprehending of his canon of design. His design for Hale Park, Hampshire, in 1638 is uniquely Jonesian in style. Yet the tragedy of Webb is that the Civil War denied him the success that he deserved as the continuator of Jones's Palladianism. Despite the stark contrast between such distinguished buildings as The Vyne, Hampshire, 1654, Lamport Hall, Northamptonshire, 1655, Belvoir Castle, Rutland, 1655, as well as Amesbury and Gunnersbury, with the great mass of Artisan-Mannerist houses, Webb's works might just as well have never existed for all the influence they exerted. Despite Greenwich and the New Gallery at Somerset House as Webb's claim to carry the Palladian style of his beloved master into the Court of Charles II, Palladianism was to be out in the cold for the next fifty years. Poor Webb would enjoy an anonymous and posthumous triumph when his buildings acted as a powerful stimulus on the neo-Palladians in the name of Inigo Jones.

Fig. 103
The Double Cube Room, Wilton House, renovated by John Webb from 1649

Fig. 104
Amesbury Abbey, Wiltshire, by John Webb, *c.* 1658. Engraving from Campbell's *Vitruvius Britannicus*, iii, 1725

Fig. 105
Gunnersbury House, Middlesex, by John Webb, *c.* 1659. Engraving from Campbell's *Vitruvius Britannicus*, i, 1715

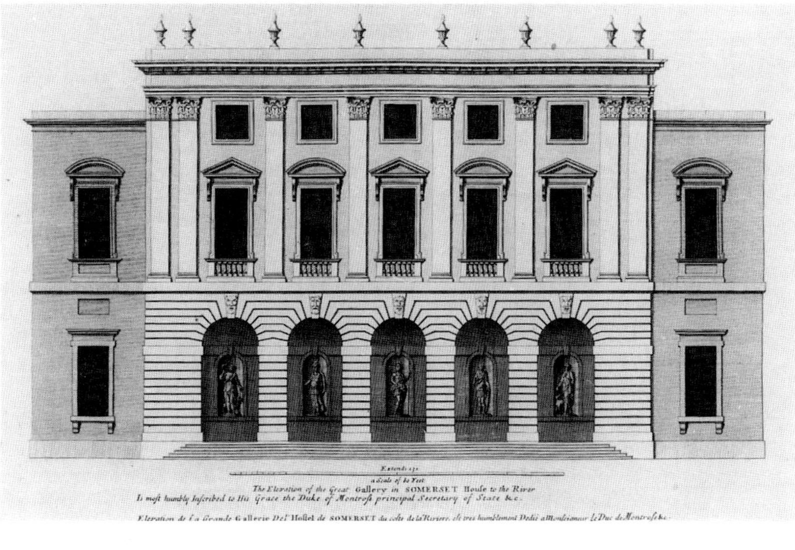

Fig. 106
The New Gallery, Somerset House, London, by John Webb, 1662. Engraving from Campbell's *Vitruvius Britannicus*, i, 1715

Appendix

Unexhibited Drawings arranged chronologically

114 Elevation for an arched doorway with voussoired surround, probably for the entrance-bay design of 1616 (cat. no. 21)

c. 1616

Pen and dark brown ink over scorelines

340 × 264 mm. Central horizontal fold

Watermark: faint, elaborate coat of arms surmounted by a coronet

Signed in bottom right-hand corner with the initial flourish of Inigo Jones's signature (rest cut off); cf. cat. no. 21

Scale: 1 ft = approx. $\frac{27}{32}$ in.

RIBA Jones & Webb 74

The voussoired surround is similar to that on the unidentified entrance-bay design of 1616 (cat. no. 21), and the initial flourish of Jones's signature in the bottom right-hand corner is the same on both drawings. This complicated flourish embodies four intertwined letters 'EXDE', signifying 'Examined' (i.e. an approved fair copy), and only occurs in Jones's signatures from 1616 to 1618 (cf. cat. nos 17, 18).

The technique is characteristic of 1616, having heavy under-scoring in a sharp point, a mixture of freehand and ruled straight lines marked by blotting and fading, and loosely handled pen shading. This type of voussoired doorway derives from Serlio and was favoured by Jones for basement entrances up until about 1630 (e.g. cat. nos 30, 31).

115 Elevation for a doorway with quoin and voussoir surround

c. 1617

Pen and dark brown ink over scorelines; black chalk additions at top

358 × 297 mm. Trimmed at top; central horizontal fold

Watermark: same as cat. no. 39; very similar to cat. no. 19

RIBA Jones & Webb 86

Although only a bare outline, this drawing can be linked in time, if not in place, with the designs for gateways at Oatlands Palace in 1617 (cat. nos 17–19). It has the heavy, experimental scorelines of dated drawings between about 1616 and 1618, and blotting, fading and overlapping in the ruled outlines. Apart from the gateways to the Vineyard, Privy Garden and park, the works at Oatlands included a 'wall about the new garden', for which no gateways are mentioned, though one or more must have been built.

Bibliography:
King's Works, iv, p. 213

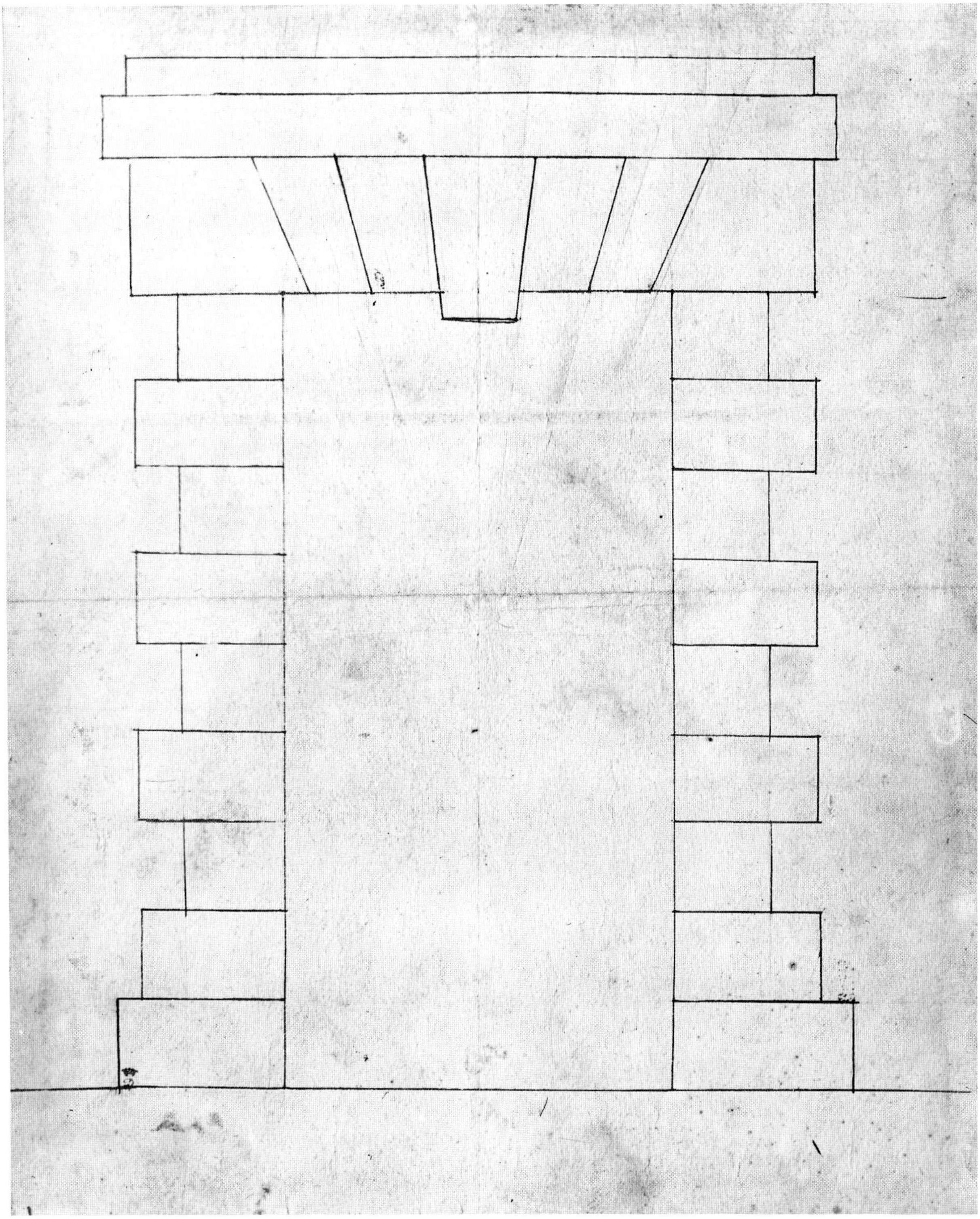

116 Elevation for an arched entrance in a wall, probably for the garden at Arundel House, Strand, London

c. 1618

Pen and grey-brown ink over scorelines

360 × 246 mm

RIBA Jones & Webb 87

A date soon after 1617 can be inferred from the technique of this simple elevation. All the straight lines are ruler-drawn and there is a tidier, more evenly handled style of penmanship than in the Oatlands Palace gateway designs of 1617 (cat. nos 17–19). Typical of the 1616–19 period are the heavy scorelines and the blotting and fading in the outlines. Jones designed two garden gateways at Arundel House the year after his Oatlands designs. John Smythson's plan of the Arundel House garden shows the Doric 'Italyan' gateway at the right end and another entrance opposite (cat. no. 40, fig. 41). He drew this second gateway on another sheet at the RIBA (fig. 107), and it appears in the background of Daniel Mytens' portrait of Aletheia, Countess of Arundel, at Arundel Castle, Sussex. Smythson depicts a rusticated arch with keystones and imposts topped by a plain fascia and three finials. Apart from the finials, Jones's design closely resembles the gate in Smythson's drawing. It has an arched opening of similar proportion to that on the Arundel House Doric gate design, and the same provision for the gate to be set in full-height flanking walls. Like the Doric design it also has a scored semi-circle around the arch, half a masonry block outwards from the opening. These scorelines seem to have indicated the wider, outer arches of each gateway, as shown in the ground-plans of the gates in Smythson's plan of the garden. The design is, then, a missing pair for cat. no. 40 and must also have been drawn in 1618.

Fig. 107
John Smythson. Record drawing of a rusticated gateway in the garden of Arundel House, Strand, London, 1619

Bibliography:
R. Strong, *The Renaissance garden in England* (London, 1979), pp. 170–4

117 Ground-plan and elevation of the front of a town house (on *verso* of a design for the 'Entry of the Augurs preceded by the Poets', for *The Masque of Augurs*, 1622)

1621

Pen and brown ink; *recto* design, pen and brown ink with brown wash over graphite

230 × 376 mm. Laid down. Sheet trimmed at bottom, cutting off top of plan (drawn upside down to *recto* design)

Chatsworth O & S 117

This is perhaps one of the most compelling designs to be used as evidence of Jones's interest in north European, particularly Augsburgian, gabled town houses, drawn on the *verso* of Orgel and Strong 117, the scene of the 'Entry of the Augurs preceded by the Poets' for *The Masque of Augurs*, performed January 1622, and again the following May. Jones provided a rough sketch of a plan, and a more detailed sketch of an elevation (the drawing is now regrettably laid down). The plan could be interpreted as follows: the line-up of spaces on the left represent some passageway with columnar screens lighting by three windows the room with the large chimney-piece on the right. This might account for the two entrances and explain the dilemma of trying to interpret this as a design for a pair of houses. A combination of domestic and commercial use is suggested. For the elevation Jones proposed on the ground floor paired entrances with a form of tripartite window in between; then a similar arrangement on the first floor where the central light is clearly pedimented; and a similar fenestration above. There is a large, broad projecting cornice with attic above and a pedimented gable. Both first and second floors have pergolas set (unusually) right across the façade. Jones is here proposing a characteristic tall four-storey house of the type found in Augsburg, or indeed any north European city. There are direct connections back to Fulke Greville's house in London of *c.* 1617 (cat. no. 22), and forward to the balconied centre-piece of the design for a seven-window house of the late 1630s (cat. no. 87).

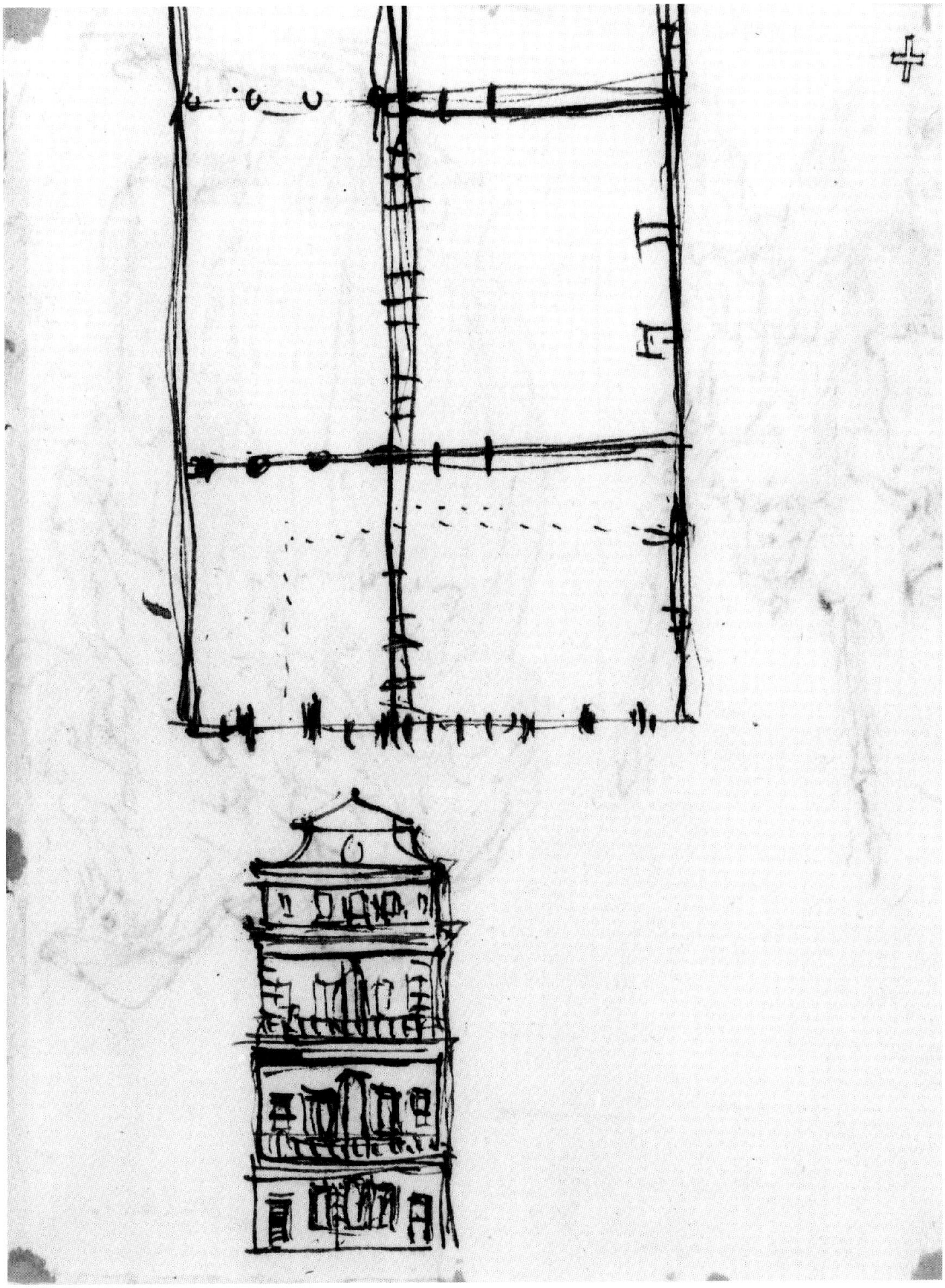

118 Sketch elevation for a three-storeyed bay, probably for the rear staircase bay of Sir Peter Killigrew's house, Blackfriars, London

c. 1630

Pen and dark brown ink over black chalk or charcoal and graphite

310 × 209 mm. Unevenly trimmed sheet of thin, grainy paper

Watermark: water-pot surmounted by four lobes, a quatrefoil and ring motif, and marked with a crescent moon above AB

Worcester College H & T 70

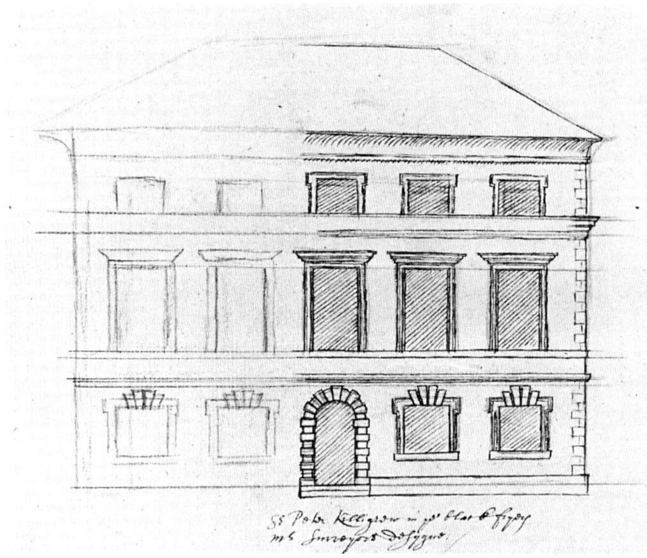

Fig. 108
John Webb. Copy elevation of Inigo Jones's design of *c.* 1630 for Sir Peter Killigrew's house, Blackfriars, London, 1640s(?)

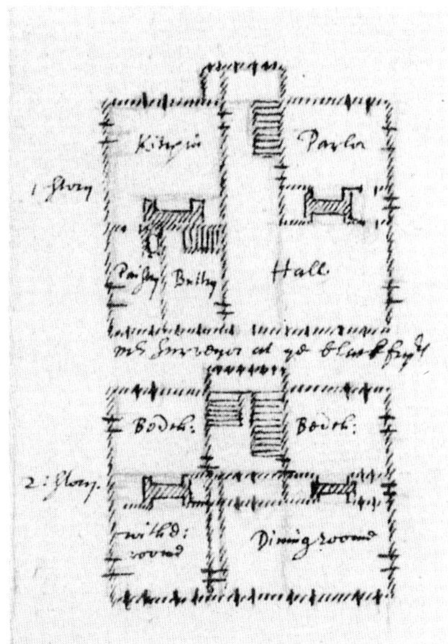

Fig. 109
John Webb. Copy plans from Jones's design for Sir Peter Killigrew's house

Jones's designs for Sir Peter Killigrew's house are known from copies by John Webb at Worcester College of the elevation (fig. 108), the ground- and first-floor plans (fig. 109), and several of the windows (fig. 110). John Newman has pointed out that this sketch corresponds in its floor divisions and architectural treatment to Webb's copy of the façade of Sir Peter Killigrew's house, and that the openings on the ground and first floor of the bay are similar to those of the rear staircase bay in Webb's thumbnail plans. Webb's first-floor plan of the stair turret (the lower of his two sketches) shows three equal openings. That these may indicate a Venetian window of the type in Jones's drawing seems to be confirmed by the sketch inscribed *windowes of ye stayrecase at S^{r} P: Kelligrews house/Blackfryers Mr Sur^{s} designe* which shows half a Venetian opening very like the one on Jones's elevation. The only inconsistency is in Webb's ground-floor plan of the turret, which shows a large central opening and two small side openings (the left one serving a kitchen annexe), whereas Jones has two equal openings – a difference sufficiently explained by the fact that Jones was sketching out a first idea for the building while Webb was drawing it completed.

The drawing probably dates near the end of the 1620s, for, as Summerson has remarked, Killigrew was knighted by Charles I soon after his accession in 1625 and is likely to have built a new house for himself not long afterwards. The thick black-chalk under-drawing technique, complemented by graphite for the under-drawing of the ground-floor arches, is characteristic of Jones's technique in the 1630s. A date near the beginning of this decade is suggested by similarities between the short pen shading around the arches and the shading on the Somerset House Chapel window design of 1632 (cat. no. 59). Although this technique resembles Webb's on the window details (fig. 110), the authorship of the drawing need not be questioned, for Webb invariably shaded within his window openings, and never used black chalk so loosely on his architectural elevations.

Jones's design for Sir Peter Killigrew's house is based on the same palazzo type as his earlier five-window courtier town house for Sir Fulke Greville of about 1617 (cat. no. 22). It has a

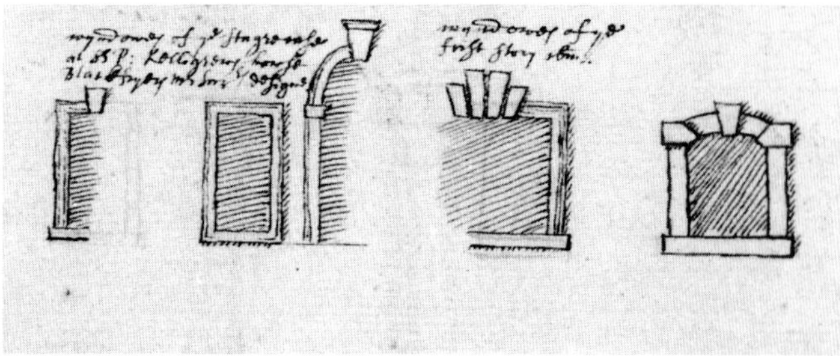

Fig. 110
John Webb. Thumbnail sketches of windows for the staircase (left) and ground floor (right) from Jones's design for Sir Peter Killigrew's house

low ground floor with quoins and voussoirs, a first floor treated as a *piano nobile* and a small attic beneath the eaves. But though the pattern of the elevation is similar, the details have been greatly reduced (e.g. the two-moulding cornices over the windows and the simple main entablature), anticipating the minimal house façades of about 1638 (cat. nos 84–7). The plan is the only evidence we have of the internal arrangement of Jones's courtier houses and shows a compromise between the traditional asymmetrical grouping of hall and service rooms and an organisation around a central axis, marked by the staircase and a through-corridor on both floors.

Bibliography:
J. Summerson, *Inigo Jones* (Harmondsworth, 1966), pp. 113–4.
J. Newman: review of J. Harris and A. A. Tait, *Catalogue of the drawings by Inigo Jones, John Webb and Isaac de Caus at Worcester College, Oxford* (Oxford, 1979) in *Society of Architectural Historians of Great Britain Newsletter*, no. 22 (Summer 1980), p. 10

119 Designs for painted or metalwork panels, including the badge of the Order of the Garter

c. 1630

Pen and brown ink with grey-brown wash, over a grid of ruled graphite lines

312 × 471 mm. Thick paper

Watermark: IHS monogram

Inscribed by Jones in pen and brown ink within left design: *HONI SOIT QVI MAL Y PENSE*

RIBA Jones & Webb 91

The Garter Star, shown in the left-hand design, was initiated by Charles I in 1630 in a revival of the ceremonies of the ancient Order of the Garter enacted at Windsor Castle. The 1630 dates seems to be incorporated in the intertwined Roman numerals of the upper panel: 'DCXXX' (for MDCXXX), the crowned 'C' being a conceit for Carolus Rex. These may be designs for panels at Windsor. The fluent pen lines and smoothly handled grey-brown wash resemble the technique on the designs of *c.* 1630 for carved or painted panels in the Ashmolean Museum (cat. nos 57, 58).

120 Sketch designs for a compartmented ceiling incorporating studies for putti, a cartouche and a reclining figure

1620s or early 1630s

Graphite, with pen and brown ink for studies

153 × 150 mm. Thin, grainy paper. Cut from larger sheet

Watermark: water-spot inscribed CH and surmounted by semicircle with five trefoils, above which is a trefoil and part of a crescent moon (rest cut off)

Inscribed on *verso* by a 17th-c. hand in pen and brown ink, partly cut off at top and on right: *to him either to night or / tomorrow morning, M^r / Jefferys wisht me to call heer / yor lovinge ffriend Humb. Thatcher.*

RIBA Jones & Webb 101

The drawing shows part of the left side of an unidentified compartmented ceiling. On the upper right is a large circular central panel; to the left is an oblong panel; and below is a broad soffit, flanked on the right by a triangular-shaped panel which is matched by another above, and on the left by a narrow vertical panel containing a mask head. The sheet has been trimmed at the top and a little on the left, but possibly not on the right, where it marks the central axis of the ceiling. The whole plan would appear to have been an oblong of roughly two squares. The ink studies fit neatly into the spaces of the ceiling, but give no clues to the purpose of the design. The largely graphite technique, the thin, grainy paper with a water-pot watermark, and the fluent figurative drawing suggest a date after about 1620. However, the loosely handled pen shading, and the absence of thick, redrawn outlines, place the drawing at least a few years earlier than Jones's vigorous interior designs of the later 1630s (e.g. cat. nos 65, 69, 76). This is one of six small study drawings at the RIBA which were once pasted on a single sheet. The others (RIBA Jones & Webb 95–100) are all studies for masque proscenium borders dating from the 1620s or 1630s.

121 Elevation for a gateway in Cannon Row, Westminster Palace, London

1634

Graphite over faint scorelines with pen and brown ink base line and scale

183 × 192 mm. (But formerly with a pasted strip at top bearing Jones's inscription, removed during restoration)

Watermark: water-pot inscribed DVL and surmounted by a five-pointed coronet, a quatrefoil and crescent moon

Formerly inscribed by Jones on an attached sheet: *for a gate to bee made from / channell row. in to y^e pallas / yarde 1634*

Scale: 10 ft = $2\frac{7}{16}$ in.

RIBA Jones & Webb 10

'Channell row' is now known as Cannon Row, and opens into Bridge Street (then called Woolstaple) opposite Big Ben. In the seventeenth century it crossed Woolstaple into Old Palace Yard – the 'Paved Yard' or 'Outer Ward' of the Palace fronted on the south by the Great Hall of Westminster. The principal entrance to the Yard was through the Great Gateway at the north-west. The gate in this design would have provided a subsidiary entrance from the north. The drawing may show the rear elevation of a columned façade (cf. cat. nos 17 and 18) and is typical of Jones's neatly ruled graphite style in the 1630s (cf. cat. no. 79). There is no record of the gateway having been built.

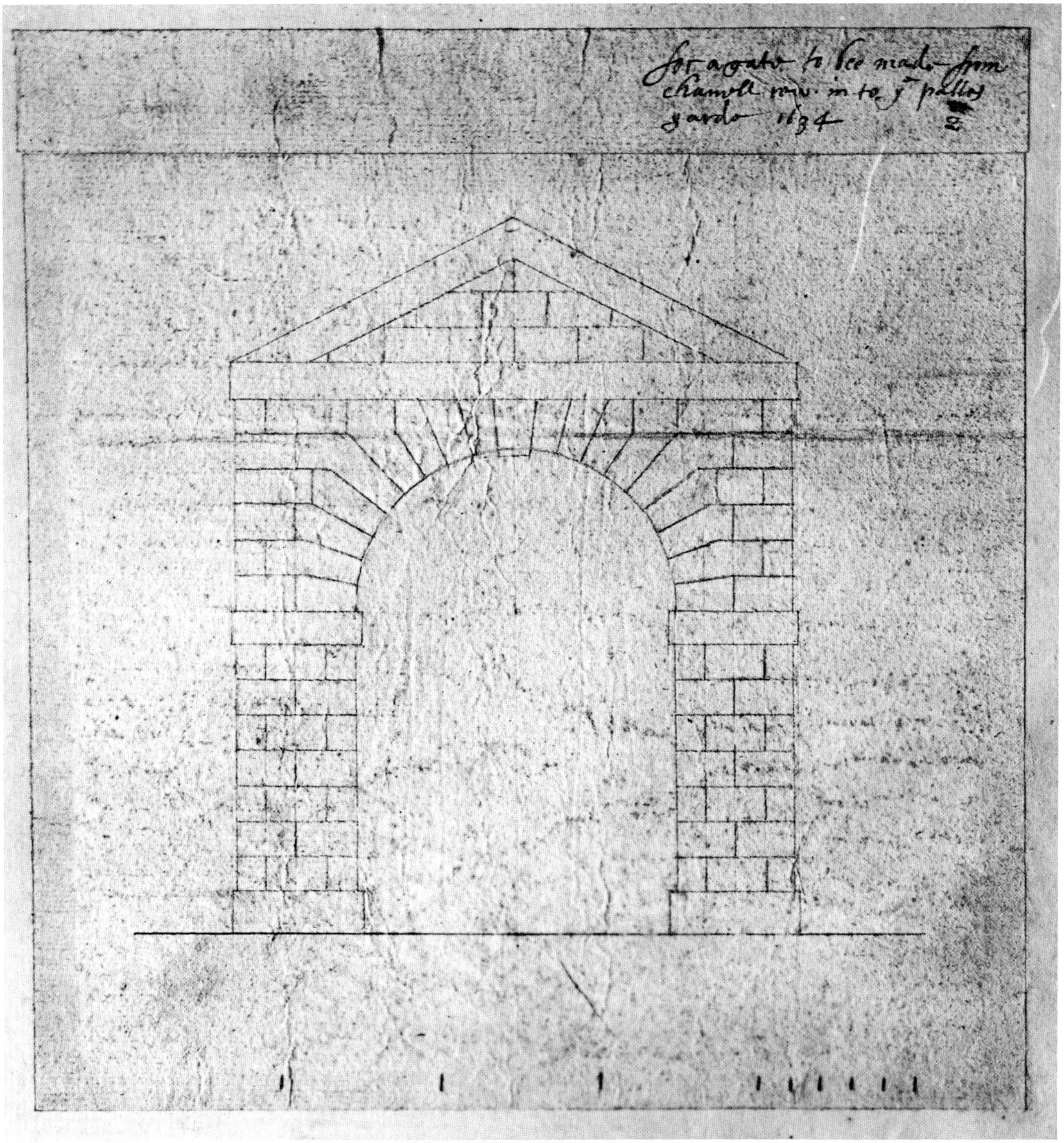
for a gate to bee made from
chanell row in to ye pallas
garde 1634
2

122 Elevation for a door with voussoired surround set in a wall

Mid-1630s

Graphite over faint scorelines, with pen and brown ink inscriptions and scale marks

251 × 187 mm. Thin, grainy paper

Inscribed by Jones in pen and brown ink within door: *3 fo., 7 fo..*

Scale: 1 ft = fractionally over $\frac{3}{4}$ in.

RIBA Jones & Webb 84

Executed on thin paper typical of the late period and drawn with neat ruled graphite outlines like those on the St Paul's north transept front, *c.* 1634 (cat. no. 79), the Cannon Row gateway design 1634 (cat. no. 121), and the section through Somerset House Chapel of about 1635 (cat. no. 123 *verso*) this elevation must date around the middle of the 1630s. As on almost all Jones's late drawings, the under-scoring is very tidy.

The design was probably made for the gardens at Oatlands Palace, where extensive works were under way between about 1631 and 1635. An arbour was built next to the Vineyard in 1631–2 and a new brick wall 19 ft 7 in. high was built to enclose an 'orrenge Garden' in 1634–5. The latter connected with the Privy Garden where the wall was probably lower. This may be a design for a door surround put into the Privy Garden wall to link the two enclosures in 1634–5.

Bibliography:

King's Works, iv, pp. 215–16

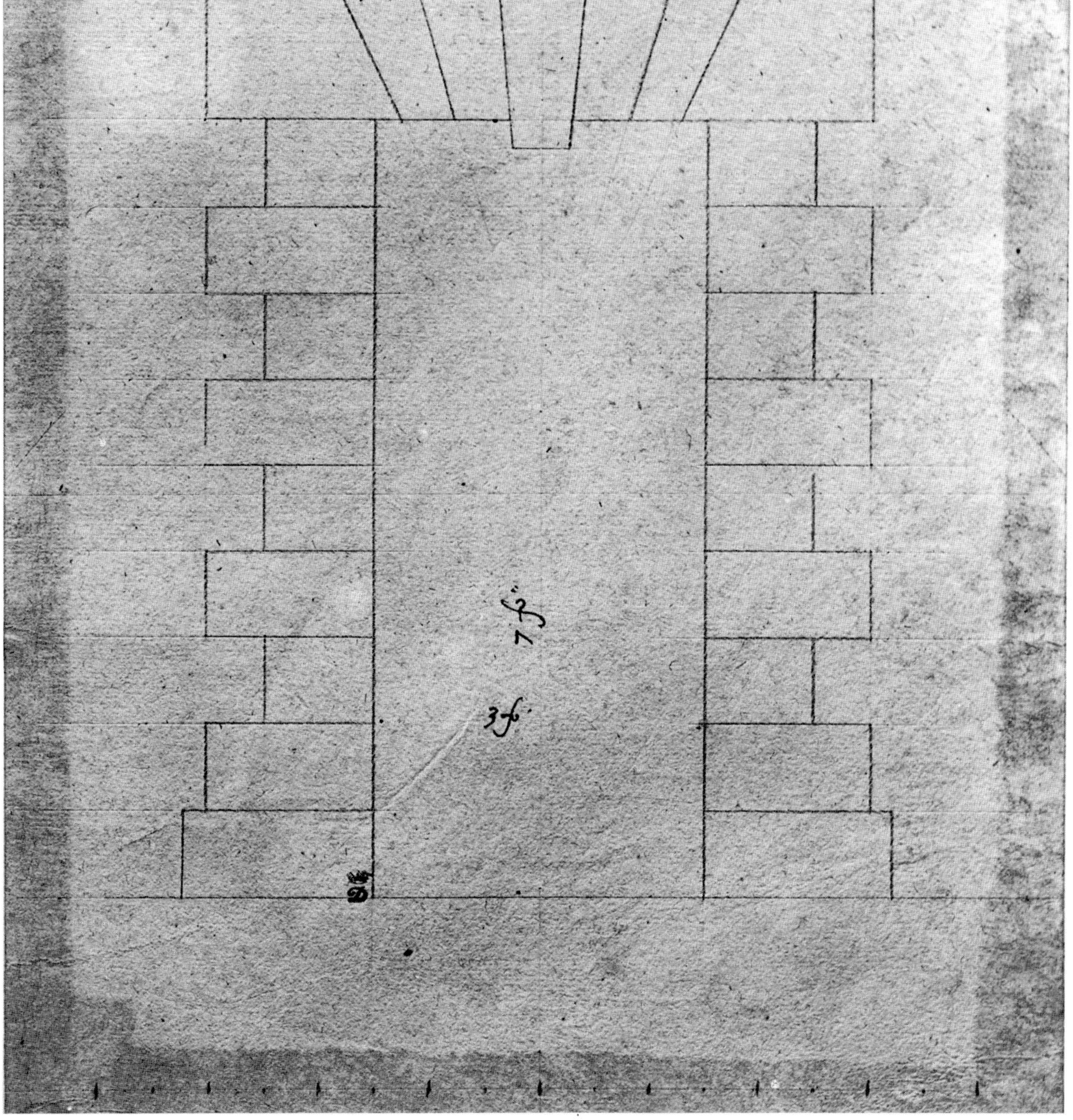

123 Sketch for a door into the terrace at the Queen's House, Greenwich, and (*verso*) section through Somerset House Chapel, London

1635

Graphite

108 × 190 mm. Trimmed sheet of thin, grainy paper

Inscribed by Jones in graphite on *recto*: *for y[e] doure in to y[e] voltes / under y[e] tarras grenwich / 1635*

RIBA Jones & Webb 20

The sketch on the *recto* of the sheet is a preparatory drawing for the arched doorway underneath the terrace on the north side of the Queen's House; it gave access to service rooms in the basement of the building. The drawing on the *verso* is a section of the Roman Catholic Chapel at Somerset House, London, 1630–5 (fig. 111). It was built on a vaulted brick undercroft and was approximately a double cube, 30 ft high, 30 ft wide and 60 ft long. At the liturgical east end there was an altar, and beyond that was a two-storey vestry. All these features are present in this drawing. There is no scale, but the height of the interior space is equivalent to the width. The doorway to the right of the altar leads into the lower vestry, while the window above is the one in the outside wall lighting the upper vestry, the floor of which is also shown. In addition, the drawing shows the external cornice and a trussed roof of the type introduced by Jones and used by him in other buildings such as the Queen's Chapel at St James's Palace.

Howard Colvin

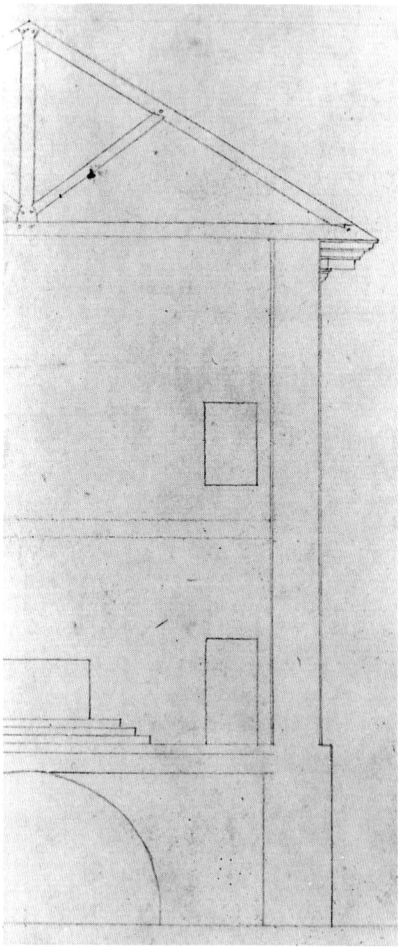

Fig. 111
Verso of cat. no. 123, showing transverse section of the Roman Catholic Chapel at Somerset House, London, 1630–5

Bibliography:
King's Works, iv, pp. 264–6
D. Yeomans, 'Inigo Jones's roof structures', *Architectural History*, xxix (1986), pp. 85–101

for ye doore in to ye volte
under ye tarras grenwich
1635
I, 21.

124 Sketch design for a chimney-piece and overmantel for the Queen's House, Greenwich, with studies for putti and two female busts

c. 1637

Pen and brown ink

281 × 195 mm. Laid down

Chatsworth. Bound volume, 'Designs by Inigo Jones: Drawings X', fo. 20, no. 121

This is one of more than 1,400 sheets of drawings by Inigo Jones in a volume at Chatsworth. The sketch in the centre of the sheet is evidently an alternative for the chimney-piece for the Queen's House in cat. no. 76.

It is based on the same source in Jean Barbet's *Livre d'architecture* (fig. 73), but has been modified through the use of a more unified form of attic, consisting of three raised sections rather than separate pedimented features.

Glossary

abacus The slab which crowns a *capital*: in the Tuscan *order*, square-sided without moulding; in the Roman Doric, square-sided surmounted by a *cymatium*; in the Roman Ionic, square or concave-sided with the lower edge moulded; in the Corinthian and Composite, a concave-sided square with the corners cut off and with hollow profile

acroterion (pl. acroteria). Plinths on the apex and lower extremities of the *pediment* to carry statuary or ornaments

aedicule The framing of an opening or niche with columns or *pilasters* carrying a lintel or *entablature* with *pediment*

architrave The lowest division of the classical *entablature*; also the moulded frame of a door or window

articulate In architecture, to distinguish the parts of a building (especially a façade) through subdivision or applied ornament

ashlar Masonry of smooth blocks in horizontal courses with vertical joints

astragal A small moulding in circular section

astylar Treatment of façade without columns or *pilasters*

atrium An inner court of a Roman house, forming an entrance hall. The roof was open to the sky in the centre, and its rim was sometimes carried on four or more columns

attic The upper storey of a building above the main *cornice*; also applied to the rooms in a roof

baluster A short pillar or column supporting a handrail or coping; a series forming a balustrade

bossed Superimposed with blocks at intervals, as on an *architrave* or column shaft (e.g. cat. no. 40)

capital The crowning feature of a column or *pilaster*

cartouche An ornamental panel, often a coat of arms, with curved and scrolled borders

cavetto A simple concave moulding

cella The main body of a classical temple, often approached through a portico

chamfered A surface made by cutting the sharp edge of a block at an angle, usually 45°

clerestory An upper storey of a building above adjacent roofs, pierced by windows

coffered Decorated with sunken square or polygonal panels

contrapposto Italian word for a pose in which one part of the body is turned in the opposite direction from that of the other

cornice The crowning or upper portion of the classical *entablature*, or any crowning and projecting ornamental moulding

corona The square projection in the upper part of a *cornice*, its *soffit* or under-surface recessed to form a drip

cove A large concave moulding, often used as a *cornice* or crowning moulding (see cat. no. 118)

cyma A moulding with double-curved profile

cyma recta A *cyma* moulding with concave profile above and convex below

cyma reversa a *cyma* moulding with convex profile above and concave below

cymatium The crowning member of a *cornice* usually in the form of a *cyma*; also applied to the topmost moulding of an *architrave* or *capital*

dado The portion of a pedestal between its base and *cornice*; also applied to the lower part of an interior wall when decorated separately

dentil A small rectangular block used in series, commonly in the lower parts of cornices

drum The upright part below a dome or cupola; it may be square, circular or polygonal

entablature The upper part of an *order* of architecture, comprising *architrave*, *frieze* and *cornice*

entasis The slight swelling or curving outwards along the outline of a column shaft, intended to correct the optical illusion of concavity if the lines were left straight

fascia A plain horizontal band, found in the divisions of an architrave and between floors on façades of buildings

frieze The middle division of the classical *entablature*

frons scenae The front of the tiring house of a theatre, forming the back scene of the stage

frontispiece The principal front of a building, or a decorated entrance, or a *pediment* over a door. Also used for the proscenium arch of a stage set (e.g. cat. no. 96)

fillet A narrow flat band between mouldings to separate them from each other, e.g. between the flutes on a column shaft

fluting Shallow, concave grooves running vertically on the shaft of a column

guttae Small cones or wedge-shaped blocks carved below the *tenia* under each *triglyph* of a Doric *frieze*

herm A pillar terminating in a head or bust (usually of Hermes)

impost A member in a wall, usually formed of mouldings, on which an arch rests

jamb The straight side of an archway, door or window

lunette A semi-circular window or wall panel

metope The space between two *triglyphs* in a Doric *frieze*

modillion A small bracket or console, frequently used beneath the *corona* of a *cornice*

module A unit of measurement, by which the proportions of a classical *order* or building are regulated; usually the diameter or half-diameter of the column at the base of its shaft

order The classical system of decoration and support comprising a column, with base (usually), shaft and *capital*, the whole supporting an *entablature*. The five principal orders are Tuscan (the simplest), Doric, Ionic, Corinthian and Composite (the most elaborate). Orders may be free-standing or applied to a wall surface

ovolo A convex moulding, often a quarter-round

pediment A low-pitched gable above a portico or pair of columns, formed by raking cornices

pergola A railed projecting balcony over a door; also a covered walk in a garden formed by double rows of posts supporting joists

peristyle A range of columns surrounding a court or building

piano nobile Italian term for the main floor of a house, containing the principal reception rooms. It is usually higher than the other floors, with a basement or ground floor below and one or more shallower floors above

pier A solid masonry support

pilaster A flattened rectangular column of shallow projection conforming with one of the *orders* of architecture

pilastrelli A small *pilaster* or strip flanking the *architrave* of a door or window

porta regia The principal door in a *frons scenae* at the back of a stage

pulvinated Convex in profile; a term usually applied to a *frieze*

quoins Dressed stones at the angles of buildings or openings, usually laid so that their faces are alternately long and short

reveal That part of a *jamb* which lies between the door or window opening and the outer wall surface

rotunda A round building or room, usually domed

rustication Masonry with rough-hewn or roughened surfaces or with deep joints

Serliana An arched opening flanked by two smaller, square-headed openings, so called because it was first illustrated by Serlio; also known as a Venetian or Palladian window, or a Palladian motif

soffit The ceiling or underside of any architectural member

stanchion A vertical supporting member, usually of iron or steel

strap-work Relief ornament consisting of interlaced bands and forms similar to fret-work or cut leather

stylus An implement with a metal, wooden, ivory or ebony tip, used to incise lines on paper as a guide for pen drawing; also called a scorer

trompe l'œil French for 'deceives the eye'; painted decoration designed to make the spectator think the objects are real

tenia The small moulding or *fillet* along the top of the *architrave* in the Doric *order*

term pilaster A *pilaster* treated like a long pedestal which merges at the top into a sculptural figure
torus A large convex moulding, used principally in the bases of columns
transept The part of a cruciform church projecting at right angles to the main building
triforium An arcaded wall-passage above the arcade in the nave of a church and below the *clerestory*
triglyph Vertically channelled blocks between the *metopes* of a Doric *frieze*. Each block normally has two vertical grooves or glyphs in the centre and half grooves at the edges
voussoir A truncated, wedge-shaped block forming an arch, or superimposed at intervals on an *architrave* or lintel

Abbreviations

Chatsworth
Chatsworth House, Derbyshire, England. Drawings loaned by the Duke of Devonshire and the Trustees of the Chatsworth Settlement

King's Arcadia
J. Harris, S. Orgel and R. Strong, *The King's Arcadia: Inigo Jones and the Stuart Court* (London, Arts Council of Great Britain, 1973)

King's Works, iii, iv, v and vi
H. M. Colvin (ed.), *The History of the King's Works* (6 vols, London, 1963–82): vol. iii, *1485–1660, Part I* (1975), by H. M. Colvin, D. R. Ransome and J. Summerson; vol. iv, *1485–1660, Part II* (1982), by H. M. Colvin, J. Summerson, M. Biddle, J. R. Hale and M. Merriman; vol. v, *1660–1782* (1976), by H. M. Colvin, J. Mordaunt Crook, K. Downes and J. Newman; vol. vi, *1782–1851* (1973) by J. Mordaunt Crook and H. M. Port

O & S
S. Orgel and R. Strong, *Inigo Jones. The Theatre of the Stuart Court* (2 vols, London and Berkeley, 1973). Numbers refer to catalogue entries

PRO
Public Record Office, London

RIBA
Royal Institute of British Architects/British Architectural Library, London

RIBA Jones & Webb
J. Harris, *Catalogue of the Drawings Collection of the Royal Institute of British Architects: Inigo Jones and John Webb* (Farnborough, 1972). Numbers refer to catalogue entries

Worcester College H & T
J. Harris and A. A. Tait, *Catalogue of the drawings by Inigo Jones, John Webb and Isaac de Caus at Worcester College, Oxford* (Oxford, 1979). Numbers refer to catalogue entries. Drawings loaned by the Provost and Fellows of Worcester College, Oxford

Bibliography

The bibliography is divided into three parts: Treatises and Sources, Inigo Jones and General Works.

1. Treatises and sources

Alberti, Leon Battista. *L'Architettura di Leon Battista Alberti tradotta in lingua Fiorentina da Cosimo Bartoli . . . La Pittura tradotta per M. Lodovico Domenichi*, Monreale, 1565 [Inigo Jones's annotated copy at Worcester College, Oxford]

Barbaro, Daniele. *I Dieci libri dell'architettura di M. Vitruvio Pollio*, Venice, 1567 [Inigo Jones's annotated copy in Devonshire Collection, Chatsworth House, Derbyshire]

Barbet, Jean. *Livre d'architecture, d'autels, et de cheminées*, Paris, 1633

Bartsch, A. von. *Le Peintre graveur*, 21 vols, Vienna, 1803–21

Bordino, Giovanni Francesco. *De Rebus praeclare gestis a Sixto V Pon. Max.*, Rome, 1588 [Inigo Jones's copy at Worcester College, Oxford (lost, 1973)]

Campbell, Colen. *Vitruvius Britannicus or the British architect*, 3 vols, London: vol. i, 1715; vol. ii 1717; vol. iii 1725

Ciardi, R. P. (ed.). *Gian Paolo Lomazzo: scritti sulle arti*, 2 vols, Florence, 1974

Collot, Pierre. *Pieces d'architecture où sont comprises plusiers sortes de cheminées*, Paris, 1633

Du Cerceau, Jacques Androuet. *Les Plus excellents bastiments de France*, Paris, 1576/9

Dugdale, William. *The History of St Paul's Cathedral*, London, 1658

Fontana, Domenico. *Della Trasportatione dell'obelisco vaticano et delle fabriche di nostro signore Papa Sisto V fatte dal Cavallier Domenico Fontana, libro primo*, Rome, 1590

Francart, Jacques. *Le Premier livre d'architecture*, Brussels, 1616

Guildhall Library, London. Works accounts for the restoration of St Paul's Cathedral, London, 1633–42; MS.25, 473 (W.A. 1–11, 13–15)

Harrison, Stephen. *Arches of triumph in London*, London, 1604

Kent, William. *Designs of Inigo Jones, with some additional designs*, 2 vols, London, 1727

Lambeth Palace Library, London. Works accounts for the restoration of St Paul's Cathedral, London: Fulham Palace 321 (W.A. 12) [one volume detached from the rest of the accounts, which are now at Guildhall Library, London]

Leoni, Giacomo. *I Quattro libri dell'architettura. The architecture of A. P. in four books to which are added several notes by Inigo Jones*, 2 vols, London, 1715–20

Lomazzo, Gian Paolo. *Trattato dell'arte, della pittura, scoltura, et architettura*, Milan, 1585 [Inigo Jones's annotated copy in a private collection]

Lorini, Buonaiuto. *Le Fortificationi*, Venice, 1609 [Inigo Jones's annotated copy of Worcester College, Oxford]

L'Orme, Philibert de. *Le Premier tome de l'architecture*, Paris, 1567 [Inigo Jones's copy at Worcester College, Oxford]

Palladio, Andrea. *I Quattro libri dell'architettura*, Venice, 1601 [Inigo Jones's annotated copy at Worcester College, Oxford]

———. *L'Antichità di Roma di M. Andrea Palladio*, Venice, 1588 [Inigo Jones's annotated copy at Worcester College, Oxford]

Peacham, Henry. *The Art of drawing with the pen, and limning in water colours*, London, 1606

Pierretz, D. Antoine. *Livre d'autels et d'épitaphes*, n.d. [but often issued with Barbet, above]

Poldo D'Albenais, Jean. *Discours historial de l'antique et illustre cité de Nismes*, Lyon, 1560

Rubens, Peter Paul. *Palazzi di Genova*, Antwerp, 1622

Rusconi, Giovanni Antonio. *Della Architettura*, Venice, 1590 [Inigo Jones's annotated copy at Worcester College, Oxford]

Scamozzi, Vincenzo. *L'Idea della architettura universale*, 2 vols, Venice, 1615 [Inigo Jones's annotated copy at Worcester College, Oxford]

Serlio, Sebastiano. *Libro primo* [to *quinto*] *d'architettura di Sebastiano Serlio Bolognese*, Venice, 1559–62 [Inigo Jones's annotated copy at Queen's College, Oxford]

———. *Extraordinario libro di architettura &c*, Venice, 1558; reprinted in *Tutte l'opera d'architettura di Sebastiano Serlio Bolognese*, Venice, 1584, Book VI, and later editions

———. *Tutte l'opere d'architettura et prospetiva*, Venice, 1600 [incomplete copy, annotated by Inigo Jones, now at Canadian Centre for Architecture, Montreal]

Vardy, John. *Some designs of Mr Inigo Jones and Mr William Kent*, London, 1744

Vasari, Giorgio. *Delle Vite de'piu eccellenti pittori, scultori, et architettori*, vol. i, part iii, Florence, 1568 [Inigo Jones's annotated copy at Worcester College, Oxford]

———. *Le Opere*, ed. Gaetano Milanese, 9 vols, Florence, 1878–85

Vignola, Giacomo Barozzi da. *Regola delli cinque ordini d'architettura*, Rome, 1607 [Inigo Jones's annotated copy at Worcester College, Oxford]

Viola Zanini, Gioseffe. *Della Architettura*, Padua, 1629 [Inigo Jones's annotated copy at Worcester College, Oxford]

Vitruvius. *The Ten books on architecture*, trans. M. H. Morgan, Harvard, 1914; repr. New York, 1960

Ware, Isaac. *Designs of Inigo Jones and others*, London, c. 1731

Webb, John. *The most notable antiquity of Great Britain, vulgarly called Stone-Heng on Salisbury Plain, restored by Inigo Jones Esq.*, London, 1655

———. *A Vindication of Stone-Heng Restored*, London, 1665

2. Inigo Jones

Allsopp, B. (ed.). *Inigo Jones on Palladio, being the notes by Inigo Jones in the copy of I Quattro libri dell'architettura di Andrea Palladio, 1601, in the Library of Worcester College, Oxford*, 2 vols, Newcastle upon Tyne, 1970

Aubrey, J. *Brief Lives*, ed. A. Clarke, 2 vols, Oxford, 1898

Bell, C. F. 'Portraits of Inigo Jones', *RIBA Journal*, xliv (1937), pp. 1007–8

Blakiston, J.M.G. 'The Inigo Jones Screen', *Winchester Cathedral Record*, nos 45–7 (1976–8)

Blayney Brown, D. *Ashmolean Museum Oxford: catalogue of the collection of drawings*, iv, Oxford, 1982

Blomfield, R. T. *A History of Renaissance architecture in England, 1500–1800*, 2 vols, London, 1897, i, pp. 99–122

Bold, J. *Wilton House and English Palladianism. Some Wiltshire houses*, London, 1988

Burman, P. 'Inigo Jones at Hale?', *Country Life*, clv (1974), pp. 263–4

Chaney, E. Review of A. C. Fusco, *Inigo Jones Vitruvius Britannicus: Jones e Palladio nella cultura architettonica inglese 1600–1740* (Rimini, 1985), *Burlington Magazine*, cxxx (1988), pp. 633–4

Charlton, J. *The Banqueting House, Whitehall*, London, 1964

———. *The Queen's House, Greenwich*, London, 1976

Chettle, G. H. *The Queen's House, Greenwich*, monograph in London Survey Committee monograph xiv, London, 1937

———. 'Marlborough House Chapel, St James's Palace', *Country Life*, lxxxiv (1938), pp. 450–3

Colvin, H. M. 'The South front of Wilton House', *Archaeological Journal*, cxi (1954), pp. 181–90

——— (ed.). *The History of the King's Works*, 6 vols, London, 1963–82: vol. iii, *1485–1660, Part I* (1975); vol. iv, *1485–1660, Part III* (1982); vol. v, *1660–1782* (1976); vol. vi, *1782–1851* (1973)

———. *A Biographical dictionary of British architects 1600–1840*, London, 1978

Cunningham, P. *Inigo Jones: a life of the architect*, London, Shakespeare Society, 1848–9; reissued 1853

De Beer, E. S. 'Notes on Inigo Jones', *Notes and Queries*, 30 December 1939 and 4 May 1940

———. 'Inigo Jones and St Paul's Cathedral', *London Topographical Record*, xviii, 1942

Dictionary of National Biography. Unsigned article, 'Inigo Jones', by A. P. Horne (1891–2)

Eisenthal, E. 'John Webb's reconstruction of the ancient house', *Architectural History*, xxviii (1985), pp. 7–31

Fisher, G. and **Newman, J.** 'A fountain design by Inigo Jones', *Burlington Magazine*, cxxvii (1985), pp. 531–2

Fraser, P. and **Harris, J.** 'A Catalogue of the drawings by Inigo Jones (1573–1652), John Webb (1611–1672) and Richard Boyle, 3rd Earl of Burlington (1694–1753), in the Burlington Devonshire Collection', RIBA typescript, London, 1960

Fusco, A. C. *Inigo Jones Vitruvius Brittanicus: Jones e Palladio nella cultura architettonica inglese 1600–1740*, Rimini, 1985

Godfrey, W. H. 'Beaufort House, Chelsea, and its neighbours', *Architectural Review*, xxix (1911), pp. 270–4

Gordon, D. J. 'Poet and architect: the intellectual setting of the quarrel between Ben Jonson and Inigo Jones', *Journal of the Warburg and Courtauld Institutes*, xii (1949), pp. 152–78

Gotch, J. A. 'The Burlington Devonshire Collection of drawings with special reference to the relations between Inigo Jones and John Webb', *RIBA Journal*, xviii (1911), pp. 317–42

———. 'The Original drawings for the Palace at Whitehall, attributed to Inigo Jones', *Architectural Review*, xxxi (1912), pp. 333–64

———. 'Catalogue of the drawings attributed to Inigo Jones preserved at Worcester College, Oxford, and at Chatsworth', *RIBA Journal*, xx (1913), pp. 349–57

——— and **Wilkinson, C. H.** 'Supplementary catalogue' to drawings by Inigo Jones, John Webb and others at Worcester College, Oxford. British Architectural Library/RIBA, MSS. 72.034(42). 5:92W + 019G, c.1919

———. 'Inigo Jones: some surviving misconceptions', *RIBA Journal*, xxxi (1924), pp. 598–9

———. *Inigo Jones*, London, 1928

———. 'The Choir Screen in Winchester Cathedral, *RIBA Journal*, xxxvi (1929), pp. 46–8

———. 'Inigo Jones's principal visit to Italy in 1614. The itinerary of his journeys', *RIBA Journal*, xlvi (1938), pp. 85–6

Harris, J. 'Inigo Jones and the Prince's Lodging at Newmarket', *Architectural History*, ii (1959), pp. 26–40

———. 'The Greenwich layout', letter in *Architectural Review*, cxxvii (1960), pp. 98–9

———. 'Raynham Hall, Norfolk', *Archaeological Journal*, cxviii (1961), pp. 180–7

———. 'Inigo Jones and his French sources', *Metropolitan Museum of Art Bulletin*, xix (May 1961), pp. 253–64

———. 'A Prospect of Whitehall by Inigo Jones', *Burlington Magazine*, cix (1967), pp. 89–90

———. *Catalogue of the Drawings Collection of the Royal Institute of British Architects: Inigo Jones & John Webb*, Farnborough, 1972

———, **Orgel, S.** and **Strong, R.** *The King's Arcadia: Inigo Jones and the Stuart Court*, London, Arts Council of Great Britain, 1973

———. 'Inigo Jones and the courtier style', *Architectural Review*, clix (1973), pp. 17–24

———. 'The link between a Roman second-century sculptor, Van Dyck, Inigo Jones and Henrietta Maria', *Burlington Magazine*, cxv (1973), pp. 526–30

———. 'The Inigo Jones exhibition', letter in *Burlington Magazine*, cxv (1973), pp. 808–9

——— and **Tait, A. A.** *Catalogue of the drawings by Inigo Jones, John Webb & Isaac de Caus at Worcester College Oxford*, Oxford, 1979

———. *The Palladians*, London, 1981

———. *The Design of the English country house, 1620–1920*, London, 1985

Higgott, G. 'Inigo Jones in Provence', *Architectural History*, xxvi (1983), pp. 24–34

———. 'The architectural drawings of Inigo Jones: attribution, dating and analysis', London University Ph.D. Diss., 1987

Higham, C. S. *Wimbledon Manor under the Cecils*, London, 1962

Howarth, D. 'Lord Arundel and Inigo Jones in Italy, *Country Life*, clvii (1975), pp. 1052–4; 1138–40

———. *Lord Arundel and his circle*, New Haven and London, 1985

Hussey, C. 'Wilton House and the Earls of Pembroke – I', *Country Life*, xcv (1944), pp. 112–15

———. 'Wilton House, Wiltshire – II', *Country Life*, cxxxiii (1963), pp. 1109–13

Isham, G. 'Inigo Jones and Northamptonshire', *Northamptonshire past and present*, v, no. 2 (1973–4), pp. 95–100

Jones-Davies, M. T. *Inigo Jones, Ben Jonson et le masque*, Paris, 1967

Keith, W. G. 'Some hitherto unknown drawings by Inigo Jones', *Burlington Magazine*, xxii (1913), pp. 218–26

———. 'The Palace of Oatlands', *Architectural Review*, xxxix (1916), pp. 76–7

———. 'A Theatre project by Inigo Jones', *Burlington Magazine*, xxxi (1917), pp. 61–70, 105–11

———. 'Inigo Jones as a collector', *RIBA Journal*, xxxiii (1925), pp. 94–108

———. 'The Queen's House, Greenwich', *RIBA Journal*, xliv (1937), pp. 943–7

Lees-Milne, J. *The Age of Inigo Jones*, London, 1953

Lethaby, W. R. 'Inigo Jones and the theatre', *Architectural Review*, xxxi (1912), pp. 189–90

———. 'New light on Inigo Jones', *Architectural Review*, xl (1916), pp. 72–3

Loftie, W. J. *Inigo Jones and Wren or the rise and decline of modern architecture in England*, London, 1893

Louw, H. J. 'Anglo-Netherlandish architectural interchange c. 1600–c. 1660', *Architectural History*, xxiv (1981), pp. 1–23

Mackintosh, I. 'Inigo Jones – theatre architect', *TABS*, xxxi (1973), pp. 99–105

Mikhailovskii, E. V. *Architektor Inigo Dzhons*, Moscow, USSR Academy of Architecture, 1939

Milizia, F. *Le Vite de'piu celebri architetti d'ogni nazione*, Rome, 1768 ['Vita di Inigo Jones', pp. 330–4]

Newman, J. 'An early drawing by Inigo Jones and a monument in Shropshire', *Burlington Magazine*, cxv (1973), pp. 360–7

———. 'The Inigo Jones centenary', *Burlington Magazine*, cxv (1973), pp. 557–61

———. 'A draft will of Lord Arundel', *Burlington Magazine*, cxxii (1980), pp. 692–6

———. 'Inigo Jones e la sua copia de *I Quattro libri* di Palladio', *Bolletino del centro internazionale di studi di architettura Andrea Palladio*, xii, 2 (1980), pp. 41–62

———. Review of J. Harris and A. A. Tait, *Catalogue of the drawings by Inigo Jones, John Webb and Isaac de Caus at Worcester College Oxford* (Oxford, 1979) in *Society of Architectural Historians of Great Britain Newsletter*, no. 22 (Summer 1980), p. 10

———. 'The dating of Inigo Jones's annotations' in 'Essays presented to Peter Murray' (London University typescript, 1980)

———. 'Strayed from the Queen's House?', *Architectural History*, xxvi (1984), pp. 33–5

———. 'Italian treatises in use: the significance of Inigo Jones's annotations' in J. Guillaume (ed.), *Les Traités de la Renaissance* (Actes du colloque tenu à Tours, 1–11 Juillet 1981), Paris, 1988, pp. 435–41

Nicoll, A. *Stuart masques and the Renaissance stage*, London, 1937

Orgel, S. 'To make boards speak: Inigo Jones's stage and the Jonsonian masque', *Renaissance Drama*, new series, i (1968), pp. 121–52

——— and **Strong, R.** *Inigo Jones. The Theatre of the Stuart Court*, 2 vols, London and Berkeley, 1973

———. 'Inigo Jones on Stonehenge', *Prose*, iii (1974)

Orrell, J. 'Inigo Jones at the Cockpit', *Shakespeare Survey*, xxx (1977), pp. 157–68

———. *The Theatres of Inigo Jones and John Webb*, Cambridge, 1985

———. *The Human stage: English theatre design, 1567–1640*, Cambridge, 1988

Palme, P. *Triumph of peace: a study of the Whitehall Banqueting House*, Stockholm, 1956

Peacock, J. 'New sources for the masque designs of Inigo Jones', *Apollo*, cvii (February 1978), pp. 98–111

———. 'Inigo Jones's stage architecture and its sources', *The Art Bulletin*, lxiv, no. 2 (1982), pp. 195–216

———. 'Inigo Jones's catafalque for James I', *Architectural History*, xxv (1982), pp. 1–5

———. 'The French element in Inigo Jones's masque designs' in D. Lindley (ed.), *The Court masque*, Manchester, 1984, pp. 148–68

———. 'Inigo Jones and the Arundel marbles', *The Journal of Medieval and Renaissance studies*, xvi, no. 1 (1986), pp. 75–90

———. 'Inigo Jones and the Florentine Court theater', *John Donne Journal*, v (1986), pp. 201–34

———. 'Jonson and Jones collaborate on *Prince Henry's Barriers*', *Word & Image*, iii, no. 2 (1987), pp. 172–94

Ramsey, S. C. *Inigo Jones*, London, 1924

Rowan, D. F. 'A neglected Jones/Webb theatre project: "Barber-Surgeon's Hall writ large"', *New theatre magazine*, ix (1969), pp. 6–15
Rowe, C. 'The Theoretical drawings of Inigo Jones, their sources and scope', London University M. A. thesis, 1947
Royal Institute of British Architects. 'Inigo Jones 1573–1652. Handlist of an exhibition of pen and ink drawings by Inigo Jones', London, RIBA, December 1952
Rykwert, J. 'Inigo Jones Architector Magnae Britanniae', *Domus*, no. 530 (January 1974), p. 54
Simpson, P. and **Bell, C. F.** 'Designs by Inigo Jones for masques and plays at Court', *Walpole Society*, xii (1924)
Stone, L. 'The Building of Hatfield House', *Archaeological Journal*, cxii (1955), pp. 100–28
———. 'Inigo Jones and the New Exchange', *Archaeological Journal*, cxiv (1957), pp. 106–21
Strong, R. *Festival designs by Inigo Jones: drawings for scenery and costume*, Washington D.C., International Exhibitions Foundation, 1967
———. *Britannia Truimphans: Inigo Jones, Rubens and Whitehall Palace*, London, 1980
Summerson, J. *Architecture in Britain, 1530–1830*, Harmondsworth, 1953; 7th ed., 1983
———. 'Inigo Jones: lecture on master mind', *Proceedings of the British Academy*, l (1965), pp. 169–92
———. *Inigo Jones*, Harmondsworth, 1966
Sumner Smith, J. 'The Italian sources of Inigo Jones's style', *Burlington Magazine*, xciv (1952), pp. 200–7
Tafuri, M. 'La fortuna del Palladio alla fine del cinquecento e l'architettura di Inigo Jones', *Bollettino CISA*, xii (Vicenza, 1970), pp. 47–62
Tait, A. A. 'Inigo Jones – architectural historian', *Burlington Magazine*, cxii (1970), p. 235
———. 'Inigo Jones's "Stone-Heng"', *Burlington Magazine*, cxx (1978), pp. 154–9
Terwen, J. J. 'De plattegronden voor het Banqueting House in Whitehall' in *Opstellen voor H. van de Waal*, Amsterdam/Leiden, 1970, pp. 203–13
Toplis, G. 'Neo-platonic aspects of the thought and work of Inigo Jones', Liverpool University School of Architecture, M.A. thesis, 1967
Triggs H.I. and **Tanner, H.** *Some architectural works by Inigo Jones*, London, 1901
Veevers, E. E. 'Sources of Inigo Jones's masquing designs', *Journal of the Warburg and Courtauld Institutes*, xxii (1959), pp. 373–4
Vinson, R. J. 'Inigo Jones disciple d'Andrea Palladio', *Les Monuments Historiques de la France*, iv (1973), pp. 1–54
Walpole, H. *Anecdotes of painting in England*, 5 vols, 1762–71 [The account of Inigo Jones is in vol. ii, pp. 142–54]
Webb, G. 'Inigo Jones tercentenary', *Country Life*, cxi (1952), pp. 1904–5
Whinney, M. 'Some church designs by John Webb', *Journal of the Warburg and Courtauld Institutes*, vi (1943), pp. 142–50
———. 'John Webb's drawings for Whitehall Palace', *Walpole Society*, xxxi (1946)
———. 'Inigo Jones, a revaluation', *RIBA Journal*, lix (1952), pp. 286–9
———. 'An unknown design for a villa by Inigo Jones' in H. M. Colvin and J. Harris (eds), *The Country Seat*, London, 1970, pp. 33–5
Wittkower, R. 'Pseudo-Palladian elements in English Neo-classical architecture', *Journal of the Warburg and Courtauld Institutes*, vi (1943), pp. 154–64; repr. in R. Wittkower, *Palladio and English Palladianism*, London, 1974
———. 'Inigo Jones, Puritanissimo fiero', *Burlington Magazine*, xc (1948), pp. 50–1; repr. in *Palladio and English Palladianism*, London, 1974.
———. 'Inigo Jones, architect and man of letters', *RIBA Journal*, lx (1953), pp. 83–90; repr. in *Palladio and English Palladianism*, London, 1974, but without the discussion which followed Wittkower's paper, delivered at the RIBA on 9 December 1952
———. Review of B. Allsopp (ed.), *Inigo Jones on Palladio* (Newcastle upon Tyne, 1970) in *Journal of the Society of Architectural Historians*, xxxi (1972), pp. 61–2
Yates, F. *Theatre of the world*, London, 1969
Yeomans, D. 'Inigo Jones's roof structures', *Architectural History*, xxix (1986), pp. 85–101
Youngblood, P. 'Royal favouritism in London building', *History Today*, xxxi (August 1981), pp. 22–7

3. General works

Auerbach, E. and **Kingsley Adams, C.** *Painting and sculpture at Hatfield House*, London, 1971
Avery, C. 'Hubert Lesueur, the "Unworthy Praxiteles" of King Charles I', *Walpole Society*, xlviii (1982)
Bentley, G. E. *The Jacobean and Caroline stage*, 7 vols, Oxford 1941–68; vi, 1968
Blunt, A. *Artistic theory in Italy, 1450–1600*, Oxford, 1940; repr. 1962
Briquet, C. M. *'Les Filigranes: dictionnaire historique des marques du papier dès leur apparition vers 1282*, 4 vols, Geneva, 1907; repr. Paris, 1970
Burns, H., in collaboration with **Fairbairn L.** and **Boucher B.** *Andrea Palladio 1508–1580: the portico and the farmyard*, London, Arts Council of Great Britain, 1975
Cevese, R. (ed.). *Mostra del Palladio; Vicenza, Basilica palladiana*, Milan/Venice, 1973
Colvin, H. M. *Royal Buildings*, London, 1968
Dawson, G. and **Kennedy Skipton, L.** *Elizabethan handwriting, 1500–1686*, London, 1968
Edmond, M. *Rare Sir William Davenant: Poet Laureate, playwright, Civil War general, Restoration theatre manager*, Manchester, 1987
Eustace, T. (ed.). *Statesmen and politicians of the Stuart age*, London, 1985
Girouard, M. 'The Smythson Collection of the Royal Institute of British Architects', *Architectural History*, v (1962)
———. *Robert Smythson and the Elizabethan country house*, New Haven and London, 1983
Goldman, P. *Looking at drawings: a guide to technical terms*, London, 1979
Gombrich, E. H. *Art and illusion*, 3rd ed., London, 1968
Gurr, A. *The Shakespearean stage, 1574–1642*, 2nd ed., Cambridge, 1980
Hambly, M. *Drawing instruments: their history, purpose and use for architectural drawings*, Cambridge, 1982 (RIBA exhibition catalogue, London, 1982)
———. *Drawing instruments, 1580–1980*, London, 1988
Harris, J. 'The Diana fountain at Hampton Court', *Burlington Magazine*, cxi (1969), pp. 444–7
Hill, O. and **Cornforth, J.** *English country houses: Caroline 1625–1685*, London, 1966
Lambert, S. *Drawing: technique and purpose*, London (V&A exhibition catalogue), 1981
Lever, J. and **Richardson, M.** *The Art of the architect*, London, 1984
Lewis, D. *The Drawings of Andrea Palladio*, Washington, D.C., International Exhibitions Foundation, 1981
Magagnato, L. and **Marini, P.** *Andrea Palladio, I quattro libri dell'architettura*, Milan, 1980 (Trattati di architettura, vol. vi)
Magueri, V. 'I manueli propedeutici al disegno, a Bologna e Venezia, agli inizi del Seicento', *Musei Ferraresi 1982, Bollettino Annuale 12*, Florence, 1984, pp. 147–56
Millar, O. *The Age of Charles I*, London, 1972
Parry, G. *The Golden Age Restor'd. The culture of the Stuart Court, 1603–42*, Manchester, 1981; repr. 1985
Reid Thompson, R. 'The Tregian Manuscripts', University of Cambridge Ph.D. Diss., forthcoming
Scott-Elliot, A. H. 'The Statues from Mantua in the collection of King Charles I', *Burlington Magazine*, ci (1959), pp. 218–27
Stainton, L. and **White, C.** *Drawing in England from Hilliard to Hogarth*, London, 1987
Stone, L. *The Crisis of the aristocracy, 1558–1641*, Oxford, 1965, repr; 1979
———. *Family and fortune*, London, 1973
Strong, R. *The Renaissance garden in England*, London, 1979
———. *Henry Prince of Wales and England's lost Renaissance*, London, 1986
Summerson, J. 'Palladio e gli inglesi', *Bollettino CISA*, xv (Vicenza, 1973), pp. 9–25
Tannenbaum, S. A. *The Handwriting of the Renaissance*, London and New York, 1931
Tomlinson, H. (ed.). *Before the English Civil War*, London, 1983
Wedgwood, C. V. *The King's Peace, 1637–1641*, London, 1955; repr. Harmondsworth, 1983
Wickham, G. *Early English stages, 1300–1660*, 3 vols, London, 1959–72; ii, part 2, London, 1972
Willson, D. H. *King James VI & I*, London, 1956

Photographic Acknowledgements

The black and white illustrations for the catalogue were supplied by the collections cited in each entry. Exceptions to this and figure illustrations were supplied by the sources listed below.

Bodleian Library, Oxford
Figs 77, 94

British Museum
Figs 6, 63, 88

A. C. Cooper Ltd
Figs 52, 80

Country Life
Figs 95, 100

Courtauld Institute of Art, Conway Library, University of London
cat. nos. 12, 22, 25, 39, 41–47, 51, 63–65, 67, 72, 73, 80, 82, 83, 89, figs 2, 3, 4, 10, 39, 43, 46, 53, 57, 65, 66, 72, 79, 82, 83, 85, 87, 101, 109, 110

Devonshire Collection Chatsworth reproduced by kind permission of the Trustees of the Chatsworth Settlement
Photograph: Courtauld Institute of Art
Frontispiece, cat. nos. 2, 7, 8, 10, 33, 34, 93–96, 98, 99a and b, 117, 124, figs 8, 9

A. F. Kersting
Figs 48, 68, 71

Magdalene College, Cambridge, by permission of the Master and Fellows
Fig. 51

Museum of London
Fig. 61

Private collection
Figs 54, 91

Royal Collection, St James's Palace, Reproduced by Gracious permission of Her Majesty the Queen
Figs 14, 15, 16, 17, 20, 50

Royal Commission on Historical Monuments of England
Figs 7, 64, 102

Royal Institute of British Architects, The British Architectural Library Drawings Collection
Figs 1, 5, 18, 19, 24, 25, 27, 29, 36, 41, 55, 56, 58, 60, 75, 84a–d, 85, 86a and b, 97, 99, 107, 111

University Museum of Archaeology and Anthropology, Cambridge
Fig. 81

Vienna National Library
Fig. 92

Woburn Abbey
Fig. 21

Worcester College, Oxford
Photograph: Courtauld Institute of Art, Conway Library
Cat. nos. 3, 4, 50, 53–55, 79, 84–88, 91, 100–113, figs 13, 30–32, 47, 49, 89

Index

Numbers in italics refer to pages on which illustrations appear. Numbers in bold italic refer to catalogue illustrations.